love letters

for the heart

Also available as
Don't Worry God Has You Covered

T. J. Nichols
(Theresa Jean Nichols)

Cover Design
John Willhite

One for each day of the year

I start with thanking God, our Father, Jesus, His Son, and the Holy Spirit. These letters are from God, inspired by the Holy Spirit, and our redemption is through Jesus. Thank you, My Lord, My Savior, My Friend.

I heard God tell me one day to give His love letters to the world. Then, I asked Him what I should call them and I heard Him say, "To Know Me" – so I have called these love letters from God, but God wants to tell you – this is to bring you to a place *to know Him.*

January 1

Ephesians 5:15-17

¹⁵ See then that ye walk circumspectly, not as fools, but as wise, ¹⁶ Redeeming the time, because the days are evil. ¹⁷ Wherefore be ye not unwise, but understanding what the will of the Lord is.

I break the chains that bind My people, holy one. My power breaks each hold, My love. When I break, and I do break open the wounds, I begin to heal from deep within. There is no compromise in Me. My ways are higher, My plans are best, and I do all things for good. I Am Your Wonderful God and I heal from deep within. All things are open before Me for I know each heart. I reveal things to you, My love, and you pray for each one. This is My will. You know in part, holy love of Mine, but I know all. I Am All and I do mighty things before your eyes. I train you and I teach you many things for I Am Your Great Teacher. Listen to Me always and obey My every whisper. I am here doing all things for I am in the midst of you. My love pours out from you in the beauty of My holiness. My world is thirsty for My drink. Give them My drink for My living waters flow through you. I refresh My dry and thirsty ones on their path I have given. You are My mighty warrior and you fight the good fight. Pray for My hurting ones, My love, for I listen to you.

January 2

1 John 1:5-7

⁵ This then is the message which we have heard of him, and declare unto you, that God is light, and in him is no darkness at all. ⁶ If we say that we have fellowship with him, and walk in darkness, we lie, and do not the truth: ⁷ But if we walk in the light, as he is in the light, we have fellowship one with another, and the blood of Jesus Christ his Son cleanseth us from all sin.

There is a light bursting forth from you. My brightness can blind and My brightness can open the eyes of those who hunger for Me. I reveal Myself to you in honor of your hunger for more of Me. There is more, My love,

3

much more. My arms are open and I draw you deeper still. My growth in you is at a rapid speed, now, My love, for My time has come to you. You are chosen, you are highly favored, you are My special treasure, you are My bride. Glorify My Name and know that I Am God. All things are Mine and only I do all things. Praise My Holy Name for I am in you revealing Myself to you. You see My hand, My mighty right hand coming down and resting on you. I Am Yours, I give you all of Me – forever and ever. I love you, holy one, and I am pleased with you. I see your faith and I know your loyal heart. Do not be discouraged, My precious one, for I am here. You know I am here, for I allow you many things. You know My presence as it hovers in you, and over you, and all around you. You see Me everywhere you go for I show Myself to you.

January 3

1 John 4:18-20

[18] There is no fear in love; but perfect love casteth out fear: because fear hath torment. He that feareth is not made perfect in love. [19] We love him, because he first loved us. [20] If a man say, I love God, and hateth his brother, he is a liar: for he that loveth not his brother whom he hath seen, how can he love God whom he hath not seen?

You are My servant. You are My child. You are My innocent one and I watch over you with My careful eye. My mercy and grace follow you all the days of your life. I Am Your Creator. You are My masterpiece. In every way, you please Me, My love. I Am Holy and I have made you holy. I Am Pure and I have made you pure. I Am Love and I have given you My love. I am coming soon and I am preparing the hearts of My chosen ones. I send you to them, My love, and I send them to you. You are My faithful one and I trust you. I Am Faithful And True and I have given Me to you. My Word lives in your heart and your heart beats one with Mine. I love you, holy one, you are very precious to Me. You are safe because I Am All Powerful. You have great peace for I Am Peace. You rejoice in My love for I rejoice over you. I am in your every thought for you have given Me your mind. My heart beats one with you for you have given Me your heart. I Am Your Strength for you have given Me your weakness. I Am The Lord God Almighty who reigns forever and ever.

January 4

1 Chronicles 29:10-12

[10] Wherefore David blessed the Lord before all the congregation: and David said, Blessed be thou, Lord God of Israel our father, for ever and ever. [11] Thine, O Lord is the greatness, and the power, and the glory, and the victory, and the majesty: for all that is in the heaven and in the earth is thine; thine is the kingdom, O Lord, and thou art exalted as head above all. [12] Both riches and honour come of thee, and thou reignest over all; and in thine hand is power and might; and in thine hand it is to make great, and to give strength unto all.

I will give you time if you pursue Me. You must continually put Me first in all you do, My chosen one, for the battle rages on. Keep yourself pure before Me. You cannot do this without Me – ever. Remain in Me for the battle is Mine. Your praise blesses Me, My love. You know the times and you know the seasons, for I have given you many signs. You are always on assignment, precious one. I give you times to rest, you must take them. My love is at work among you. I take each one on their journey and I teach them. Do not be discouraged, for they are not blind. I will show them My great and awesome love. Keep your eyes on only Me, for I have called you out from among them. I am in you, holy one, do not doubt My call upon you. Remember the things I have shown you. Keep Me in your every thought, for I am here. All is well, My love, all is well.

January 5

John 17:9-11

[9] I pray for them: I pray not for the world, but for them which thou hast given me; for they are thine. [10] And all mine are thine, and thine are mine; and I am glorified in them. [11] And now I am no more in the world, but these are in the world, and I come to thee. Holy Father, keep through thine own

name those whom thou hast given me, that they may be one, as we are.

There are no words to adequately describe My love for you – there are no words. I have shown you My love in many ways. I created the world just for you, My love. I gave you My only Son to redeem you. I love you with all that I Am – and I Am GOD, The Almighty One Who Is And Was And Is To Come. I Am The Holy One Of Israel and I love My people. Pray for My people, holy one, for I love them so. Tell them of My great love. Oh beloved, My beloved, hear My words for they are true. I Am Love and I live inside of you. I am closer than close, My love. My heart beats for you and your heart beats in Mine, for we are one and I love you so. I take good care of you, continually. I protect you and surround you in My great and awesome love. You are My obedient one and I trust you with My precious people. I love them, precious one, I love them so. Tell them I love them, tell them I gave them life, tell them I gave them My everything, tell them I Am Truth and I Am Life. Only I bring freedom, only I am their God who loves them so.

January 6

Joel 2:25-27

²⁵ And I will restore to you the years that the locust hath eaten, the cankerworm, and the caterpiller, and the palmerworm, my great army which I sent among you. ²⁶ And ye shall eat in plenty, and be satisfied, and praise the name of the Lord your God, that hath dealt wondrously with you: and my people shall never be ashamed. ²⁷ And ye shall know that I am in the midst of Israel, and that I am the Lord your God, and none else: and my people shall never be ashamed.

You are My place of beauty. I rapture your beauty into Me and behold your love. Your heart lay open before Me in the beauty of My holiness. I receive your heart and enclose it in Mine. You beat in Me and we are one. I fill you with My mighty things as you come to Me there. My peace like rivers flood your soul and My joy is beyond measure. I give these to you with strength and wisdom and compassion for My hurting ones. I give you love beyond compare and Truth to set you free. I give you honor and gentle touches that only come from Me. I give you grace, and mercy too, for it is My joy to give. My peace comes rushing in during the whirlwinds of your life. It gives you strength to endure the race and bring My loved ones home to Me. I sent you to My hurting world to gather up My sheep. They are lost, and live in fear and hate, and chained in selfish ways. Help them know I set them free to walk in peaceful ways. I Am Their God who loves them so – oh tell them how I heal.

January 7

1 Peter 5:6-9

⁶ Humble yourselves therefore under the mighty hand of God, that he may exalt you in due time: ⁷ Casting all your care upon him; for he careth for you. ⁸ Be sober, be vigilant; because your adversary the devil, as a roaring lion, walketh about, seeking whom he may devour: ⁹ Whom resist stedfast in the faith, knowing that the same afflictions are accomplished in your brethren that are in the world.

You have not sinned against Me, holy one. You ask Me to reveal Myself to you and to teach you My ways. I just revealed this thing to you. Now, obey Me. I do not hold your not knowing against you, My love. It was not time, it was not time. The time for you to know this is now. I will give you the strength and the wisdom to do this. Believe in Me in all you do. Know that I am with you. Know that I Am GOD, The Almighty One, who helps you. I want you to know this one thing, precious one, you are in My holy presence at all times and I commune with you. You are My beloved one, My chosen one who brings Me glory and honor and praise. All things are in order and under My control. Never forget, all things are under My control and are working for good. I am at work among you, holy one. Never doubt My presence for I am here. You are Mine and I am guiding you in all things. You are Mine and I show you many things in My perfect timing. I strengthen you for more of Me and refine you to My perfect ways. I love you, mighty one. I honor you, for I love you so. You are very precious to Me. Keep your eyes on only Me.

January 8

Song of Solomon 4:9-11

9 Thou hast ravished my heart, my sister, my spouse; thou hast ravished my heart with one of thine eyes, with one chain of thy neck. 10 How fair is thy love, my sister, my spouse! how much better is thy love than wine! and the smell of thine ointments than all spices! 11 Thy lips, O my spouse, drop as the honeycomb: honey and milk are under thy tongue; and the smell of thy garments is like the smell of Lebanon.

I will protect them, My love. I have always protected them. I hear you, My love. I breathe with you, I am one with you. I know your every thought! My how you please Me so! I have taken you into My holiness and I surround you there. Oh breathe deeply from My holiness and let My great peace reign in your heart. My love is in you. My favor rests on you, for you bring Me glory and honor and praise. My fairest flower in My field, how your blossoms glow from My kiss. Your aroma reaches up to My heavens and permeates the air with your sweetness. I have given you much, holy one. You will not disappoint Me, for you love Me so. My power and My might strengthen you and keep you from the former things. I am here, precious one, always. My love pours, My love breathes, My love dances, My love sings, My love honors, My love blesses, and My love heals. My love walks among you in My gentle fields. My love gives you fresh air to breathe. My love sends you and My love keeps you – forever and ever – you are Mine.

January 9

Jeremiah 31:35-37

35 Thus saith the Lord, which giveth the sun for a light by day, and the ordinances of the moon and of the stars for a light by night, which divideth the sea when the waves thereof roar; The Lord of hosts is his name: 36 If those ordinances depart from before me, saith the Lord, then the seed of Israel also shall cease from being a nation before me for ever. 37 Thus saith the Lord; If heaven above can be

measured, and the foundations of the earth searched out beneath, I will also cast off all the seed of Israel for all that they have done, saith the Lord.

My rivers flow mightily in you, rushing in and rushing out! My how you glow in My presence. I love you, mighty one! My lips burst forth in song over you for you refresh Me with your praise! I give you more for this new day and take you deeper still. I am with you, precious love of Mine and I keep you safe within. My work is great and almost through – the finish line in sight! Hold tightly to all you know and love for I am mighty in this fight! I fight the battles as you praise My Name and worship Me, My love. I am in control, and victory is running through My blood. Oh precious one, this is but a small thing for Me, for I Am Owner of All That Is And Was And Is To Be. I Am Almighty God and I am in you. Worship Me, My holy one, for I love to behold your beauty. I smile upon you the entire time, for you have captured My heart in your song. Oh sing of your great love for Me, sing deeply from your soul! My heart is filled with all of you and I enjoy you so!

January 10

Ephesians 1:3-6

3 Blessed be the God and Father of our Lord Jesus Christ, who hath blessed us with all spiritual blessings in heavenly places in Christ: 4 According as he hath chosen us in him before the foundation of the world, that we should be holy and without blame before him in love: 5 Having predestinated us unto the adoption of children by Jesus Christ to himself, according to the good pleasure of his will, 6 To the praise of the glory of his grace, wherein he hath made us accepted in the beloved.

I Am Your Abba when you cry out to Me. I Am Your Healer for you are very precious to Me. I Am The Mighty One who shines out in you, The Holy One of Israel is My Name. Raise your hands toward My Holy Throne and glorify My Name for what I have done! All power and honor and glory are in My Name. Blessed be the day of your salvation for you bring honor and glory to My Name. I have a plan, precious one, I have a great

9

and awesome plan! Speak in My Name, holy one, for I have chosen you to represent Me. Speak in The Name of The All Sufficient One. Tell them I can do all things, oh tell them I will do all things – tell them, My love. I have deposited My power in you, mighty one. My Name, The Name Above All Names is at work among you. My kindness rests in you and I fill you with wisdom and understanding. Watch Me, My love, for I unfold My mysteries for you to behold. I Am The Lord, The Lord Your God, and it pleases Me to bless you.

January 11

Revelation 3:20-22

[20] Behold, I stand at the door, and knock: if any man hear my voice, and open the door, I will come in to him, and will sup with him, and he with me. [21] To him that overcometh will I grant to sit with me in my throne, even as I also overcame, and am set down with my Father in his throne. [22] He that hath an ear, let him hear what the Spirit saith unto the churches.

The rivers rush in and the rivers rush out. My tide takes them out, oh but My tide brings them back! I Am, oh yes I Am The Great I Am, listening to you, hearing you, working in you, speaking to you, and gathering you to My secret place where My power reigns in victory forevermore! All glory and honor and praise to My Name, My Holy Name sees all, knows all, is all – forever and ever! I hear you, oh yes, I hear your every whisper and I, The All Powerful Mighty One says "Yes" to you. I give you My "Yes and Amen!" I give you My love, My great and awesome love and I honor you. My favor is upon you for My glory and honor and praise! I have touched My world with My light, holy one. Shine out in Me and brighten the darkened places for I have given you My power and might! Praise My Holy Name for I Am Your God who loves you so. Look around you and see My touch, look around you and watch and see My mighty right hand at work among you.

January 12

2 Chronicles 20:15-17

[15] And he said, Hearken ye, all Judah, and ye inhabitants of Jerusalem, and thou king Jehoshaphat, Thus saith the Lord unto you, Be not afraid nor dismayed by reason of this great multitude; for the battle is not yours, but God's. [16] To morrow go ye down against them: behold, they come up by the cliff of Ziz; and ye shall find them at the end of the brook, before the wilderness of Jeruel. [17] Ye shall not need to fight in this battle: set yourselves, stand ye still, and see the salvation of theLord with you, O Judah and Jerusalem: fear not, nor be dismayed; to morrow go out against them: for the Lord will be with you.

I hear the stirrings of your heart and listen to your pleas. I reign in you with power and might for the entire world to see. I am with the ones who hurt so deeply and I send My love to them. There is not one who is unnoticed by Me! I see each heart from deep within and I come to them in love. My love is powerful, you will see what all I do for you. Oh glory to My Name on high for I shine out in the places I send you. I want you to know these things, My love, for you are very precious to Me. I send you to My hurting ones for I came to set them free. I walk in you and guide you in Me for all eternity. Do not lose sight of My great power for I do all things for you. You can cry out to Me, Your Mighty One, and I do answer you. There is a way, I have a plan, just keep your trust in Me. I Am Your King, I've told you so and you can plainly see My mighty right hand is resting its favor on you.

January 13

Daniel 2:20-23

[20] Daniel answered and said, Blessed be the name of God for ever and ever: for wisdom and might are his: [21] And he changeth the times and the seasons: he removeth kings, and setteth up kings: he giveth wisdom unto the wise, and knowledge to them that know understanding: [22] He revealeth the deep and secret things: he knoweth what is in

the darkness, and the light dwelleth with him. [23] I thank thee, and praise thee, O thou God of my fathers, who hast given me wisdom and might, and hast made known unto me now what we desired of thee: for thou hast now made known unto us the king's matter.

Holy one, precious one, listen to Me for I speak and it is so. I Am The Almighty One who works among you leading the way for all things. All things are coming together, working together for My suddenly. Cry out for My people, My holy ones, My chosen ones, for My time is at hand. Obey Me for My mighty right hand is upon you. Obey Me for My Spirit is in you working all things. Do not ask another, you ask only Me. Do not go to another, you come to only Me. Do not look around you, for I have taken you up to My holy place and I meet you there. I Am Your King and you are to come to only Me. I will not share you with another, ever. All you need is in Me. All your answers are in Me. All your questions are in Me. I control your every step. Do not go back to the former things, for that is not My will. Press on, mighty one, for I am pleased with you. Keep your eyes on Me and My promises for I am smiling on you. It is here, you can see the rain coming, bursting through the clouds. You can smell the rain coming for it is here.

January 14

Daniel 4:34-35

[34] And at the end of the days I Nebuchadnezzar lifted up mine eyes unto heaven, and mine understanding returned unto me, and I blessed the most High, and I praised and honoured him that liveth for ever, whose dominion is an everlasting dominion, and his kingdom is from generation to generation: [35] And all the inhabitants of the earth are reputed as nothing: and he doeth according to his will in the army of heaven, and among the inhabitants of the earth: and none can stay his hand, or say unto him, What doest thou?

Take the steps toward the door. I'll open the door, for My time has come. As you step forward, I see your faith and am pleased with you. Do not be afraid, precious one, for I am with you. Your obedience brings out My favor upon you. Your obedience pleases Me, holy one. I watch you as you sleep and I have My mighty ones guarding you all the days of your life. You are My treasure, My priceless one who has captured My heart. The evil one has tried to kill you, but I have said "No." You are Mine and I take good care of you. I Am Your King, Your Protector and Provider. I enjoy our alone times, holy one. I refresh you in our precious times. Our time is holy and sacred for I have blessed it. It is in those times that I strengthen you and take you deeper still. There is more of Me, My holy one – much more I want to show you. Give Me more alone time, My love, for I love to commune with you. I hunger for more of you, My love. Come spend more time with Me and fill Me with your love.

January 15

Acts 4:31-33

[31] And when they had prayed, the place was shaken where they were assembled together; and they were all filled with the Holy Ghost, and they spake the word of God with boldness. [32] And the multitude of them that believed were of one heart and of one soul: neither said any of them that ought of the things which he possessed was his own; but they had all things common. [33] And with great power gave the apostles witness of the resurrection of the Lord Jesus: and great grace was upon them all.

The power is in Me, My beloved and I hear your request. The power is in My Name, holy one. You honor and glorify My Holy Name and I send My power upon you. My power shakes the very foundation of the earth and moves each heart I choose. I know the hearts of those who love Me. I know all things, mighty one. Do not be dismayed at the large numbers, and do not be dismayed at the overwhelming circumstances. I Am Your Overwhelming King! I Am The Conqueror Of All for victory is My Name. Oh how you please Me with your great requests for I Am Your Great King who loves to show you who I Am! I will show My mighty power among My people and heal them of their diseases. I will show My mighty power

13

among My people and I will give them courage and boldness as they stand in My Holy Name. I give all things and I take away all things. All things are under My control, at all times, forever and ever. Ask of Me, My love, for I am here.

January 16

1 Samuel 20:41-42

41 And as soon as the lad was gone, David arose out of a place toward the south, and fell on his face to the ground, and bowed himself three times: and they kissed one another, and wept one with another, until David exceeded. 42 And Jonathan said to David, Go in peace, forasmuch as we have sworn both of us in the name of the Lord, saying, The Lord be between me and thee, and between my seed and thy seed for ever. And he arose and departed: and Jonathan went into the city.

Yes, My love, things as you have known them are changing now. I give you My vow, My solemn vow, I will take care of the ones you love. No harm will come, for My protective hand is upon them. I Am Your Trusted One who shows My faithfulness to you all the days of your life. I send My workers into My field and gather My people back to Me. My plan continues strong in the face of My enemy and I am strengthened in your love. The time is now to worship Me and enter into Me more. I keep you in My safe, strong place and hide you deep within. I promise you My safe, strong place and hold you in My love. Do not be afraid, My precious one, for I am with you everywhere you go. Hold on to what you know in Me and keep Me in your heart. I surround you in love, strength, and power, and keep you safe within. Rise up to the challenge I set before you, for I have called you out by name.

January 17

Philippians 4:6-8

6 Be careful for nothing; but in every thing by prayer and supplication with thanksgiving let your requests be made known unto God. 7 And the peace of God, which passeth all

understanding, shall keep your hearts and minds through Christ Jesus. [8] Finally, brethren, whatsoever things are true, whatsoever things are honest, whatsoever things are just, whatsoever things are pure, whatsoever things are lovely, whatsoever things are of good report; if there be any virtue, and if there be any praise, think on these things.

I hear you when you speak, holy one. I hear you when you think, My love. I know your heart for I Am Your Creator. I know the thoughts I have for you, My beloved. I am doing all things for you that are wonderful and good for I love you so. My how I love you so! Never doubt My love for you, precious one. I am here working all things for good. Keep your mind on My wonderful things, holy one. Remember the cross – remember Me. When My precious creation forgot Me and did not honor Me, I sent My Beloved Son to redeem them back to Me. The price has been paid, My love, the victory has been won. Pray for them, My love, for they are My hurting ones. Show them My love, for I Am Love. Speak to them in kindness and cry out to Me for help. I will help you, for you are My beloved. I open the eyes of the blind and I soften the hearts of the hardened. I heal the sick and I raise the dead. I Am The Alpha and Omega – The Beginning And The End.

January 18

Revelation 3:7-8

[7] And to the angel of the church in Philadelphia write; These things saith he that is holy, he that is true, he that hath the key of David, he that openeth, and no man shutteth; and shutteth, and no man openeth; [8] I know thy works: behold, I have set before thee an open door, and no man can shut it: for thou hast a little strength, and hast kept my word, and hast not denied my name.

I search you daily, My love. I search you continually for I protect your heart. I keep you in My loving embrace and call you pure and righteous. My love has cleansed you and My love has taken you deeper still. My holiness reigns and rules in your heart, My tender one. Drink from the richness of our secret place and let My bounty fill you. The times are evil,

My holy one, and you need My abundance to stand. I fill you with My power, mighty one, and strengthen you for the times. I guard you with My fiercest love and take you deeper still. You are safe, My love, for you obey Me with your love. You walk in Me as I direct, and you hold fast to what I say. I honor you, My holy one, for you have shown Me all your love. I watch you take your steps of faith and lavish you in love. How sweet is your name upon My lips as I fill Myself with your love. I created you to love Me more and more each day. I breathe deeply into you and give you life so full and overflowing. I reveal Myself in deeper ways as you read My Holy Word. Your beauty fills My holy place when you come into My presence. I love you, precious one – I love you so.

January 19

Revelation 4:3-6

³ And he that sat was to look upon like a jasper and a sardine stone: and there was a rainbow round about the throne, in sight like unto an emerald. ⁴ And round about the throne were four and twenty seats: and upon the seats I saw four and twenty elders sitting, clothed in white raiment; and they had on their heads crowns of gold. ⁵ And out of the throne proceeded lightnings and thunderings and voices: and there were seven lamps of fire burning before the throne, which are the seven Spirits of God. ⁶ And before the throne there was a sea of glass like unto crystal: and in the midst of the throne, and round about the throne, were four beasts full of eyes before and behind.

I Am All Powerful and I Am Almighty. I Am Forever And Ever and I sit on My Throne. All of creation calls Me holy and bows to My Holy Name. I Am Creator of All That Is And Was And Is To Be. I give you all of My love and I give you My great wisdom to honor Me in the beauty of My holiness. You are My precious one, My holy one, who comes before My Throne. I listen with power and I send forth My answer – and I give you the desires of your heart. You are Mine, My beloved, and I answer you from My all powerful place, with all of My love, for you have captured My heart. I bless the day of your creation for you honor and glorify My Holy Name. Let all of heaven and earth rejoice as I shake the foundations of the earth and come to rescue you! Glorify My Holy Name. Honor Me with your praise, for I am coming to rescue you from the hour of My wrath.

January 20

Genesis 12:1-3

12 Now the Lord had said unto Abram, Get thee out of thy country, and from thy kindred, and from thy father's house, unto a land that I will shew thee: ² And I will make of thee a great nation, and I will bless thee, and make thy name great; and thou shalt be a blessing: ³ And I will bless them that bless thee, and curse him that curseth thee: and in thee shall all families of the earth be blessed.

You come before My Throne, holy one and sit at My feet. I pick you up, My child, and hold you close to Me. I breathe My deep peace into you as I hold you closer still. Our hearts beat as one and you rest your love in Me. Let My love sustain you for this new day. Draw from My wells of depth and let Me take you deeper still. Meditate on My Word and live in My love, holy one. Breathe deeply from My love and fill your mind and heart with all things wonderful and good. I Am All Things Wonderful And Good and I love you so. I will send you to My hurting ones and give you what you need. Keep crying out to Me for more and I will use you mightily. I lavish you each new day in the power of My love. Walk in the light of My Word and the darkness must flee. I Am Your Redeemer who paid the price upon that tree. It is yours, My love, My precious one, freedom is full and rich in Me. Praise My Holy Name and worship Me for all eternity. I keep you safe inside of Me, don't look around to see the world that beckons strong for you, keep your eyes on only Me. I Am The Way, The Only Way and I want all of you. I will take nothing less from you for I have given you all of Me.

January 21

Psalm 55:16-18

[16] As for me, I will call upon God; and the Lord shall save me. [17] Evening, and morning, and at noon, will I pray, and cry aloud: and he shall hear my voice. [18] He hath delivered my soul in peace from the battle that was against me: for there were many with me.

My light is in you, holy one. My presence goes before you, My presence hovers over you, and My presence is behind you. You are My beloved one and I am with you always. I send you to My hurting ones and I give you what you need. I Am Almighty God and you are My beloved. I keep you in My secret place and delight Myself in you. I commune with you and hold you close and strengthen you for each new day. When the panic starts to rise, My love, sing out your songs of praise. My songs of love refresh you and peace will flood your soul. I am here, My precious holy one, and I take good care of you, for you belong to only Me, Your Faithful One. I speak My words of love to you and protect you mightily. I Am Your God of spoken truths and My heart belongs to you. My Lamb was slain for you, My love, so you could live with Me. Behold My Son who died for you and brought you back to Me. The power of our love in you shines brightly for all to see. Bring them to us, holy one, for we have our trust in you. I receive your love, My holy one, come and worship Me.

January 22

Genesis 14:18-20

[18] And Melchizedek king of Salem brought forth bread and wine: and he was the priest of the most high God. [19] And he blessed him, and said, Blessed be Abram of the most high God, possessor of heaven and earth: [20] And blessed be the most high God, which hath delivered thine enemies into thy hand. And he gave him tithes of all.

Your roots grow deep into My fertile soil, for I have enriched you in My living waters, holy one. Drink deeply, yes, My love, there is plenty, drink all you want for I am here and I Am Your More. I satisfy your thirst and send you out to give. I bring you back to Me and replenish you again. I love the flow of Me in you, oh precious one, My love rests so sweetly in you. You are My refreshing one who comforts many, for you are My love, My heart, My bride. I give to you, My precious one, I give to you much more, for you please Me in your obedience to seek Me even more. I bless you, precious love of Mine and take you deeper still. I will not share you with another, no My love, I never will. You are My beloved, My holy one, to serve Me 'til the end. I take you places you have never been and watch over you tenderly. Feel My touch, My warm embrace and rest your love in Me. I take good care of you, My love, and hold you tenderly. You have seen My hand upon your life, for I have never left your side. The time is now, My precious one, come sit before My Throne. I look upon your beauty and I lavish you in love.

January 23

Romans 8:37-39

[37] Nay, in all these things we are more than conquerors through him that loved us. [38] For I am persuaded, that neither death, nor life, nor angels, nor principalities, nor powers, nor things present, nor things to come, [39] Nor height, nor depth, nor any other creature, shall be able to separate us from the love of God, which is in Christ Jesus our Lord.

I fill you in our quiet times and reveal Myself to you. I Am Mighty And Strong and I walk in victory among My enemies. But, with you I Am Tender, Gentle And Kind. I fill you with My beauty and give you all My love. You do not lack for anything, for I Am Your God Above. I reach My mighty right hand out and send My love, My song. My songs of love dwell deeply in you and I give you every one. I love you precious one and protect you in My love. You are safe within My hiding place and given so much more. I gently take your hand in Mine and teach you tenderly. We walk in love and perfect peace for you have honored Me. Sometimes we pause along the way and I hold you close in Me. I refresh you in these times of pause and love you tenderly. Oh the light that beams in you as you look upon My face, I fill you with My light, My love, and hold you in My embrace. My power thunders all about and keeps all harm from you. There is none greater in the world, for I Am Your King Of Victory. Enjoy My love and lavish Me in all you say and do. I love to watch you loving Me and I remember you. I take your "Yes" upon My lips and bless you greatly. Come soar with Me, My love, My life, and live in fullness of Me.

January 24

Psalm 25:11-15

[11] For thy name's sake, O Lord, pardon mine iniquity; for it is great. [12] What man is he that feareth the Lord? him shall he teach in the way that he shall choose. [13] His soul shall dwell at ease; and his seed shall inherit the earth. [14] The secret of the Lord is with them that fear him; and he will shew them his covenant. [15] Mine eyes are ever toward the Lord; for he shall pluck my feet out of the net.

I Am The Mighty Roar Of The Ocean. I Am The Giver Of Life and I Am The Taker Of Life. All things are Mine. All things belong to Me – The One And Only who does as I please, for I Am Almighty God – God Most High. I will reveal Myself to you for it is My will to bless you in every way. I have given you your children and I bless them for a thousand generations. My peace will rest upon your household, for you have put your trust in Me. Only I can save you, and only I have saved you from the darkness that lurks behind every corner. I Am Holy, oh yes, and I Am True. There is none but Me and I Am The One And Only who comes to your rescue. You recognize Me, My love, oh yes, you will recognize Me, for I Am Your Love, Your Only Love, who comes to you in all of My passion and sets you in places where only I can. I will keep you, My holy one, My love, for I do as I please, and I have chosen you to be Mine forever and ever. I drink deeply from your praises and I give back what the evil one has taken.

January 25

2 Chronicles 20:15

[15] And he said, Hearken ye, all Judah, and ye inhabitants of Jerusalem, and thou king Jehoshaphat, Thus saith

the Lord unto you, Be not afraid nor dismayed by reason of this great multitude; for the battle is not yours, but God's.

Precious one, My precious one, I hold you dear to My heart. I listen to your requests for My hurting ones with much love, much love. Blessed one, I say "Yes" to you, for you stand on My promises and claim each one. You refresh Me in your love and you bring a smile to My lips. My love, My image, My likeness, you please Me so. I have given you My heart and I show you many things. I fill your heart with great peace and require much from you. I have strengthened you for this time and I have prepared your feet for the journey. You are My tender one, My precious one, the one in whom I trust. My Kingdom is before you as I give you all My love. Come, work with Me in fields unknown and bless My hurting ones. I Am The One And Only One who knows your heart and mind. I created you to come to Me for every single need. I am here with you, by your side, for all eternity. I have called you forth out of the darkness and shown you My bright light. Oh beam of Mine, shine out in Me and draw deeply from My streams. I flow in you, My holy one, I flow in you indeed! I love you, precious light of Mine, I hold you closely in Me. I Am The One who gives you peace, The Only One who takes good care of you.

January 26

Genesis 17:7-8
⁷ And I will establish my covenant between me and thee and thy seed after thee in their generations for an everlasting covenant, to be a God unto thee, and to thy seed after thee. ⁸ And I will give unto thee, and to thy seed after thee, the land wherein thou art a stranger, all the land of Canaan, for an everlasting possession; and I will be their God.

Loving Me this deeply has come from a process, My love, My breath. You can reflect on times present and times past to know My mighty right hand rests on you. You have strength for today and hope for tomorrow in My great and awesome process. I breathe deeply into you, My love. I take you into My secret place and show you more of Me. I love the process, My precious one, for I Am Your Teacher. I saturate your soul in My holiness and delight in revealing Myself to you. Oh how I love to take you there. My love, My smile, My holy one. Take in all you want of Me for I love to take you deeper still. You know Me, My love, you are ready. I will speak My Words through you. Do not be afraid, for many will come and I will protect you. You know Me, I Am Greater. Do not fear, for their words cannot penetrate what I have built in you. I have taken you through My process, holy one, and it cannot be crushed. You are strong in Me, My love. My process does not fail. I have taken you through My holy fire and purified you to shine in Me. Oh how you shine, My beloved – oh how you shine! You know Me, precious lamb of Mine, you know My voice. They will not take you from My love, for I Am greater in you.

January 27

Zephaniah 3:19-20

[19] Behold, at that time I will undo all that afflict thee: and I will save her that halteth, and gather her that was driven out; and I will get them praise and fame in every land where they have been put to shame. [20] At that time will I bring you again, even in the time that I gather you: for I will make you a name and a praise among all people of the earth, when I turn back your captivity before your eyes, saith theLord.

My people are hurting, holy one, and My heart cries out to you. Pray for My people, My love, for they need Me so! I will open their eyes and reveal Myself to My hurting ones. I show you My heart, My tender place of love for My lost and hurting people. Oh cry out for them before My Throne and ask Me for much more. I answer you, My chosen one, I listen for your cries. Let the nations turn to Me, Their Savior and Their God. Pray for those I have put in places high above the rest. I will open eyes to those who see My glory that abounds. I Am Your God who loves you so. I seek the lost among the found and bring them back to Me. I unveil the love that is in you and send you in My Name. The holiness of God Himself rests upon My Name. Holy, holy, holy, describes My Throne above. My power shakes the heavens and earth, and all will bow before My Name. There is no matter too great or small that stops My answer to you. I answer you, My obedient one, with My "Yes" and My "Amen." I have given you authority in My Holy Name. Cry out to Me for all the souls you see and do not see!

January 28

Daniel 10:10-12

10 And, behold, an hand touched me, which set me upon my knees and upon the palms of my hands. 11 And he said unto me, O Daniel, a man greatly beloved, understand the words that I speak unto thee, and stand upright: for unto thee am I now sent. And when he had spoken this word unto me, I stood trembling. 12 Then said he unto me, Fear not, Daniel: for from the first day that thou didst set thine heart to understand, and to chasten thyself before thy God, thy words were heard, and I am come for thy words.

The river is running its course, My love. The river is running. Its mighty current runs strong on your behalf. I will not let them be swept away, My love. I have said "Yes" to you. I have all power to do all things. I give you My "Yes" for those you have requested. I sent you into a hurricane to command the storm to cease, My chosen one. I have given you My Name and you have used it well. My rivers pour out from you and save each one, for you cling to Me, Your Mighty Rock. Your anchor holds, My love, your anchor holds. You know Me, holy one, you know Me. The power is in My love. I strengthen you in My love for each new day and hold you closely in Me. I show Myself to you, My love, and keep you calm in Me. You rest inside the palm of My hand and you are in the center of My heart. I delight Myself upon your face and hold you closer in Me. We walk the storms in perfect peace for your eyes are on only Me.

January 29

1 Samuel 3:11-13

11 And the Lord said to Samuel, Behold, I will do a thing in Israel, at which both the ears of every one that heareth it shall tingle. 12 In that day I will perform against Eli all things which I have spoken concerning his house: when I begin, I will also make an end. 13 For I have told him that I will judge

his house for ever for the iniquity which he knoweth; because his sons made themselves vile, and he restrained them not.

I will protect you from the sons of Eli, My holy one, for they are many, My love. My path will be clear for you, for you have pleased Me with your request. I Am Your God and I will keep you close in My heart, for you have come to Me, The One And Only Who Is Faithful And True. I breathe deeply into you and bless every part. I leave nothing unattended for the evil that lurks to pounce. I take you deeply within My secret place and protect you with My might! I Am Your King, Your Mighty One who is in control of all things. My heart, My love, My precious child, I devote Myself to you. I bless you from the depths of Me and hold you tenderly. I will heal the broken ones you see, each one you cry out to Me. I open your eyes to see the hurt and listen for your cries. I heal them, holy one of Mine, for I honor your requests. I place great burdens on your heart and wait for you to come and bring them back to Me, My love – each and every one. I give you more and more of Me each hour and each day – sit before My Throne with Me and lavish Me today. I take your heart inside of Mine and love you tenderly.

January 30

Psalm 46:4-7

4 There is a river, the streams whereof shall make glad the city of God, the holy place of the tabernacles of the most High. **5** God is in the midst of her; she shall not be moved: God shall help her, and that right early. **6** The heathen raged, the kingdoms were moved: he uttered his voice, the earth melted. **7** The Lord of hosts is with us; the God of Jacob is our refuge. Selah.

My love for you has no bounds and continues on and on. I look upon your face so sweet, I never tire of you, My refreshing drink, My soul delights in you! Your trust and love have no bounds and continues on and on. I bless you, precious love of Mine, My tender, holy one. I Am Almighty God and I speak to you alone, within My chambers deep within, and draw you closer to Me. I love your presence, holy one, and keep you in My love. You love

24

My holy presence and always linger there. I keep you in Me longer, and longer, each new time, for I love to give you more of Me and fill you with My love. I created you for only Me and sing to you, My love. You know the song within My heart for I sing it in your soul. I set before you eternity, My love, My life, My song. The song I sing to you, My love, is our wedding song. Rejoice in Me, My holy one, and dance before My Throne. I fill you in the joy of Me and watch you tenderly. Your King is captive in your laugh and smiles upon His Throne. I delight in you, My treasured one, and protect you mightily.

January 31

Haggai 2:4, 23

4 Yet now be strong, O Zerubbabel, saith the Lord; and be strong, O Joshua, son of Josedech, the high priest; and be strong, all ye people of the land, saith the Lord, and work: for I am with you, saith theLord of hosts:...
23 In that day, saith the Lord of hosts, will I take thee, O Zerubbabel, my servant, the son of Shealtiel, saith the Lord, and will make thee as a signet: for I have chosen thee, saith the Lord of hosts.

It is all Me, My love – all of it. I live in the midst of you. You feel My sorrow, My laughter too, and all the love I have for you. I Am Your Hunger And Your Thirst. I draw you closer in Me. You have entered the door inside of Me that has given you so much more. The place is safe in Me, My love, for you live on holy ground. I have given you My love, My Word, My power in My truth. You stand in Me, and I in you, for we are one indeed! Blessed be My Name for all eternity, for My bride has come to walk in Me and live in My great peace. I bless you there, My precious one, for you have come to know Me more. I honor you, My holy one who lets My rivers flow. Oh mighty one who flows in Me, My rivers run deeply in you. You have turned to Me, Your Only One, and I have responded to your plea. Oh precious one, My lamb, My bride, I take good care of you. I respond to you each time you ask, and give you so much more. There is no greater place to be than deep inside of Me. I smile upon your face so sweet and hold you tenderly.

February 1

1 Peter 2:4-5

[4] To whom coming, as unto a living stone, disallowed indeed of men, but chosen of God, and precious, [5] Ye also, as lively stones, are built up a spiritual house, an holy priesthood, to offer up spiritual sacrifices, acceptable to God by Jesus Christ.

Enjoy this day, beloved, for I am in this day. I whisper in your spirit the things you need to know. My Word is real and alive in you for you recognize My touch. You see My mighty right hand in every detail of your life. This pleases Me, oh precious one, for you know I am here with you. Enjoy the peace of My great love, I give you what you need. My revelation comes to you in surprises, holy one, I watch your delight as I unfold another surprise from Me to you. My Word has deeper meaning still, oh delight in its great richness. The mysteries unfold for you and teach you what you need. Oh the need for more of Me is created in your soul. You hunger for the deeper things, I give you your great hunger. I satisfy the depths of you with one piece at a time, and watch you relish in the moment, you delight Me, precious one! I long to show you who I Am, oh how I long to give you more. There is always more of Me, My love, I will always give you more. The level of Me in you has saturated you. Your mind, your heart, your soul, and strength, loves Me totally. Now the time has come, My love, to reveal to you some more, not to establish you in Me for that part is now done. This part takes you forward, beyond your thinking ways.

February 2

1 Peter 4:1-2

[4] Forasmuch then as Christ hath suffered for us in the flesh, arm yourselves likewise with the same mind: for he that hath suffered in the flesh hath ceased from sin; [2] That he no longer should live the rest of his time in the flesh to the lusts of men, but to the will of God.

Oh the power of My Word, how it heals, how it pours peace into your soul. My Word is sweet, eat it, My love. My Word satisfies the hunger in your soul. My favor is upon you. My Word has spoken it, for you are My obedient one and I have given you My promises. Oh drink from My fountains and drink from My wells, live in My river for it flows in you, My love. Never will you wither, never will you dry out, for My healing waters nourish you and replenish you always. The hungry and the thirsty are coming, blessed one, feed them of My pleasures, My Word has come upon you. Stand in Me, oh holy one, you know that I am here. How you please Me, precious one, stand in Me, My love. I pour My great strength in you, the battle is Mine only, stand in Me, My holy one, for I am here, and I have ended this dry season. Praise My Holy Name, My love, for I have come forth in this new season. I empower you, oh holy one, go forth inside My love. Oh vessel, My sweet vessel, how I have emptied you of things, the earthly things have vanished, and My new things have now entered. Oh glory to My Holy Name, for I have My chosen few! You fill yourself with Me, My love, and I have come to you. Your vessel overflows in Me, My beloved, holy one. I use you in My mighty ways. This new season has begun!

February 3

Isaiah 54:4-5

⁴ Fear not; for thou shalt not be ashamed: neither be thou confounded; for thou shalt not be put to shame: for thou shalt forget the shame of thy youth, and shalt not remember the reproach of thy widowhood any more. ⁵ For thy Maker is thine husband; the Lord of hosts is his name; and thy Redeemer the Holy One of Israel; The God of the whole earth shall he be called.

You are holy. You are pure. I cleanse you and keep you forever for I love you so. I know the things you suffer. I sent My Son to know, and live and breathe and feel, the mortal man in you. I know you do not know the things I have hidden deep in you. I know, My love, I know, you are still human wrapped in mortality. I reveal Myself in different ways and teach you about Me. I want to show you more of Me so I must separate you to see. The world cannot have your thoughts for I protect you closely. I hold you close in My secret place and tenderly speak to you. My chosen ones have much to do and need Me more and more. The time is short, oh precious one, I need you more and more. Dig deeper into My Word, My love, and keep your thoughts in Me. I balance you in Me alone, My scales are set for you. I do not share you with the world, I give assignments to you. You are My love, My holy one, set aside for only Me. Trust Me only, do not doubt, for I have plans for you. My plans include your times of rest as I replenish you in My strength. Oh love of Mine, do not forget My power rests in you. My love flows deeply within your soul and holds you closely in Me.

February 4

2 Corinthians 4:16-18

[16] For which cause we faint not; but though our outward man perish, yet the inward man is renewed day by day. [17] For our light affliction, which is but for a moment, worketh for us a far more exceeding and eternal weight of glory; [18] While we look not at the things which are seen, but at the things which are not seen: for the things which are seen are temporal; but the things which are not seen are eternal.

You have seen the detail of My favor, holy one. You have seen My mighty right hand delicately work in every situation to bring favor upon you. My favor rests on you and all you love, for you are holy and righteous before Me. I drink deeply from your love and open My heart to your every desire. It is My perfect will to give you all the desires of your heart for your desires are My desires. I love My precious people and I draw them into My love. Precious love of Mine, hear My passionate "Yes" to you, for I Am Your God who loves you so. I have stretched forth My mighty right hand across My heavens and spread out My table before you. I give you all of My blessings. Come, dine with Me and take all you want. I set before you life for any you choose. My heart trusts you, for I have given you My heart. My love flows and enriches all who come near you. My passionate love for you has no bounds. I give you authority in My Holy Name for you are Mine, chosen and set apart, to declare My love to the nations. My power, My love, My powerful love, washes hearts clean with My Word.

February 5

Matthew 5:13-16

[13] Ye are the salt of the earth: but if the salt have lost his savour, wherewith shall it be salted? it is thenceforth good for nothing, but to be cast out, and to be trodden under foot of men. [14] Ye are the light of the world. A city that is set on an hill cannot be hid. [15] Neither do men light a candle, and put it under a bushel, but on a candlestick; and it giveth light unto all that are in the house. [16] Let your light so shine before men, that they may see your good works, and glorify your Father which is in heaven.

I am here, My love. I am here. My presence will help you get through this day. I see your affliction and I know your thoughts. I see your determination. Keep pressing further and remember – I am here. You know Me, My love. I do not abandon you. Do not let this affliction stop you. Stay alert, holy one – stay alert. I have given you this duty, My love, you must press forward. One step at a time, My love, one step at a time. Do not be discouraged by the evil that abounds. The time is short, My love, the time is short. Remain in My love and keep your eyes on only Me. I am not a hard taskmaster if you remain in Me. You cannot do this without Me, My holy one. Do not look around you – ever. Keep your eyes on Me and the goal that I have set before you, and do not be overwhelmed, My love. I strengthen you with each step. Keep your songs of love to Me in your heart and know that I am here. You have My promise, holy one, I will not put more on you than you can stand. Keep moving deeper and deeper into Me and take your rest in My love.

February 6

1 John 3:22-24

[22] And whatsoever we ask, we receive of him, because we keep his commandments, and do those things that are pleasing in his sight. [23] And this is his commandment, That we should believe on the name of his Son Jesus Christ, and love one another, as he gave us commandment. [24] And he that keepeth his commandments dwelleth in him, and

he in him. And hereby we know that he abideth in us, by the Spirit which he hath given us.

You will see My hand upon you today, My love. It is the day of promise – it is the day of healing. The dawn has come and bursts through My eastern skies. Let your heart rejoice, for today is the day that I have made and set before you. Your strength is returning in this day and I have lifted you up into My great arms and strengthened you. Breathe deeply, for My healing has come. I have tested you, searched you, and cleansed you through and through. You know My voice, you know My power, and you trust Me completely in all you do. You know I Am Faithful and you know I Am True. I have spoken to you and shown you My ways that are set in the heavenlies for you to take. I will bring relief to those you love and I set the captives free. You have obeyed My voice, My holy one, and I have drawn you near to Me. You have My heart, My tender heart and you love My people so. Keep them close within your heart and pray for them, My love. The evil tries to keep them discouraged and beaten down. Remind them of My love for them and show them how I love them so.

February 7

Romans 8:18-21

¹⁸ For I reckon that the sufferings of this present time are not worthy to be compared with the glory which shall be revealed in us. ¹⁹ For the earnest expectation of the creature waiteth for the manifestation of the sons of God. ²⁰ For the creature was made subject to vanity, not willingly, but by reason of him who hath subjected the same in hope, ²¹ Because the creature itself also shall be delivered from the bondage of corruption into the glorious liberty of the children of God.

You have not sinned against Me. I would reveal it to you, holy one. Do not be discouraged in this fight, for I am on your side. I direct your every step, and sometimes you do not understand. My ways are higher than what you can know, that is why you must trust Me so. My plan is in My total control and your path has been set by Me alone. My timing is perfect, steadfast and sure – I will show you what to do. My hand is moving, mighty one, constantly churning the work to be done. Never doubt the constant in Me – forever working for My eternity. I have set you free, completely in Me, to show My dear people, how they have need of Me! I have broken the bonds that held you captive and taken you places where My people need Me. Your mind is a precious place I own. Meditate on My Word and let your mind roam on the goodness of Me and the splendor of My love. Your heart and soul belong to Me, for you have given them to Me. I give you your strength for each new day, remain in My Word and sing Me your song.

February 8

Judges 3:1-3

3 Now these are the nations which the Lord left, to prove Israel by them, even as many of Israel as had not known all the wars of Canaan; **²** Only that the generations of the children of Israel might know, to teach them war, at the least such as before knew nothing thereof; **³** Namely, five lords of the Philistines, and all the Canaanites, and the Sidonians, and the Hivites that dwelt in mount Lebanon, from mount Baalhermon unto the entering in of Hamath.

The times are evil, holy one, but I control it. I do not put more on you than you can stand. I watch you very carefully and I know the Spirit I have given you. I know your every need, My love, and I know your every desire. I know you walk by faith, and do not see My full plan. This is why I will break forth like the dawning of My new day for you, precious one. The new day has come, your soul sees the light. Your heart knows what I have spoken, and oh how I have spoken. My time of taking is over and My time of giving has come. You are My faithful one who has delighted My heart with your love. You have been refined to know My voice and you have seen the works of My mighty hand on you. Nothing can stop the flow of My hand, whether it takes or gives, the power is Mine. I do not allow things that would destroy your soul, only to strengthen and make you bold. You stand in My presence each step of the way, more sure of My presence with each new day.

February 9

Psalm 75:1-3

75 Unto thee, O God, do we give thanks, unto thee do we give thanks: for that thy name is near thy wondrous works declare. ² When I shall receive the congregation I will judge uprightly. ³ The earth and all the inhabitants thereof are dissolved: I bear up the pillars of it. Selah.

The attacks are constant, from every angle they come. You must stay protected in the fullness of Me. I show you the things that blind another and require you to pray and cry out to Me. I do not weary of you telling Me, I wait for your plea so I can answer you. Do not doubt My powerful love that opens the eyes so they can see. Hold tightly to My promises and remain in Me, for you cannot do this without Me. The tasks will not overtake you when you stay in Me, let Me guide you to bring My chosen unto Me. The evil is much and fights this way and that, oh but you know you are in combat. Stay alert and abound in the fullness of Me and walk each day in My victory. Keep your eyes on Me, My eternal things to see, and do not let the little things take hold of you. Do not be weary in the midst of the fight for I have My faithful ones upholding the fight. I hear the cries of My faithful and true who cry out for help and I rescue them. You are not alone in the battle, holy one, and you must always remember, the victory is won! The price has been paid to give you My peace, My joy overflowing as you live in Me. Love Me the most and love all the others. Pray for each other out of the depths of your love and you will see Me bring you the victory.

February 10

Isaiah 37:31-33

³¹ And the remnant that is escaped of the house of Judah shall again take root downward, and bear fruit upward: ³² For out of Jerusalem shall go forth a remnant, and they that escape out of mount Zion: the zeal of the Lord of hosts shall do this. ³³ Therefore thus saith the Lord concerning the king of Assyria, He shall not come into this city, nor

shoot an arrow there, nor come before it with shields, nor cast a bank against it.

My mercy flows, My mercy abounds in the lives of those you love. My love pours into them and My tenderness settles in their hearts. My love flows continually and never stagnates. My love washes and cleans, purifies and forgives, and draws My chosen ones back to Me. My peace flows for all who will receive. Let My joy flow abundantly from you as you sing praises to My Holy Name. I Am God, I Am Your God and I love you so. Praise My Holy Name for I created you to worship Me. Serve Me, serve only Me. Love Me, love only Me. Let My abundance flow in you, show them My love and great mercies too. Tell them, My love, what happens to you when you serve Me completely in humbleness too. I exalt the humble and I bring down the proud. My vessels must be emptied of earthly desires, for My eternal plan must dwell in their hearts. There is no other way to walk in victory but to die to yourself and walk humbly before Me. Then I can work and use you for Me, to bring back My chosen ones into Me eternally.

February 11

Psalm 71:19-21

[19] Thy righteousness also, O God, is very high, who hast done great things: O God, who is like unto thee! [20] Thou, which hast shewed me great and sore troubles, shalt quicken me again, and shalt bring me up again from the depths of the earth. [21] Thou shalt increase my greatness, and comfort me on every side.

My love will prevail for you, holy one. You have My Word, precious one, it will not return void, ever. You have My Holy Spirit, My power that lives in you – always. Let Me hear you sing, rest in Me, with your songs of love to Me. Fill My heart with your allegiance and praise My Holy Name. My love for you is deeper than the deepest seas. I take you into the depths of Me, for I am deeper still. My cleansing love has purified you to serve Me far beyond what you thought you could. There is no greater power in all of the earth than what I have placed inside of you. The Name of My Son, so holy and pure, has paid the great price to see you through. Shout for joy, for the price was so great, nothing can stop you when on Me you wait. Keep pressing on, for you have been called to battle with Me, for their souls I do long. I want them, My love, to enter Me into My great peace where they long to be. You are My light shining brightly for Me. Keep your oil burning for I am using you. I long for our times when we sit all alone and dine with each other and sing our love songs. You are My beauty I love to behold and I whisper to you which way you should go. You hear My soft voice, oh you know it well, for I have redeemed you for Me alone.

February 12

John 8:27-30

[27] They understood not that he spake to them of the Father. [28] Then said Jesus unto them, When ye have lifted up the Son of man, then shall ye know that I am he, and that I do nothing of myself; but as my Father hath taught me, I speak these things. [29] And he that sent me is with me: the Father hath not left me alone; for I do always those things that please him. [30] As he spake these words, many believed on him.

My people know My voice, precious one. I Am The Father of Truth and I reveal Myself to My people. My Spirit, My power is here at work among you, guiding and strengthening you all the days of your life. Hold on to My Truth and cling to Me, Your Rock, for I Am Steadfast and True. I show you each day the steps that you take and fill you with wisdom each step of the way. I Am The One who teaches you and holds you tightly all through the night. No darkness can touch you each day and each night for My brightness illumines each path that you take. You are My chosen one who is faithful and true, your obedience pleases Me and I smile upon you. I have placed you deeply in the midst of the storm to bring peace to the hurting and hope to the forlorn. Oh treasure of Mine, My heart you have captured and I trust you, My love, for you obey My commands. You know who I Am and you consult with Me before each step, for you represent Me. I can use you, My love, for My glory can shine in your vessel that is pure and sanctified. I give you My love and My blessing too, oh shine out in My love for I am using you.

February 13

2 Timothy 4:1-2

4 I charge thee therefore before God, and the Lord Jesus Christ, who shall judge the quick and the dead at his appearing and his kingdom; **2** Preach the word; be instant in season, out of season; reprove, rebuke, exhort with all long suffering and doctrine.

I replenish your soul daily, My holy one, and fill you in My love. My love pours deeply in the marrow and runs through your veins. Your thoughts are My thoughts and our hearts beat as one. My precious delight, I love you so. My grace and My mercy abound in you all the days of your life. You bring forth a smile upon My lips when you serve Me in love and steadfastness. I give you My strength, it is surrounding you, for many have walked and have stumbled too. But I hold you up in My mighty right hand and I say "No" to the evil one who wants you to weaken and weary and quit. You are My beloved who is devoted to Me. I Am Your One And Only and I am in love with you. Till death do us part is what they say, but with Me, My love, death cannot get in the way. I have pledged My love to you forever and ever throughout eternity that has no end. I am always beside you each step of the way. I never leave your side, I stand strong and alert beside you, My love. You live a life filled with victory, for you know all My promises I have given you. Come dance in My joy and let your heart be filled with song, for I Am Your Savior, Your Redeemer, Your Strongest One.

February 14

Matthew 11:28-30

28 Come unto me, all ye that labour and are heavy laden, and I will give you rest. **29** Take my yoke upon you, and learn of me; for I am meek and lowly in heart: and ye shall find rest unto your souls. **30** For my yoke is easy, and my burden is light.

My plan will prevail. Human frailties do not stop My plan. I have set forth My Word and it is fulfilled. There is no greater power than Mine, holy one. What I say is truth, for I Am Truth. My plan is not compromised, it is not delayed, it is effective in all that it is designed to be. My Word establishes all that is, all that was, and all that is to be. I Am Omnipotent, Your Holy Father, Creator Of All, and I, and only I, have control of everything. I direct your paths and I have set My plans for you from before the creation of the world. You are Mine, My chosen one, My beloved one, and I keep you and protect you all the days of your life. I have given you My heart, My only Son, My Word filled with promises, and all of My love. You are My precious one, My priceless treasure, My pleasure, and My bride. I take you to My holy mountain and fill you with My peace. I strengthen you in My holy place, My secret place, and I comfort you in My love. Never doubt My Holy Word, for I have promised you many things. Remain in Me each step of the way and take each blessing I have bestowed. I bless you in My loving favor and rest My hand on you. My peace runs deeply within your veins.

February 15

Hebrews 9:11-12

[11] But Christ being come an high priest of good things to come, by a greater and more perfect tabernacle, not made with hands, that is to say, not of this building; [12] Neither by the blood of goats and calves, but by his own blood he entered in once into the holy place, having obtained eternal redemption for us.

I wanted you to need Me, precious one. I created you to need Me. I wanted you to depend on Me for your every need, for I Am Your King. I have you in the palm of My hand and hold you closely all the days of your life. I Am Your Protector. I have given you My Name for I Am Your Redeemer. I have cleansed and purified you, My love, for I love your presence before Me. I have allowed you to come into My holy presence, for you are My righteous one. I have given you My heart of mercy, and you represent Me well, holy one. My plans require much of you, for I Am Much. My fullness flows in you and radiates My abundance for I love you so. Your heart is filled with compassion, for you have My heart. My heart beats one with you, My love, for we are one. Your gifts do not go unnoticed for they are gifts to Me. I love your gifts, My holy one, they are very precious to Me. I guide you every step of the way, hold tightly to My hand. I am in each place, I send you there and guide you every day. Keep your eyes on only Me each step in every day.

February 16

Genesis 32:26-28

²⁶ And he said, Let me go, for the day breaketh. And he said, I will not let thee go, except thou bless me. ²⁷ And he said unto him, What is thy name? And he said, Jacob. ²⁸ And he said, Thy name shall be called no more Jacob, but Israel: for as a prince hast thou power with God and with men, and hast prevailed.

I have given you My Word. You know where I stand. I do not compromise My holiness – ever. My love prevails – always. My way, in My time – forever and ever. My time is now to reconcile My people back to Me, My way, for I am returning to take My bride home to Me. Nothing can stop Me for My love presses on. No one can harm Me for I Am GOD, The Almighty One. None go before Me, none go after Me – none. I Am The Omnipotent One and the price has been paid. Holy one, stand back and watch your King, for I am here. I have listened and I have come to carry out My great and awesome plan. I come in power. I come swiftly and I come in My honor and My glory. I come filled with righteousness and love. All Powerful is My Name. Let Me hear your rejoicing for the victory is Mine and I come and take it. I will not be mocked, I will not be shamed – ever. My Kingdom reigns forever and ever. Angelic hosts sing praises to My Holy Name for all glory and honor and power are in My Holy Name. The heavens ring out their harmony in Me. I come to complete the harmony in all the earth, for it is Mine. I take what is Mine in gentle love, in quiet whispers, until My time has come.

February 17

1 Corinthians 2:7-10

⁷ But we speak the wisdom of God in a mystery, even the hidden wisdom, which God ordained before the world unto our glory: ⁸ Which none of the princes of this world knew: for had they known it, they would not have crucified the

Lord of glory. [9] But as it is written, Eye hath not seen, nor ear heard, neither have entered into the heart of man, the things which God hath prepared for them that love him. [10] But God hath revealed them unto us by his Spirit: for the Spirit searcheth all things, yea, the deep things of God.

I have set My path before you, My love, walk in it. I Am The Way, The Only Way, follow Me. Empty yourself before Me and let Me fill you with all of Me. Let My Spirit increase in you and show you My wonderful ways. I am not a hard taskmaster. I require obedience, My love. If you love Me, you will obey. Let My love abound in you and flow richly in the souls I send to you. Your strength will come from the joy I bring when you serve Me fully. Let My abundant life bless you as you walk in My ways, precious one. Walk in Me, My love, for there is no other way. Teach them My gentleness and kindness too for that is what I have called you to do. Never forget the reason I came, to save the lost and bring hope where there is none. It is My desire to help them, My love, and I have chosen you to be My feet and hands. I require this of you and to love them too, for only My love can see them through.

February 18

Psalm 34:7-10, 15, 17

[7] The angel of the Lord encampeth round about them that fear him, and delivereth them. [8] O taste and see that the Lord is good: blessed is the man that trusteth in him. [9] O fear the Lord, ye his saints: for there is no want to them that fear him. [10] The young lions do lack, and suffer hunger: but they that seek the Lord shall not want any good thing…
[15] The eyes of the Lord are upon the righteous, and his ears are open unto their cry…
[17] The righteous cry, and the Lord heareth, and delivereth them out of all their troubles.

You will speak of My love everywhere I send you. I want them to know of My great and awesome love. I pour My love into you, pour My love into them. I am rich in mercy and I am rich in grace. My favor abounds in My obedient ones. My great peace settles them for they love Me so. I trust you with them, the closest to My heart, for I have equipped you, and tested you, and trained you for the journey, holy one. I set you apart and call you by name and hold tightly to you in the pouring rain. My rains are now pouring for all to see, I cherish the ones who serve only Me. I Am All You Need, no matter the cost, cling tightly to Me and bring Me My lost. I fill your mind with My Holy Word and you walk in My love with My peace from above. You are devoted to Me, no matter the cost, and cry out to Me for the souls who are lost. I gave you your heart, so tender and true, and I honor your love for I Am Faithful to you. I paid a great price to redeem you to Me.

February 19

Psalm 74:12-17

[12] For God is my King of old, working salvation in the midst of the earth. [13] Thou didst divide the sea by thy strength: thou brakest the heads of the dragons in the waters. [14] Thou brakest the heads of leviathan in pieces, and gavest him to be meat to the people inhabiting the wilderness. [15] Thou didst cleave the fountain and the flood: thou driedst up mighty rivers. [16] The day is thine, the night also is thine: thou hast prepared the light and the sun. [17] Thou hast set all the borders of the earth: thou hast made summer and winter.

My Holy Spirit lives in you and breathes in you and prays for you, My love. I do not leave you unattended to fight this battle. I have My mightiest ones in this battle, holy one. The rivers run deep and My process does not fail. I show you My ways for you seek Me. I give you what you need to know when you need to know it. I have never failed you, My love. I will never fail you. I do not fail – ever. Trust in Me for I am here, guiding all things, in all ways, at all times. You are pure and righteous before Me and I honor you. I Am Your King and I Am The King of All Kings – forever and ever. My plans for you are for good and not for harm. I never take My watchful eye off of you. I am very attentive to your every need, My love, for you are very dear to My heart. I hold you close and closer still, for you are Mine and Mine alone. My holy blood paid the price for you and I have redeemed you to Me.

February 20

Zechariah 2:3-5, 13

³ And, behold, the angel that talked with me went forth, and another angel went out to meet him, ⁴ And said unto him, Run, speak to this young man, saying, Jerusalem shall be inhabited as towns without walls for the multitude of men and cattle therein: ⁵ For I, saith the Lord, will be unto her a wall of fire round about, and will be the glory in the midst of her...
¹³ Be silent, O all flesh, before the Lord: for he is raised up out of his holy habitation.

I have deposited My rivers in you, My love. You flow in My power and My great peace. The storms are stilled as My rivers flow. The power of My love is active in My flowing rivers. There is none in all the earth that can stop the flow of Me in you, for you obey My voice. You know Me, My holy love, and you have seen what I can do. Go forth, My precious one, for you honor My Holy Name in all that you do. You are the apple of My eye, chosen to represent My love. I Am Your Refreshing Drink in a dry, parched land. I bring healing in My wings and comfort you there. I cleanse you and wash you each day in My love and refresh your spirit along the way. I have chosen you to represent Me and I take you into the deeper places in Me. I speak to you gently and whisper your name and I call you forth and I teach you My ways. Wherever I send you, you feel at home, for I am in you and I Am Your Home. I have scattered My people to go to My lost and show them My love, no matter the cost.

February 21

Psalm 104:27-30

²⁷ These wait all upon thee; that thou mayest give them their meat in due season. ²⁸ That thou givest them they gather: thou openest thine hand, they are filled with good.
²⁹ Thou hidest thy face, they are troubled: thou takest away their breath, they die, and return to their dust. ³⁰ Thou

sendest forth thy spirit, they are created: and thou renewest the face of the earth.

I am doing many things, holy one, for you are My obedient one. I send you to them and I reveal My will to your heart. My people are hurting, precious one, pray earnestly for My precious ones, for they are very dear to My heart. My angels work among you, side by side, for My Kingdom reigns in the eternal realm. My power is great and I distribute it among many. You are My worker, My chosen one who represents Me, at all times, in all ways. It is harvest time, My love, it is harvest time. Busy are the hands of those who love Me so. I give you rest on your journey from the load you carry, for I Am Your Tender God who loves you with My compassionate heart. You know My love is true for I Am Faithful in all I do. Remember My promise to you, precious one, I will not put more on you than you can stand. I have strengthened you for much, mighty warrior, and I smile upon your face, for you please Me so. I created you for Me long before you knew, and I placed My special heart deep inside of you. You come forth like a lion yet gentle as a lamb, for My Holy Spirit lives in you and brings back to Me what is Mine – for I Am The Great I AM.

February 22

Daniel 2:19-22

[19] Then was the secret revealed unto Daniel in a night vision. Then Daniel blessed the God of heaven. [20] Daniel answered and said, Blessed be the name of God for ever and ever: for wisdom and might are his: [21] And he changeth the times and the seasons: he removeth kings, and setteth up kings: he giveth wisdom unto the wise, and knowledge to them that know understanding: [22] He revealeth the deep and secret things: he knoweth what is in the darkness, and the light dwelleth with him.

When you run to Me, My love, I run faster to you. When you seek My face, I take you deeper still. When you reach for Me, I take your hand and hold you tightly. I am found by you, holy one, you know My touch, you know My Name, you hear My voice, My friend. I walk in you so rich and free, oh what a blessing you are to Me. I take you in and fill you full of

41

Me and send you out to those you see. Run back to Me, My precious love, and let Me give you more from the depths of Me. I have called you My bride, My helpmate to Me, I chose you to be by My side, eternally. Come, dance in My love, drink deeply of Me for you are My beloved and I honor you. From your mouth, speak My Word, speak My Name all day long, let My power flow out to My hurting ones. There are many, My love, who cannot find Me, oh show them, My love, how to come to Me. I give you My power for strength for this day, delight in My love, I'll show you the way. The time has approached for the entire world to see My love shining forth inside of you.

February 23

Romans 13:10-12

¹⁰ Love worketh no ill to his neighbour: therefore love is the fulfilling of the law. ¹¹ And that, knowing the time, that now it is high time to awake out of sleep: for now is our salvation nearer than when we believed. ¹² The night is far spent, the day is at hand: let us therefore cast off the works of darkness, and let us put on the armour of light.

Some love the world more than Me, precious one. Some love themselves more than Me, My love. Some love their children more than Me, holy one. But there are some, My love, yes there are some, who love Me most of all. You are not alone in this fight you see. I have shown you My angel working beside of you. My love does not stop and never does it rest, for I am gathering My lost and hurting ones home to Me. I give you My love for each new day and send you My loved ones to encourage you along the way. Keep fast to My promises, each and every one, for they are yours, My love, My tender one. I walk beside you each step of the way and I control all things in every day. I use you, My love, in various ways and I protect you from those along the way. I keep you humble and tender in Me, and hide certain things that is not good for you. You can trust Me completely in all that you do, for you know My holy presence is surrounding you. You are precious to Me, so close to My heart, I'll love you forever, I'll never depart. Delight yourself in My holiness, for pure is your heart and I love your sweet presence. I delight Myself in all you are, My creation, My love, My beautiful bride.

February 24

1 John 4:11, 16-17

11 Beloved, if God so loved us, we ought also to love one another…

16 And we have known and believed the love that God hath to us. God is love; and he that dwelleth in love dwelleth in God, and God in him. **17** Herein is our love made perfect, that we may have boldness in the day of judgment: because as he is, so are we in this world.

I have heard your cry to look through the eyes of the hurting ones who pass you by. Tell them I love them as much as the rest, and I dispatch all of My workers to bring them to Me. I heal the sick and bring comfort to those who especially have need of Me. Tell them I love them as much as the rest for they are the closest inside of My heart. Tell them I mend their broken heart and I give them My love, never to depart. Tell them I hold them tightly to Me and I protect them and care for their every need. Tell them I died many years ago to set them free from their lives of woe. Tell them I hear every word they speak and I run to them when they call out to Me. Tell them about the peace I bring and the hope for the future of eternity with Me. Tell them I created them to worship Me for I love to hear them sing praises to Me. Tell them I smile when they whisper My Name and I smile when I whisper their precious name. Tell them I gave them all I own and I never regret the love I have. Tell them I teach them along the way and show them My love in various ways.

February 25

Isaiah 49:10-12

10 They shall not hunger nor thirst; neither shall the heat nor sun smite them: for he that hath mercy on them shall lead them, even by the springs of water shall he guide them. **11** And I will make all my mountains a way, and my highways shall be exalted. **12** Behold, these shall come from far: and, lo, these from the north and from the west; and these from the land of Sinim.

I lift up your head and restore you to Me for I Am Your Savior who satisfies you. I give you My presence each step of the way for I delight in your love with each new day. I have magnetized you to Me, for I draw you nearer and nearer for you to see. I love you completely and saturate you in My holy presence and power too. Hold tightly to Me, do not look at another, I show you My love in various ways. You recognize Me in many of them, oh but I still have My mystery hidden. I delight Myself in giving you more for I love to surprise you with My gifts galore. I Am Your Wonderful King who never forgets My promises to you of greater things. Your loyalty brings honor to My Holy Name and I will reward you in My holy ways. I love you, My treasure, I do not forget for I Am Your Master who trusts you so. Listen to My Words for I am whispering to you. You need not worry, I am taking good care of you. Breathe deeply from Me, for I am here filling your soul with all of Me. I have moved mountains for only you. I crush each one with My little finger and walk forward with you in My holy splendor. Delight yourself in all of Me for I am strong on your behalf.

February 26

Genesis 41:39-42

³⁹ And Pharaoh said unto Joseph, Forasmuch as God hath shewed thee all this, there is none so discreet and wise as thou art: ⁴⁰ Thou shalt be over my house, and according unto thy word shall all my people be ruled: only in the throne will I be greater than thou. ⁴¹ And Pharaoh said unto Joseph, See, I have set thee over all the land of Egypt. ⁴² And Pharaoh took off his ring from his hand, and put it upon Joseph's hand, and arrayed him in vestures of fine linen, and put a gold chain about his neck;

There is no end to My rivers of love, holy one. I will satisfy you with wonders and awe all the days of your life. I love to show you My tender, sweet ways. I love to show you My almighty power and work among you. It is My pleasure, My great pleasure, to reveal Myself to you, in My way, in My appointed times. I encourage you with My loving reminders along the way. I am here, I am with you, I am in love with you, and I take good care of you, forever and ever. I smile as I touch your sweet, holy face, and I draw you into Me, deeper still. I hear you when you pray, My love, and I answer each precious prayer. I have drawn your heart into one with Mine and given you My desires, My worker, My friend, My precious one. I see your loyal heart. I bless you, My love, in all you do, for your love has touched My tender heart. My blessings rain down in abundance, My love, for you are obedient in all you do. I stand strong in you and walk beside you each day, for I am coming soon, it will not be long.

February 27

1 Kings 22:19-21

¹⁹ And he said, Hear thou therefore the word of the Lord: I saw the Lord sitting on his throne, and all the host of heaven standing by him on his right hand and on his left. ²⁰ And the Lord said, Who shall persuade Ahab, that he may go up and fall at Ramothgilead? And one said on this manner, and another said on that manner. ²¹ And there came forth a spirit, and stood before the Lord, and said, I will persuade him.

I took you back to the piercing of My heart that day to remind you, My people are suffering today. The pain was so strong, it weakened you, but I strengthen you back to where you were. Rejection is painful, no matter the loss, it lashes and whips from the depths of the heart. The hurricane winds hit all in its path, protect yourself, My love, from its great destructive path. Remember Me and keep full in My armor and never forget, I walk beside you. They will come to you from many different places and try to corrupt you, My holy living vessel. I will protect you fully as you remain in Me and seek Me consistently in all you do. I will guide you and teach you with every new thing and tell you I love you continually. I have secured you to Me all the days of your life. Do not worry, My love, I have paid the great price. There is no one greater in all the world, and I live inside of you. Go forth in My Name, in all the power it brings, and tell them I love them eternally. My mighty ones are sent to surround you and protect you in Me.

February 28

Hebrews 10:19-22

[19] Having therefore, brethren, boldness to enter into the holiest by the blood of Jesus, [20] By a new and living way, which he hath consecrated for us, through the veil, that is to say, his flesh; [21] And having an high priest over the house of God; [22] Let us draw near with a true heart in full assurance of faith, having our hearts sprinkled from an evil conscience, and our bodies washed with pure water.

I have allowed you to feel the pain in My life. But I have protected you all the days of your life. My pain comes from love of the deepest kind and it rips and it tears and it heals and it mends. Go forth in My Name and pray for each one for the ravages of sin have left holes in each heart. The heart is designed to be filled with Me and My love, to heal and to mend with My tender touch. You are a lamb among wolves, that is planned by Me so My glory and honor will come forth in you. My mighty right hand is on all you do. I'll speak through you, do not worry. I am in all things, doing much you do not see, for that is My plan at work among you. Never give up, the fight is worth every cost, for My loved ones are perishing and feeling My loss. They cry out to Me from the darkest of places and I hear every one and I send you to them. I let your heart see what is important to Me and I teach you My ways to follow Me. Let your voice go public on behalf of Me and tell them I love them and they can come to Me. I love them all and I have a reminder of My love for them in the palm of My hand. Tell them I am greater than all they see.

February 29 Leap Year!

Luke 22:1-6

22 Now the feast of unleavened bread drew nigh, which is called the Passover. ² And the chief priests and scribes sought how they might kill him; for they feared the people.

³ Then entered Satan into Judas surnamed Iscariot, being of the number of the twelve. ⁴ And he went his way, and communed with the chief priests and captains, how he might betray him unto them. ⁵ And they were glad, and covenanted to give him money. ⁶ And he promised, and sought opportunity to betray him unto them in the absence of the multitude.

The thief has been found out, love of Mine, for I have revealed this thing to you. I give to you the inheritance that is allotted to you, My love. This is not a hard thing for Me! I am in this manifestation, holy one. Receive My greater things, My awesome things, for My angels are among you doing My good and perfect work. I am seen by you, oh glory to My Name, I am seen by you. I love you, My bride, My beautiful one. Come, dance with Me on this higher plane. I am in you, My love. Enjoy the depths of Me, for you are in Me. I never stop thinking about you. My plans are unfolding, the season has come, the full circle is complete, come higher and higher. Be gone insignificant things, be gone! My beloved has come to My fountain and taken the deeper drink. Rejoice, rejoice, for it is harvest time!

March 1

Psalm 105:42-45

[42] For he remembered his holy promise, and Abraham his servant. [43] And he brought forth his people with joy, and his chosen with gladness: [44] And gave them the lands of the heathen: and they inherited the labour of the people; [45] That they might observe his statutes, and keep his laws. Praise ye the Lord.

Settle into Me, My love. Breathe deeply from the aroma of My sweet presence. I am in the midst of you – you walk on holy ground. Let My holiness fill you, saturate yourself in My love. I Am Your Tender God who loves you so. Drink from My rivers of bounty and feel My cool breeze refresh you on your journey. Come, let Me hold you in the warmth of My embrace. Lift high your head to worship Me and feel our hearts, they beat as one. You comfort Me in your warm embrace when you pray for one another. I hear your plea to comfort them and My heart is lifted up. I set before you life and death and your choice has thrilled My heart. Come walk in Me much deeper still for I am ready to take you higher. I trust you, holy love of Mine. I take you to My lost and tell you what to say to them in love and wisdom too. My anointing rests upon your head as I speak My words to you. Never fear, rest your love in Me for I am closer than you know. You have seen and you will know, I never abandon you. You are My precious treasure I have called My very own. I have searched your tender heart and washed you clean in Me. You are purified to do this service unto Me. Take hold of My hand and follow Me, you are on the right path I have set for you.

March 2

1 Corinthians 15:46-49

[46] Howbeit that was not first which is spiritual, but that which is natural; and afterward that which is spiritual. [47] The first man is of the earth, earthy; the second man is the Lord from heaven. [48] As is the earthy, such are they also that are earthy: and as is the heavenly, such are they also that are

heavenly. [49] And as we have borne the image of the earthy, we shall also bear the image of the heavenly.

A treasure is buried. Sometimes it is buried deeper than others. I unfold the mystery in you, My buried treasure. I dig deep – deeper than you want and I purify the scars and I wash them clean. You come forth with a shine from the inside out with all the delights of a fresh spirit and a brand new start. You have My glow set upon your face and you resemble Me more and more – Your Father Of Mercy And Grace. I knew you, My treasure, before the crust came on and I determined to come and rescue you. I have set you free, but you still do not know, all of the things I have stored up for you. I Am Your God, full of mystery and pleasure, and I lead you in ways to help you discover. I delight Myself in watching you grow into the knowledge of Me for I love you so. Oh treasure of Mine, buried deep from within, I gather you up and redeem you to Me. I set you apart for a little while and I clean you up gently and carefully, so you don't break from it all. I mold you and shape you with My loving embrace, and I step back and look upon you with a smile on My face.

March 3

John 17:20-22

[20] Neither pray I for these alone, but for them also which shall believe on me through their word; [21] That they all may be one; as thou, Father, art in me, and I in thee, that they also may be one in us: that the world may believe that thou hast sent me. [22] And the glory which thou gavest me I have given them; that they may be one, even as we are one:

My holy blood runs through your veins, for you are My beloved and you walk in My Name. I have given you a family, I have united you into My family, for you belong to Me. The gifts flow in My family, and they teach and correct gently, then love you endlessly, and fight the good fight with you. Beloved one, I have designed you for My holy purpose, and I have set you apart for My Kingdom plan. I have given you a family, a unity of power in My loving Name to help you along your journey. Pray for them, My love, for they need Me. They pray for you, My love, for you need Me. This is My design, My holiness works among My members, and stands united with Me to fight the good fight. Do not feel abandoned, for you are not abandoned. You have My promise, I never leave you nor forsake you. You know Me, My love, for My blood runs through you and My holy family stands. Sing out your praises to Me, for I do mighty things in all the world! Rejoice in My presence for I show Myself mighty on your behalf. I Am Your Father and I have given you My Name, with My honor and glory forever and ever. I rest My love on you. I give you great and mighty things.

March 4

Deuteronomy 32:1-4

32 Give ear, O ye heavens, and I will speak; and hear, O earth, the words of my mouth. ² My doctrine shall drop as the rain, my speech shall distil as the dew, as the small rain upon the tender herb, and as the showers upon the grass: ³ Because I will publish the name of the Lord: ascribe ye greatness unto our God. ⁴ He is the Rock, his work is perfect: for all his ways are judgment: a God of truth and without iniquity, just and right is he.

Know yourself in Me, holy one. When you know who you are in Me, you can bless others. Jacob, My Israel, knew who he was in Me when he blessed Pharaoh that day long ago. You are Mine, you represent Me, I have given you My mighty right hand of blessings, for you have chosen life. Bring life to My hurting ones, teach them, show them, love them into Me. Bless them in My Name, for you have My power and you have My blessings. I have prepared you to step out and bless others, My beloved. The times are evil and My power is much. Do not delay for My power burns inside of you, go help My hurting ones. I have given you My tender touch, My grace beyond measure and My mercy overflowing. Set forth to speak My blessings upon My people and bring them back to Me. My love rests in you. My love trusts in you. My love beats one in you. Love My people, tell them they can trust Me, tell them of My harmony, the rhythm of My peace. I love you in times of loss, I love you in times of plenty, and I love you in-between. I give you My heart, I give you My Name, I give you My blessings in My abundant rains.

March 5

Daniel 2:48-49

⁴⁸ Then the king made Daniel a great man, and gave him many great gifts, and made him ruler over the whole province of Babylon, and chief of the governors over all the wise men of Babylon. ⁴⁹ Then Daniel requested of the king, and he set Shadrach, Meshach, and Abednego, over the affairs of the province of Babylon: but Daniel sat in the gate of the king.

Come, rest your mind in Me. Come, let My love wash you in peace. I love you, precious one, rest awhile, for I give you rest. Strengthen yourself in My love, for I am here. Do not be discouraged, love of Mine, for I use you in mighty ways and I keep you humble before Me. You have My heart, My humble heart, and My tender ways. I require you to speak out boldly from your heart filled with love. My people are perishing, My treasures are hidden, there are so many, there are so many. Speak of My love, you who walk in My fullness. Show mercy on My people and show them My love. When you love another, you love Me. I Am God, The Almighty One and I call Myself the God of Abraham, Isaac, and Jacob. I Am Your God, I call Myself Your God for you are Mine and I send you out to bring My people back to Me. My Spirit lives in you, My Spirit breathes in you, for I have given you life, you know what I require of you for I have spoken. You are My creation and I have called you forth for such a time as this. Position yourself and stand strong. I am moving you into a larger place for My time is now.

March 6

2 Timothy 3:16-17

¹⁶ All scripture is given by inspiration of God, and is profitable for doctrine, for reproof, for correction, for instruction in righteousness: ¹⁷ That the man of God may be perfect, thoroughly furnished unto all good works.

I show Myself strong in your weakness. I Am Your Mighty God who is strong on your behalf. I swirl My mighty protection about you and keep you alert. The evil prowls about seeking to find a way, but I warn you and you obey. You are protected by your obedience and you are My mighty one, for you are loyal to Me and obedient to My commands. No harm can touch you, My love. No harm can touch the ones you love, for I have come forth strong for you. I protect the minds of My children until they are strong. I do not leave My young unattended, precious one. You are on good soil, holy one, your roots run deeply in the richness of Me. I Am Your Protector and I guard your walls. I never sleep, I never slumber, I watch you with My jealous eye. You are Mine. You belong to Me. I paid the price and it is done. There is no weapon – none – that can stand against you, for I AM. Creation from My heart, I love you with My passion, I love you with My actions, I love you. My mighty river runs, flowing in and out, for My people need Me, precious one. Eternity waits and sits nearby in the hearts of all creation. My design is not temporary – ever. There is no end. I Am The Alpha And Omega – The Beginning And The End – and I give eternity that has no end. Never forget the souls at stake.

March 7

Nehemiah 4:13-14

[13] Therefore set I in the lower places behind the wall, and on the higher places, I even set the people after their families with their swords, their spears, and their bows. [14] And I looked, and rose up, and said unto the nobles, and to the rulers, and to the rest of the people, Be not ye afraid of them: remember the Lord, which is great and terrible, and fight for your brethren, your sons, and your daughters, your wives, and your houses.

You breathe in Me, you see in Me, you hear in Me, for I have taken all of you into the depths of Me. I enclose you in My love, I embrace you in My love for I Am Love. My heart beats in you, My blood flows in you, salt of My earth. Drink from My rivers, eat from My table for I have My banner over you. I bless you, My precious one, I reveal Myself to you, My holy one, and I walk among you for you obey Me. My feet, My hands, My temple, My vessel, I fill you in My fullness and I honor you, My faithful one, I honor you, precious love of Mine. You sit at My feet and bring glory and honor to My Holy Name. I bless you in My rich sweet ways, with My tenderness of touch, for you have captured My heart. I Am Your God who loves you so. I mend the broken through you, I touch the deepest needs, for I have heard your cries. Your heart is true and your mind is pure for I keep you closely in Me. You will not depart from My ways, for you cling to Me, Your Solid Rock. The canker worm withers under the power of My touch. I touch them through you, My chosen one, My beloved.

March 8

Ephesians 1:3-4

³ Blessed be the God and Father of our Lord Jesus Christ, who hath blessed us with all spiritual blessings in heavenly places in Christ: ⁴ According as he hath chosen us in him before the foundation of the world, that we should be holy and without blame before him in love:

I speak to you from My most tender place, holy one. I speak to you from the depths of My love. I am pleased with your love and I satisfy Myself in the pleasure of you. You are My tender one whose roots grow deeply inside of Me. No storm will ravage you, for you put your trust in Me. I Am Your Mighty Fortress and I stand strong on your behalf. You are My beloved and I Am Your Tower of Strength. KING of Kings and LORD of Lords is My Name. No forces that come against you can stand – for I am here and I never leave your side. Blessed are you in My eyes. I have called you holy, set apart for Me and My Kingdom. You encourage My heart and bring gladness to My soul. As the days grow shorter, your beauty shines brighter. Oh that My people would draw near to Me! I search for the hearts that do not exalt another. I search for the hearts that love Me and walk in My ways. I bless My obedient ones and I honor them for they bring Me such pleasure. Work in My fields, bring My people back to Me. Tell them I love them, holy one – show them My love. Tell them My love endures forever and it has no end. I have given you My heart, I have given you My gifts, I have given you My body, I have given you My Name, I have given you the tools, go work in My fields for My time is near. Go in My blessings and all of My love.

53

March 9

1 John 2:3-5

³ And hereby we do know that we know him, if we keep his commandments. ⁴ He that saith, I know him, and keepeth not his commandments, is a liar, and the truth is not in him. ⁵ But whoso keepeth his word, in him verily is the love of God perfected: hereby know we that we are in him.

Lift up your head and receive from Me, Your Mighty One who loves you so. Lift high your head and praise Me, Your Faithful and True. Rise up and stand strong for I have done great and awesome things in My love for you. No power can stand against you – no weapon formed against you can stand. I alert you to the weapons and I keep you on your guard. I Am Your God who fights for you and teaches you many things along the way. You obey Me, precious one, My how you obey Me so. You refresh Me in your obedience and I love your songs of praise. I have come forth on your behalf for you have shown Me your love. I know your heart, I know your mind, I search you and keep you pure and righteous before Me. You have My heart, you have My mind, you have My blessings – every one. I adore you, My love, My tender flower. Your radiance fills My field as you encourage the ones who are weary. Teach them My joy, show them My strength is in the joy. I Am God, I never fail them or abandon them – ever. I am close to the brokenhearted, closer than they know. Walk in My glory, walk in My honor, for I have given you My Name and I trust you with My Name. My power lives in you, and My Holy Spirit hovers over you.

March 10

Deuteronomy 28:12-13

¹² The Lord shall open unto thee his good treasure, the heaven to give the rain unto thy land in his season, and to bless all the work of thine hand: and thou shalt lend unto many nations, and thou shalt not borrow. ¹³ And the Lord shall make thee the head, and not the tail; and thou shalt be above only, and thou shalt not be beneath; if that thou hearken unto the commandments of the Lord thy God, which I command thee this day, to observe and to do them:

I Am The God of Generations. I Am The God of Abraham, Isaac, and Jacob. I give blessings for generations and I give curses for generations. Here My voice those who love My Name. I have given you the power in My love to bind the demons of generations. I have given you the authority in My Name to choose blessings for generations. Listen to you, search your heart, do you see beyond your now? Now is the time to set your house in order for generations to come. I Am The God of Today, Yesterday, and Forever. Your life brings blessings or curses for generations. Listen to Me, do you know who I Am? I Am Your God who listens to you. Cast down your imaginations, do not exalt another above Me. I do not compromise – ever. Let the generations see the sins of their fathers. Unite in the power of My love, unite together family of Mine and break forth in blessings, not curses, for generations to come. Cast down the evil that so easily besets you. I have given you My Name. Take back what I have given you. I Am Your Father, The God of Abraham, Isaac, and Jacob.

March 11

Psalm 18:16-19

[16] He sent from above, he took me, he drew me out of many waters. [17] He delivered me from my strong enemy, and from them which hated me: for they were too strong for me. [18] They prevented me in the day of my calamity: but the Lord was my stay. [19] He brought me forth also into a large place; he delivered me, because he delighted in me.

The time has come for revelation of more of Me, holy one. You see Me clearer everyday. The fog is lifting and My power is revealed. I stretch forth My mighty right hand on your behalf, My love. I hear your cries for another and I heal you when you pray. I open My heart to you and reveal Myself to you. You know My tender mercies and you know My gentle ways. I see your thankful heart as you enter My gates of praise. Beloved, it is with joy I answer you. Speak of My great love and let your hearts be filled with joy. Mighty Am I when I come forth on your behalf. My presence lives in the blessings of obedience. The lonely will know that they are not alone. The wounds that lie so deeply are mended with My touch. Your beauty bursts forth like the dawn when you speak of My love. I heal the hurts, I mend the wounds, I set the captives free – for I abound in all you say and do. My peace runs through you and My joy floods your soul.

Fill yourself with all of Me, drink deeply from My well. I have enough to go around for every dry and parched land. My waters run freely in every way when you stop to listen and then you obey. My beauty runs through you and shines from within to brighten the path when the way seems too dim.

March 12

Matthew 7:24-25

[24] Therefore whosoever heareth these sayings of mine, and doeth them, I will liken him unto a wise man, which built his house upon a rock: [25] And the rain descended, and the floods came, and the winds blew, and beat upon that house; and it fell not: for it was founded upon a rock.

My holiness touched you with the pureness of My peace. My love pours into every place I send it. I Am Love and only I bring peace and joy from the depths of Me into you. My creation is designed to love My touch. My creation responds to My touch. I Am All Powerful and I can restore or destroy with one touch. I have restored you to Me, holy one, and I have set My righteousness upon you. The desire of your heart is for Me because I want you. My desire is for you, My treasure, My bride. I love you in My holiness and I wrap you in My love. You are surrounded by My power and you are protected in My fierce love for you. I Am Your Almighty God who has chosen you to be with Me. I take you to My place where no harm can touch you. My love resonates in you and My power is upon you as you live in My Word and love Me completely. Oh the joy you have given Me – I bless you in every way. My obedient one, I bless you My faithful servant, for your heart is faithful to Me. I give you strength to remain faithful and I forgive you of your sins. I see your repentant heart and I unfold your beauty that is within. I do not condemn you, I bless you. I do not keep a record of wrongs, I forgive you. My love is pure, My love is true, My love is faithful and I give you My love. Come, rejoice in our love for now is the time of rejoicing.

March 13

Hebrews 10:19-22

[19] Having therefore, brethren, boldness to enter into the holiest by the blood of Jesus, [20] By a new and living way, which he hath consecrated for us, through the veil, that is to say, his flesh; [21] And having an high priest over the house of God; [22] Let us draw near with a true heart in full assurance of faith, having our hearts sprinkled from an evil conscience, and our bodies washed with pure water.

I protect you completely, My love. I tenderly guide you in the paths of greater good. You know the beat of My heart, you know the direction to follow, for My presence goes with you. I Am Gentle and Kind on your behalf and I have redeemed you unto Me. No lie set before you will stand, for I stand in your midst and I defend you. Let all of heaven and earth hear My voice, I declare My love for you forever, My beloved, My bride. You want this mountain removed? Ask Me, My love, and it is gone. The mountains crumble into the sea at My command. You want your children to walk in Me? Ask Me, My love and I will give you a thousand generations, for you are Mine and I Am Yours. My covenant is with you, every promise is sure, for I Am Your Faithful God who does not lie. You know My mighty love for you, My Spirit lives in you. Fight with love, this battle will be won no other way, for love is the key to walking in victory. I know your frailties; I have allowed each one, to show Myself strong on your behalf. My glory abounds in all you do, and My love overflows in the midst of you.

March 14

Romans 3:22-24

[22] Even the righteousness of God which is by faith of Jesus Christ unto all and upon all them that believe: for there is no difference: [23] For all have sinned, and come short of the glory of God; [24] Being justified freely by his grace through the redemption that is in Christ Jesus:

My power lives in you, mighty warrior. I have chosen you to come in My Name and walk in My ways. I have given you My authority, representative of Mine. Do not walk in defeat – I Am Not Defeated. Be encouraged by My Word, let My love fill you with My power. Stand firm in Me and watch Me fight for you. There is no name greater than My Name. Lift high your head as you shout your victory song, and praise My Holy Name. No weapon formed against you will stand. You are the head and not the tail. You are Mine and I Am Yours – forever and ever. My wings shelter you, My armor protects you, My love empowers you, My Holy Spirit lives in you. Grab hold of My promises. Cling to every one, for they are yours. Take them. You have My strength for I have given it to you – use it. Cast down all strongholds – they are demolished in My Name. I Am Truth and I stand strong on your behalf. Hold to what I have said and do not let go – ever. Grasp My Word and speak in its power for it will not return void. You know Me, you are from My Kingdom and you are in My plans.

March 15

Hosea 11:8-9

8 How shall I give thee up, Ephraim? how shall I deliver thee, Israel? how shall I make thee as Admah? how shall I set thee as Zeboim? mine heart is turned within me, my repentings are kindled together. 9 I will not execute the fierceness of mine anger, I will not return to destroy Ephraim: for I am God, and not man; the Holy One in the midst of thee: and I will not enter into the city.

You have captured My heart, My beautiful one – for you have seen My ways and you honor Me. I honor you in the assembly for you have been given wisdom from above. My love has entered your heart and drawn you close to Me. I sing over you, My love, and you live in My peace. Your faith has been tested in every way, and you have grown deeper in Me each day. I have taken you to the depths of your fears and healed you, My love, in all the deep places. I nurture you and sustain you in Me, and teach you of pleasures you have never seen. I Am Your Delight, Your Greatest of Treasures, and I have captured your heart with My tender touches. My power protects you each day and each night, for My love for you will never depart. I took you through things you did not understand, but you leaned closer to Me and you took My hand. You please Me, My love, in every way and I smile upon you as I walk with you. I show you My ways to see you through. You do not doubt Me, you know Me by name, you feel My touch when you call out My Name. I hear you, My love, from the depths of Me, and I come forth for you in every way. I sing and rejoice, for you have seen My love, and accepted My offer to serve Me in love.

March 16

1 Corinthians 15:37-38

³⁷ And that which thou sowest, thou sowest not that body that shall be, but bare grain, it may chance of wheat, or of some other grain: ³⁸ But God giveth it a body as it hath pleased him, and to every seed his own body.

Blessed are you I call holy. Honored are you, My love, for I Am Your Beloved. I go before you and pave the way of righteousness and justice I have designed just for you. No eye has seen the beauty of what I have stored up for you. No ear has heard what I have prepared for you. No one can stop what I have done for you, My precious love. I behold your beauty and I breathe deeply from your love. You fill Me with pleasure when I drink from your praises. I give you My love, My beloved, and I give you back what the evil one has taken. Rejoice in Me for today is the day that I have made. Behold My beauty in today, for it is yours. I give you life, rich and full, blessings not curses – for you are Mine and I Am Yours. My treasure, My treasure, My hidden most treasure, my how you shine in My love! My brightest of gems, filled with richness of color, you satisfy Me as you drink from My fountains. Oh river of Mine flowing out from within, I give you My blessings with fruit overflowing. Our hearts beat as one as you breathe in My Name and drink from My pureness without refrain. Sing Hosanna to Me, for I Am Your King, Your Creator, Your Savior, Your Everything. I protect you My love, for you have entered My rest and you lean on Me for all of your needs. I supply you with plenty as you serve only Me and I take you to places deep inside of Me.

March 17

Romans 13:10-13

[10] Love worketh no ill to his neighbour: therefore love is the fulfilling of the law. [11] And that, knowing the time, that now it is high time to awake out of sleep: for now is our salvation nearer than when we believed. [12] The night is far spent, the day is at hand: let us therefore cast off the works of darkness, and let us put on the armour of light. [13] Let us walk honestly, as in the day; not in rioting and drunkenness, not in chambering and wantonness, not in strife and envying.

You see Me coming to your rescue, holy one. It is time to bring all things together for good. Your steadfast love and your obedient heart have brought Me forth on your behalf. Precious one, I am here tending to your every need. I am here walking in the midst of every detail. You see Me, My love, and you watch Me with the sweetest smile upon your lips. I am smiling upon you, My chosen one. I love you, precious bride. My hand is mighty, My hand is tender, My hand is gentle and My hand is strong. I control all things and I rebuild My temple that has been devastated from within. I heal her broken heart and I mend the deepest wounds. My healing touch has come and My restoration is here. Sing to Me, My precious one, for I Am Your King who restores and mends, and refreshes your heart. Today is the day for rejoicing, for I have lifted My heavy hand from upon you. I call you blessed and I give you My glory and honor, for you have come to Me for your safety. I cover you in My love and I take good care of you. You know Me, My love. I Am Faithful And True.

March 18

Luke 10:2-3

[2] Therefore said he unto them, The harvest truly is great, but the labourers are few: pray ye therefore the Lord of the harvest, that he would send forth labourers into his harvest. [3] Go your ways: behold, I send you forth as lambs among wolves.

The rivers are flowing for all to see. I have reached down My hand and rescued you. From the depths of My soul, you have stirred in Me a "Yes and Amen," for I honor you. Let My light shine and rejoice in Me, for I Am Your Holy Father who has come forth for you. The time has come for the world to know how I honor the ones who love Me so. Sing unto Me for I have lifted you up and healed all your wounds and fears from above. I have reached deep inside, and I bring you forth, in healing, completely. You are My love, I chose you for Me and I give you My love – faithfully. I cherish your love you have given Me and I sing My great love song over you. Blessed are you who comes in My Name and speaks of My love to the world. Cry out to Me for your every need for I say "Yes" to you – I say "Yes indeed!" My tender, gentle touch, has captured your heart, and I rejoice and I sing with a very glad heart. Glory to My Name, for the world will see My light shining brightly inside of you. I love you, My treasure, let My glory shine, for I come to your rescue in just the right time. I love all My treasures, My brightest of gems – the ones who obey Me and love Me from within.

March 19

1 Kings 22:21-22

21 And there came forth a spirit, and stood before the Lord, and said, I will persuade him. 22 And the Lord said unto him, Wherewith? And he said, I will go forth, and I will be a lying spirit in the mouth of all his prophets. And he said, Thou shalt persuade him, and prevail also: go forth, and do so.

The spirits are many that live among My people. Stay close in Me and know that I Am God. My Spirit in you discerns each one, you know Me, My love, My precious one. Do not be deceived, for many will come and try to persuade you, each to their own. You know Me, My love, I have prepared you in Me, My process does not fail, as you will see. I have strengthened your nets and I have walked with you through the struggles and pain, and I have set you free. Your love is complete for it is sustained in Me, Your Rock and Your Savior and Protector of You. I stand strong by your side and keep you in Me, forever and ever, as you will see. Do not be afraid, for many will come, remain in My love, I'll show you each one. You will know by their fruit, with discernment too, who serves only Me and obeys My commands. You know Me, My love, for I have introduced you to the deeper things that come from above. I give you My blessings as I set you free! Come, fly on My wings of abundance. I give you My laughter and joy in this place of deepest devotion to fight in this race. My rivers of peace run deeply from within, you are safe in My love and protected within.

March 20

Hosea 2:14-16

[14] Therefore, behold, I will allure her, and bring her into the wilderness, and speak comfortably unto her. [15] And I will give her her vineyards from thence, and the valley of Achor for a door of hope: and she shall sing there, as in the days of her youth, and as in the day when she came up out of the land of Egypt. [16] And it shall be at that day, saith the Lord, that thou shalt call me Ishi; and shalt call me no more Baali.

I took you aside a long time ago and held you as My bride and loved you so. I sent you to earth in a flesh and bone cover, to tell of My love to one another. You serve only Me for that is My will and I love you, My bride, My holy treasure. Your beauty within grows brighter each day, and shines in My glory in all of your ways. Your life speaks of Me in every way as you live in My love, and trust and obey. I have protected our love from the day you were born and scattered your enemies, each and every one. I stand by your side, My sword fully drawn, and remain on alert all of the time. I cover you in love and My power too, for many will come and try to attack you. You stand firm in My love, for you know Me so well, you have been through My process to see you through. You know I come when you call on My Name for I Am Your Redeemer, Your Savior and Friend.

March 21

Psalm 112:1-3

112 Praise ye the Lord. Blessed is the man that feareth the Lord, that delighteth greatly in his commandments. ² His seed shall be mighty upon earth: the generation of the upright shall be blessed. ³ Wealth and riches shall be in his house: and his righteousness endureth for ever.

The rain begins to drip from My heavy cloud – lift up your head and taste the rain, for it is here to stay. Let your voice ring out to Me, Your Beloved, for I am here and I rest My love on you. Comfort My hurting ones, sing your songs of comfort, for many need My touch. Let My light stretch forth from you for generations to come. My light separates you. My light permeates you as I walk with you each day. I take you to My secret place and I refresh your heavy heart. I give you burdens upon your heart, and ask you to pray – touch the sick and mend their hearts, renew their minds you say. I hear you, precious love of Mine, and I answer you today. Love My people along your path and lift them up to Me. I count each tear, I hear each prayer, and I hold them dear to Me. Oh love of Mine, you do not know the things I say and do. You know in part, but only then you see through mortal view. I have so much to share with you, so much more I want to say. Stay true to Me in all you do, for I want to speak these things to you. I have a plan to see you through, My love. You are My treasure, My greatest prize, My creation and My friend.

March 22

Isaiah 54:13-14

¹³ And all thy children shall be taught of the Lord; and great shall be the peace of thy children. ¹⁴ In righteousness shalt thou be established: thou shalt be far from oppression; for thou shalt not fear: and from terror; for it shall not come near thee.

My persistent one, My obedient one, I am here. Rest your mind, rest your heart, lean on Me, I am here. My love does not fail, My promises are true. My holiness surrounds you, My love is in you, and I protect you – forever and ever. I call you Mine. Keep your eyes on Me, precious one, do not look about the calamity on every side. I am in you, I am here. I am in control and you please Me, you delight Me, and I never tire of you. Listen closely to what I say, I speak to you in My tender way. Your ears do hear, your mind is on Me, and I have your heart for eternity. There is none but Me, no not one, Your God and Your Savior, The Only One. My hand is strong holding yours so tightly, I will not let go, I am holding you closely. The dawn is breaking, My light bursts through, the darkness around you is leaving you. I have stretched forth My hand and said it is enough, rejoice in My love for I have lifted your load. The days are now full of the evil last days, rejoice, My dear love, for My power is greater. Remain in My Word, let it penetrate deeply, and watch how I reveal Myself to you. I delight you in love, My greatest of treasures, and bring peace to your soul. You see the evil inhabit another, but it cannot touch you in any way.

March 23

Psalms 89:1-4

89 I will sing of the mercies of the Lord for ever: with my mouth will I make known thy faithfulness to all generations. ² For I have said, Mercy shall be built up for ever: thy faithfulness shalt thou establish in the very heavens. ³ I have made a covenant with my chosen, I have sworn unto David my servant, ⁴ Thy seed will I establish for ever, and build up thy throne to all generations. Selah.

They will come to you, precious one, you will not go to them. I rest My favor upon you for you obey Me, My love. The river flows deeply and will not be stopped. The signs are clear for each path you take, for you know My peace and My joy. I comfort you and I love you so. You are in My thoughts filled with good and wonderful things! I shine out in you and I smile down upon you, for you are My beloved and I Am Yours. My heart is tender and gentle with you. My heart is filled with passion for you. I protect you in My passion and I care for your every need. Many have been sent out on your behalf. Many are at work on your behalf. My love does not fail you, My Word does not lie, and I stand beside you all of the time. You have given Me your cares, each and every one, and I take them from you as I answer each one. I loose all My power from heaven to earth to cover you completely in My fullness, My love. I saturate you in My holy splendor and take you in Me as you live in surrender. My plans are for good and not for your harm, you realize this, My love, and run into My arms.

March 24

Matthew 12:18-21

18 Behold my servant, whom I have chosen; my beloved, in whom my soul is well pleased: I will put my spirit upon him, and he shall shew judgment to the Gentiles. 19 He shall not strive, nor cry; neither shall any man hear his voice in the streets. 20 A bruised reed shall he not break, and smoking flax shall he not quench, till he send forth judgment unto victory. 21 And in his name shall the Gentiles trust.

It is My desire to take you into My secret place. I long to spend more time with you there, My precious holy one. I draw you closer to Me for I hunger for more of you. Your desire for Me grows as I take you deeper still. I Am Wonderful, My love, and you want more of Me. I Am Faithful and True and filled with kindness too. I never leave you nor forsake you – My heart belongs to you. I take good care of all your needs and bless you with an abundance of Me. I give you time inside of Me for you delight in My presence and I delight in you. My love has no end, it gets stronger each day and I fill you with My richness in every way. Obedient heart who loves only Me, I come to you completely. The hour is soon and every tear will be dry, for My Son is returning in the twinkling of an eye. Look up to the heavens and let your heart be encouraged – I am coming soon and I hear you say hurry. My chosen ones will all be together forever, and I fill you with perfection and joyous reunions. The earth has its sorrows; I know that is true, but look up to the heavens for I am coming for you.

March 25

John 4:23-24

23 But the hour cometh, and now is, when the true worshippers shall worship the Father in spirit and in truth: for the Father seeketh such to worship him. 24 God is a

Spirit: and they that worship him must worship him in spirit and in truth.

Absorb Me for I am here, My love. Drink deeply from My well for it never runs dry. Linger in My presence and let Me refresh you on your journey. I empower you with My wisdom and strengthen you in My love, My rich love soothes, and heals, and mends, and tends to each and every care. I speak to you in My tender love and I accept your praises to Me. I receive your love and fill you with My ease. Oh love of Mine, I hold you closely and draw you deeper still. Do you want more of Me, My love? Open wide your heart and mind. Let Me fill you with My love sincere and My wisdom in My Word. Listen closely to My desires and know My hungry heart. I long for more of you, My love, linger here awhile. The daily things of life must be, but more importantly, spend more time with Me, and let Me speak to you. Keep your mind on eternal things for daily things come and go. Let them come, then let them go and remain in Me, My love. I Am Your God who created you to come and love Me so. Walk in Me and love My ways and I will see you through, and take you home with Me, My love, someday very soon. The end is near, My heart beats faster with anticipation to return. Keep looking up to Me alone, Your Redeemer and Your Friend. I have made room for you, My love.

March 26

Matthew 4:14-16

[14] That it might be fulfilled which was spoken by Esaias the prophet, saying, [15] The land of Zabulon, and the land of Nephthalim, by the way of the sea, beyond Jordan, Galilee of the Gentiles; [16] The people which sat in darkness saw great light; and to them which sat in the region and shadow of death light is sprung up.

The dawn is breaking for the new day is here. Glory to My Name for I have come to you. I Am Your Redeemer and I have come to you. I do not rest. I am at work continually on your behalf. I Am Your Creator and I watch over you with all of My love. My thoughts are on you continually, for I Am Your Everything. I love the way you love Me, holy one. I love to hear you worship Me. Oh what beauty I behold when I look upon your sincere heart. You are very precious to Me. I am bringing all things together to delight you, My love. My how you please Me so! What a refreshing drink you are, My obedient one. I have placed My great peace inside of you and whispered your name I hold so dear. Your love will grow stronger in Me every day, for I want to delight you in your earthly stay. I fill you with joy, now and forever, and teach you My victorious ways. Abound in Me, for there is no other, who gives you your love for one another. Tell of My goodness for all will see I have rested My blessings upon you.

March 27

Matthew 25:20-21

20 And so he that had received five talents came and brought other five talents, saying, Lord, thou deliveredst unto me five talents: behold, I have gained beside them five talents more. 21 His lord said unto him, Well done, thou good and faithful servant: thou hast been faithful over a few things, I will make thee ruler over many things: enter thou into the joy of thy lord.

I have prepared you, My process continues as you grow deeper into Me. Your roots are attached strongly, and bound tightly to Me, for you are ready, My precious love, you are ready. I have tested you, oh yes, you have been through the fire. The dross has been cleared and My reflection shines out. I call you righteous, for you believe Me and have obeyed. Let all of heaven rejoice, for I sing My victory song over you! Let My glory shine, My love, My treasure, and My bride, for I am here and now is the time for greater things. You know what pleases Me, My love – it is much fruit. Bring them to Me, holy one, and teach them of My love. Give to them the wisdom I have placed within your soul. My process never fails, My love, My process will unfold. I give you extra in this day, the day of My return. I never leave you without strength, and I fill you with My power, never ceasing in My love, never ceasing is My work. The harvest is ripe and it is time to reap the plenty in My love. Bring to Me My chosen ones with power and with love.

March 28

1 Samuel 2:1-2

2 And Hannah prayed, and said, My heart rejoiceth in the Lord, mine horn is exalted in the Lord: my mouth is enlarged over mine enemies; because I rejoice in thy salvation. ² There is none holy as the Lord: for there is none beside thee: neither is there any rock like our God.

As you sit at My feet, My love, you see the scars in each. The scars remain and My light shines through to remind you of My love for you. You may touch My feet and worship Me in the beauty of My love. I pick you up, with scars inside My hands, and touch your broken life. You feel My touch, you see the scars that I have kept for you. I show you what you mean to Me so you will never forget. The price is paid — you have been set free, for I have paid your debt. Oh precious one, come dance with Me, for you are free indeed! I live in you, you live in Me, together we are one. I call you friend, My confidant, and precious love of Mine. I tell you of My precious love and show you all day long. I bring to you My chosen ones and give you strength to bring them home. You work for Me in heartfelt love. I see you, My precious holy love. I see your love at work for Me in all you say and do. I am pleased with you. Come rest in Me, and let Me strengthen you. I give you more for each new day, spend time with Me, My love. You cannot do this, not one day, without My strength and love. I fill you full for each new day for My tasks are not too hard. I love you, precious treasure, come look upon My scars.

March 29

Acts 8:4-6

⁴ Therefore they that were scattered abroad went every where preaching the word. ⁵ Then Philip went down to the city of Samaria, and preached Christ unto them. ⁶ And the people with one accord gave heed unto those things which Philip spake, hearing and seeing the miracles which he did.

My mercies are great and My heart is tender. My love endures forever and I do not slumber. I know your needs, your encouragement too, and I meet each one to see you through. My love rests on you from beginning to end in eternity with Me – never to end. Oh love of Mine, you seem so surprised when I reach forth My hand and come to your side. I Am Your Companion, your sweetest of all, I'll come every time when I hear you call. My love does not weary when you call out My Name. I delight in you coming and I show you the way. I want you to know I walk beside you, and I honor you, My treasure, in all that you do. I use you in ways you do not ever know and I keep you humble for I love you so. Your love for Me grows, deeper still, for there is more of Me and I want more of you. I Am Above All Things and I am in control. I hear your every whisper, I see each tear fall. I Am Your Friend and Your Father too, who sends you to those who comfort you. I Am Your God, full of comfort and love, and I lavish you from My Throne Room above. I pour out My gifts, and I give much to you, from My abundance of love.

March 30

Acts 7:30-32

30 And when forty years were expired, there appeared to him in the wilderness of mount Sina an angel of the Lord in a flame of fire in a bush. 31 When Moses saw it, he wondered at the sight: and as he drew near to behold it, the voice of theLord came unto him, 32 Saying, I am the God of thy fathers, the God of Abraham, and the God of Isaac, and the God of Jacob. Then Moses trembled, and durst not behold.

The veil has been torn, your eyes have been opened and now I show you many things. Some things are for you alone to know, some are for others. I will guide you in all things, do not be afraid of the things I show you. I hold your hand tightly as I carry you through, for you are helpless without Me in all you say and do. It is separation time, holy one, it is separation time. The wheat and the chaff are sifted through, the wheat will hold up and be gathered to Me. I know all things, I search each heart, and I am in control of every thing. My process is at work and it never fails, My love. Stay in My richness, remain in My love. The evil one snares with plots and schemes, but I Am God, holy one, and I control all things. I send to your rescue each one you need and they encourage your heart in the attack upon you. I stand by your side, My power in you, and all swords are drawn to defend you, My love. There are many about you full of My Spirit and the victory is won – you will not perish. I keep you in Me in the closest of places, you live in My heart for I am in love with you.

March 31

Luke 7:47-48

[47] Wherefore I say unto thee, Her sins, which are many, are forgiven; for she loved much: but to whom little is forgiven, the same loveth little. [48] And he said unto her, Thy sins are forgiven.

You see the beams of light shooting out all around. You see the signs of blessings stepping forth for My Renown. Oh precious one, I show you My touch along the way, to fill your heart with much delight, for you are Mine to stay. The love we share cannot compare with another, holy one. I Am Your Great Delightful One who surprises you in many ways. I am not boring, not at all, My plan is exciting, precious one. It is a plan of teamwork, for blessings rest on all. I made you one inside of Me, our unity is sure. I gave you many chosen ones to lift the load you bear. I give you rest along the way – much refreshing is in Me. I fill your heart with laughter and I rest My peace in you. Oh precious one, I call you blessed, holy and righteous too. Come with Me on this journey, I will see you through. I laugh with you, I cry with you, and I hold you oh so closely. I give you all of Me, My love, come with Me – hold on tightly. I Am All Power And All Might, nothing stops Me from My plan. I reveal to you the plot of man – the evil that abounds. I show you how to flee from all the danger that is plotted to stop the flow of Me in you, oh holy one. Lift high your head and spirit too, and soar within My heights – far beyond what man can touch or any evil that is devised.

April 1

Acts 7:54-55

⁵⁴ When they heard these things, they were cut to the heart, and they gnashed on him with their teeth. ⁵⁵ But he, being full of the Holy Ghost, looked up stedfastly into heaven, and saw the glory of God, and Jesus standing on the right hand of God,

No eye has seen, no ear has heard what I have stored up for you, My love, My delight. I have taken you through and I am bringing you back, for there is much work to do, holy one. I have brought you to My place of obedience and I have restored you back to Me. Oh precious one, the time is now and much will be your fruit. You saw My hand in all of it and you knew I was at your side. You clung to Me, and did not let go, no matter what the cost. Now watch Me show Myself to you in response to you, My love, for you held on to Me and did not let go! My Word is true and speaks to you with love and much compassion. It is Me, My love, My holy one, giving you My direction. I love you and I fill you with My gifts and strong devotion. You will produce much fruit for Me, for you love Me, precious one. I knew your heart before corruption – I made it just for Me. I have cleansed you from your fears, My love, and I have given you perfect peace. My perfect love is inside you and gives you strength for each new day. You are My love, My holy one, I know your love will stay. I have shown you many things, My love, and whispered in your ear.

April 2

Ephesians 5:8-12

⁸ For ye were sometimes darkness, but now are ye light in the Lord: walk as children of light: ⁹ (For the fruit of the Spirit is in all goodness and righteousness and truth;) ¹⁰ Proving what is acceptable unto the Lord. ¹¹ And have no fellowship with the unfruitful works of darkness, but rather reprove them. ¹² For it is a shame even to speak of those things which are done of them in secret.

Patience is a fruit I cultivate in you, My love. You must pursue and persevere, never to give up, for I have covered you with My righteousness. The battle is won with My full armor on – nothing less will do. Joy is a benefit I give to you and I speak of its importance. It must abound, this gift from Me to you, for it is your strength, My love. You will not run the race without it in My victorious ways. Your strength will fade in every way without My joy, My love. I give you rest in My great peace, your soul was created for it. My peace is flowing in your soul and your face shines forth. My love is in you and it stills your heart and keeps away all fear. My perfect peace is trust in Me, it is My perfect will. The storms rage on, but not in you, for you are My holy one. You see the storms, how they rage about, but they have no affect on you. Soar higher than the world can see and keep your eyes on only Me. You know My love, My perfect peace, and My strength in the joy. I flow through you, My mighty one, for I have untangled you from the cares of the world.

April 3

Psalm 1:1-3

1 Blessed is the man that walketh not in the counsel of the ungodly, nor standeth in the way of sinners, nor sitteth in the seat of the scornful. ² But his delight is in the law of the Lord; and in his law doth he meditate day and night. ³ And he shall be like a tree planted by the rivers of water, that bringeth forth his fruit in his season; his leaf also shall not wither; and whatsoever he doeth shall prosper.

The tides are turning, My love, now I bring in what I have ebbed out. I have the power to do all things. These things had to be, My love, for a part of the world still had a string it could pull. I have snapped the chord and made you walk in total submission to Me. I have protected you from the chords that have tried to wrap themselves around you. I separated you for a season. This was no accident. I have protected you, unengaged you, and spun you into Me. I spin My chords in and around you and I have fastened them with My hand. The chords I have that hold you tightly to Me cannot be snapped or broken. I can send you now, for you are ready to help My entangled ones. I give you all My kindness and love to help you. You are Mine. I have sealed you with My kiss. I have bound you to Me

72

and set you free – go bind My people unto Me. I am sending them to you and I send you to them for there is much work for you to do. Rest when I send you, to the one who has your heart, and let My love replenish you in this great fight. It is not soon, My love, it is now, it is here, and you are ready. Come – fly higher with Me.

April 4

1 Samuel 25:40-41

⁴⁰ And when the servants of David were come to Abigail to Carmel, they spake unto her, saying, David sent us unto thee, to take thee to him to wife. ⁴¹ And she arose, and bowed herself on her face to the earth, and said, Behold, let thine handmaid be a servant to wash the feet of the servants of my lord.

My love is tender, My love is strong, My love endures, My love has a song. I sing over you in My great love, and I rejoice in your love for Me. I rest My love upon your face – oh how you shine for Me! You have tasted the bitter, but now it is sweet, your beauty has come forth from the evil one's ash heap. Praise My Name, for you have come forth, and you have clung to Me, My love. I Am Your Rock, Your Solid Rock, who is your steadfast love. You are protected in My great love, I hold you tightly in Me. Stand tall for Me, My forgiven one, and boldly come to Me for those I send you on your path toward eternity. I give you My "Yes and Amen" – so be it done in Me. I give you power in My Great Name and great responsibility! Hold on to My Words deep within your heart and let them grow deeper in you. Refresh yourself in My cool fresh streams and let My breezes blow. I give you times of refreshing, and I tend to each wound you receive. Come walk in My healing and perfect love, and rest your cares in Me. I Am Mighty, I Am Strong, and I come forth in all My splendor to rescue you, My love. You have given Me your tender heart and I have made you strong.

April 5

Psalm 47:5-9

[5] God is gone up with a shout, the Lord with the sound of a trumpet. [6] Sing praises to God, sing praises: sing praises unto our King, sing praises. [7] For God is the King of all the earth: sing ye praises with understanding. [8] God reigneth over the heathen: God sitteth upon the throne of his holiness. [9] The princes of the people are gathered together, even the people of the God of Abraham: for the shields of the earth belong unto God: he is greatly exalted.

The flowers wither and die, but My love for you will never fade, wither or die. I breathe deeply inside of you and hold you closely in Me. You are safe in My love, for I have surrounded you. I wrap you in My warm embrace, and I hold you close in Me. Come, let Me take you higher, for there is much I want you to see. With every breath I take, you are on My mind. I have My ways, My unique ways, to show you My great love. You see Me in the smallest touch – oh yes, My love, it is Me, even in the smallest things, for My heart is drawn to you. I want to show you how I feel, I am with you every day. I watch over you at night, My love, as you sleep and get your rest. I place My hand upon your face and bless you in your rest. My heart is full; My love is great, as I look upon your face. I take in all of you, My love, and I inhabit all your praise. I come in all My fullness as I hear your sweet love songs, and I listen as you worship Me and love Me all day long. I love to hear you praise Me – I love your sweet love songs. I hear your voice I gave you – how it pleases Me, My love.

April 6

Luke 1:68-71

[68] Blessed be the Lord God of Israel; for he hath visited and redeemed his people, [69] And hath raised up an horn of salvation for us in the house of his servant David; [70] As he spake by the mouth of his holy prophets, which have been since the world began:

71 That we should be saved from our enemies, and from the hand of all that hate us;

You want Me, you need Me, you hunger for more of Me because I long to draw you closer – come into Me, My love. I Am Your God who created you to love Me with all your might. I love you, holy one, your presence is My delight. I have waited for this moment to call you Mine, My love. You have received My love into you, and thrilled Me with delight! Oh precious one, the one I love, I take you into Me, and love you with My tender touch that comes from only Me. I look upon your countenance and see My smile in you. Oh praise My Holy Name, My love, for there is much for you to do. Bring My people back to Me and show them My great ways. There is no peace within their hearts – no peace in all their days. Oh tell them how I love them so and speak of My great love. Show them all My beauty and joy within your soul. My gift is free, oh tell them, it is paid with My great price. I sacrificed My Son for them and gave them My gift of life. The time is short, the days go by, and each is numbered in its time. My day of wrath is coming, oh tell them – there is not much time. I breathe in you, breathe out in them, and love them back to Me.

April 7

2 Timothy 3:16-17

16 All scripture is given by inspiration of God, and is profitable for doctrine, for reproof, for correction, for instruction in righteousness: **17** That the man of God may be perfect, thoroughly furnished unto all good works.

My holy one, My lovely one, I smile upon your face. I take you in My warm embrace and keep you there, My love. My presence is around you, oh sing a sweet love song. You know the beat of My heart, you know the rhythm of Me, for we are one, My love, your heart beats inside of Me. The flow of Me inside of you comes forth for each new day, for I have replenished you in Me each step along the way. I fill you with My steadfast love each and every day and whisper how I love you and tell you what to say. I show you what to say and do for I live inside of you. My power and My love are inside of you to stay. You trust Me in the simple things and you trust Me in My complex ways. You trust Me with a little and you trust Me with much more. I give you My abundance for you trust Me in our love. I reign in you – I inhabit all your praise. I love your thankful heart, My treasure, and I hold you closely inside of Me. I love to take your heartbeat and let it rest its beat in Mine. I carry you upon My wings and take you higher still. Come soar with Me and hold Me close for I am always here. I will do whatever it takes to come to your rescue, for I Am GOD, The Holy One, who comes to see you through. You need not fear of anything, for I am by your side.

April 8

2 John 1:6-7

⁶ And this is love, that we walk after his commandments. This is the commandment, That, as ye have heard from the beginning, ye should walk in it. ⁷ For many deceivers are entered into the world, who confess not that Jesus Christ is come in the flesh. This is a deceiver and an antichrist.

Taste Me, for I Am Sweet, drink of Me, for I Am Refreshing. Dine with Me, for My banquet is before you. I love you, precious one. Come, join Me in our love song. Let Me behold your beauty, sit before Me, My love. My heart beats one with you, My love. Come, rest your love in Me. I Am Your Good And Loving King, and I give you all you need. I fill you with My sweetest love. Come, behold My beauty – I give it all to you. You are My greatest treasure, I created you for Me. I take your love into My heart and saturate you in Me. Oh the pleasure you bring to Me, My holy one! You have received My Word inside of you and received Me with such love. I take you deeper still, My love, for I have much more for you. Develop all your senses to see Me, holy one. I created you to behold Me when you search for Me, My love. Behold My beauty before you, it is yours, My love, it is yours. Your desire is to please Me, I am pleased, My precious one. My desire is to give you all the things you ask of Me. Ask of Me, My precious one, for I am meeting every need. I love you in our secret place, so holy and so pure.

April 9

Jeremiah 32 NLT

But this is what the LORD, the God of Israel, says: [37]I will certainly bring my people back again from all the countries where I will scatter them in my fury. I will bring them back to this very city and let them live in peace and safety. [38]They will be my people, and I will be their God.

I will rest My personal touch on all you ask of Me, holy one. I will come to those intimately and let them know who I Am. They will not walk in distance from Me, for I will hold them close. It is done. Rejoice in Me and praise My Holy Name for I have come to you and I have said "Yes" to you. There is no power in all of heaven and earth that can prevent Me from giving you the desires of your heart. Your desires are My desires for we are one. You are blessed by Me, holy one, for I have clothed you in My righteousness and I have set you free. You will enjoy all the plans I have for you, for I have shown you mercy, and My grace abounds in all you say and do. I have gone before you and prepared the way. You are heard by Me, oh yes, every word. I come to you today and I whisper to you – I honor you in every way, for you are Mine – forever to stay. Rejoice all you people in all of the lands for My mighty right hand is upon the face of the earth. I have come forth in My splendor to rescue you from the tempter's snares. You are My people, My chosen ones, and I have sealed you to Me, for the victory is won. Come dance in My joy, and sing your love songs, for I Am Your Redeemer all the day long.

April 10

Hosea 14:4-6

[4] I will heal their backsliding, I will love them freely: for mine anger is turned away from him. [5] I will be as the dew unto Israel: he shall grow as the lily, and cast forth his roots as Lebanon. [6] His branches shall spread, and his beauty shall be as the olive tree, and his smell as Lebanon.

Let My children come unto Me. They need to know Me – they need My touch. You are My touch upon their lives for I live in you. I breathe in you and I take you to My tender place. Breathe My life into them, for they will die without Me. Go forth in My Name and tell them of My great love. Show them My great love, live in Me, for I Am Love. Protect your joy, I will lead you – pay close attention. The strength is in Me. Dread and fear are not from Me, holy one – pay close attention. You know Me, rest in Me, let My Word lighten your load. It is Me, My love, here at your side. You are on My path, the one I have chosen, listen closely to Me and not another. Stay in My Word, lean into Me, climb higher with Me, beyond what you can see. You will love the heights as we climb even higher, rest in My love and behold all My splendor. Breathe deeply in My pureness, let it saturate you, as you drink in My beauty and holiness too. Let your love be for Me, and not for another, for I do not share this place in your heart – you are created to love Me the most. I Am Your Creator, Your Father, Your God, Your Greatest Love, and I stand by your side.

April 11

James 3:17-18

¹⁷ But the wisdom that is from above is first pure, then peaceable, gentle, and easy to be intreated, full of mercy and good fruits, without partiality, and without hypocrisy. ¹⁸ And the fruit of righteousness is sown in peace of them that make peace.

My blessings are upon you, holy one, they will overtake you and lift you up. Your heart belongs to Me and only Me all the days of your life. My integrity rings out from you with My beauty and harmony too. Praise Me, precious one, for I have heard you. Praise My Holy Name for I bring healing in My wings. I bestow mercy on those who call on My Name and I listen to the pleas of those who love Me. Let your words be few as you behold My splendor. Let your awe be great, for I am among you. Reverence Me in this holy time, for I am doing many wonderful things on your behalf. I Am Holy and I Am Pure. I have purified you in Me and I have made you holy. Righteous are you in My eyes. I hold you so closely, I am right by your side. You may dance and you may sing in the beauty of My love for you. I delight you, I sing over you – my how I love you so! Let all of heaven rejoice, for My love is in you and around you, all the days of your life. My chosen one, My blessed one, all the powers of darkness cannot touch you, for I have said "No." You are Mine, you walk in Me, you will not fear the days of great sorrow, for I Am Your King who has come to rescue you. My love, My precious love, I give you My heart.

April 12

1 Kings 19:15-18

[15] And the Lord said unto him, Go, return on thy way to the wilderness of Damascus: and when thou comest, anoint Hazael to be king over Syria: [16] And Jehu the son of Nimshi shalt thou anoint to be king over Israel: and Elisha the son of Shaphat of Abelmeholah shalt thou anoint to be prophet in thy room. [17] And it shall come to pass, that him that escapeth the sword of Hazael shall Jehu slay: and him that escapeth from the sword of Jehu shall Elisha slay. [18] Yet I have left me seven thousand in Israel, all the knees which have not bowed unto Baal, and every mouth which hath not kissed him.

The time of My favor has come. Let it rain My abundance upon you. I give you strength to endure, for the work is great and the harvest is ripe. Oh My people, My precious people, they need Me so! I have prepared your heart to love only Me. You are ready to work in My field. My love abounds in you, precious one – walk in My ways. I Am Good and I Am Kind, I Am Tender at Heart and I Am Patient and Strong. Keep your eyes on only Me, holy one. You know Me, you know My love. My love will keep you and sustain you all the days of your life. Bring them to Me, My love, I want them, they are Mine and I love them so. Tell them of My great love, and show them My ways. I created you for My loving heart. I love you, holy one, I call you My precious treasure. No harm will come to you, My love, for I have promised you forever. I am here, you know My touch. You hear Me whisper My great love inside your deepest places, I have captured you, My love.

April 13

Acts 10:28-29

[28] And he said unto them, Ye know how that it is an unlawful thing for a man that is a Jew to keep company, or come unto one of another nation; but God hath shewed me that I should not call any man common or unclean. [29] Therefore came I unto you without gainsaying, as soon as I was sent for: I ask therefore for what intent ye have sent for me?

My light has come to those around you – show them My great ways. Tell them of My mercy and tender loving ways. I take you to the darkness and speak through you, My love. I give you all the desires of your heart you ask of Me. You know My tender mercies, I have given you each one. I took your broken body and I healed you of all wounds. I mended them in My pure gold and let them shine for Me. Oh precious one, you know My voice for I call you by your Name. I walk with you and talk with you each and every day. I give you all of Me, My love, and I lavish you in love. I Am Love, Your Only One, who died for you that day. I brought you life, and gave you hope upon that tree. Come dance in My delight, My love, and let Me sing to you. I brought you out of darkness and I looked upon your face – I placed My smile upon your lips and gave you My embrace. My light shines brightly from inside you, and glows upon your face. My hand has been upon you and I kept you in My grasp. I would not let them have you – no matter what the cost. I would bankrupt heaven to keep you at My side. I live in you and breathe in you, because I want to, holy one. I love you, My creation, I love you, precious one.

April 14

Romans 12:9-12

[9] Let love be without dissimulation. Abhor that which is evil; cleave to that which is good. [10] Be kindly affectioned one to another with brotherly love; in honour preferring one another; [11] Not slothful in business; fervent in spirit; serving the Lord; [12] Rejoicing in hope; patient in tribulation; continuing instant in prayer;

There is room for you, My love. There is room. It comes quickly and it comes with My passion. I do what I do with passion. I Am Your Passionate God. I am not idle and I am not tamed by any. My ways are My ways – I do not conform to the ways of the world. I Am Your Zealous God and I have a zealous plan. Hot or cold is what I say. I want all of your love – not halfway. When I give to you, I give you all of Me. I take nothing less from you. I Am Your First Love and there is no other. I created you for Me and I require you to love Me first, honor Me and worship Me, My love. I Am Good and I Am Kind and I will meet your every need. Lavish Me in all your love and let My beauty shine. I give to you from My deep wells and I have called you Mine. Never doubt My steadfast hand upon you all the time. I take you to My better place, the one I made for you. Come walk among My beauty and let Me behold all of you. My heart holds you so closely in Mine and I love you tenderly. Behold Me, precious love of Mine, for I am here to show you more.

April 15

Isaiah 55:3-5

³ Incline your ear, and come unto me: hear, and your soul shall live; and I will make an everlasting covenant with you, even the sure mercies of David. ⁴ Behold, I have given him for a witness to the people, a leader and commander to the people. ⁵ Behold, thou shalt call a nation that thou knowest not, and nations that knew not thee shall run unto thee because of the Lord thy God, and for the Holy One of Israel; for he hath glorified thee.

There is a world of silence, they cannot hear at all, for people are too busy to look around and see. The needs are there, and many go untouched, My love. Reach out your arms about them and tell them I am here. I give you strength in each new need and show you what to do. My people are too busy to see the silent ones. I hear the silent ones, My love, I see each tear that falls, I hold their broken heart in Mine and I send you to their side. My love abides inside of you and fills you with great peace and joy that overflows in you. Feed the hungry, heal the sick, and love the unlovable ones. Give to them My richness and guide them in My light. I Am your Rock, Your Solid Rock, and you are safe in Me. Go to My hurting ones and call them out to Me. I listen for your cries to Me about the ones I send. Pray for each one with fervency and let My love descend. I hear you every time you speak and I send My love to them. My richness flows upon them and I heal them of their sins.

April 16

Ephesians 1:5-7

5 Having predestinated us unto the adoption of children by Jesus Christ to himself, according to the good pleasure of his will, 6 To the praise of the glory of his grace, wherein he hath made us accepted in the beloved. 7 In whom we have redemption through his blood, the forgiveness of sins, according to the riches of his grace;

My hand has come upon you, My holy precious one. I dance upon your face – with light and love, and joy in Me, and it leaves My holy glow. I smile upon your countenance and hold you close in Me. I protect you from the evil one who tries to take your love from Me. I said "No" many years ago when I hung upon the tree. I redeemed you back to Me in love when I came back from death's dark door. The way is paved in purest gold when you submit to Me. I keep you from the evil that plans and schemes and seethes. You are My royal bride, My love, the one who walks with Me. There is no greater power than The One who lives in you. It is My Holy Spirit who lives inside of you. Praise My Name from the heart and soul of you. I listen to your sweet love songs and smile on you, My love. I created you for Me, love Me in this day. I strengthen you for more of Me in these evil times. I hold you closely upon My breast and tell you it is time. Dance upon My clouds so high and soar with Me, My love.

April 17

2 Corinthians 6:1-2

6 We then, as workers together with him, beseech you also that ye receive not the grace of God in vain.

[2] (For he saith, I have heard thee in a time accepted, and in the day of salvation have I succoured thee: behold, now is the accepted time; behold, now is the day of salvation.)

The flowers are blooming in My garden of plenty. My rains come down upon them in My due season. They live in Me and breathe in Me and radiate My love. Their aroma fills My nostrils and warms Me in their love. My garden has My flowers that grow in My great love. I tend to each with loving care and watch them as they grow. Oh the beauty I behold when I look upon each one. My colors are so vibrant in each and every one. I come to them alone each day and give them of My touch. Oh tender one, I love you so, grow rich in My deep soil. I give you all you need to grow and flourish inside Me. Come to Me when you want something; I am here to meet your need. I love you in My holy place – the climate is just right. I protect you from the elements and I give you of My light. Grow in Me, My tender one – inside My holy place, and let Me breathe your fragrance as I look upon your face. Behold the face of Your Creator, I love you tenderly. See My smile upon My face as I walk in My garden, among My ones, My chosen ones, and feel My warm embrace. Radiate in Me, My love, and let the world behold a garden so much better. Come, let Me plant you in My richest soil of peace and joy and love.

April 18

Isaiah 43:3-5

[3] For I am the Lord thy God, the Holy One of Israel, thy Saviour: I gave Egypt for thy ransom, Ethiopia and Seba for thee. [4] Since thou wast precious in my sight, thou hast been honourable, and I have loved thee: therefore will I give men for thee, and people for thy life. [5] Fear not: for I am with thee: I will bring thy seed from the east, and gather thee from the west;

I Am Your Faithful Savior, I have called you out by name. I have given you My favor, go forth in My Holy Name. I bless you in My marketplace, at home and abroad, I bless you, precious treasure, come walk in My pure love. I reach My hand across the skies and I lift up My fallen ones. Bring them to Me, holy one, I have called you from above. Take them by My tender hand and guide them in My love. Give them the answer to their questions – they just have need of Me. I put the hole within their heart that can be satisfied by only Me. Tell them of My love for them and I yearn for them, My love. I miss them in My holy place of peace and joy and love. I want to give them fullness when they fall in love with Me. I want to give them much delight and life eternally. Oh tell them of My power – how I heal with just one touch. It is a small thing for Me, My love, to meet their every need. Prepare yourself in Me, My love, don't worry about tomorrow. I am here beside you guiding you, My love. I give you all of Me, My love, with hope in life eternal. The path is paved before you with My light that shines so brightly.

April 19

1 Peter 2:1-5

Wherefore laying aside all malice, and all guile, and hypocrisies, and envies, and all evil speakings, [2] As newborn babes, desire the sincere milk of the word, that ye may grow thereby: [3] If so be ye have tasted that the Lord is gracious. [4] To whom coming, as unto a living stone, disallowed indeed of men, but chosen of God, and precious, [5] Ye also, as lively stones, are built up a spiritual house, an holy priesthood, to offer up spiritual sacrifices, acceptable to God by Jesus Christ.

You serve Me well, My precious one, you serve Me well. I accept your gifts of worship in My holy secret place. You fill Me with your presence – enter into Me, My love. My heart is yours with compassion, love and mercy too – in all My ways of devotion, I have given Me to you. I bless you from My Mountain of ever flowing rain and teach you of My wonders and My all sufficient ways. Lift high your head to Me, My love, and raise your holy hands, as you worship Me with all your might, and let Me wash you in My love. My Word rests deeply within your soul and teaches you My ways. Keep yourself informed of Me and let Me delight you in My ways. I never tire of you My love, My time is never ending. Worship Me, oh holy one, and let Me bless you in My love. I fill the holes within your heart with peace and strength and joy. I created you for Me to love, let Me show you so much more.

84

April 20

John 17:20-22

20 Neither pray I for these alone, but for them also which shall believe on me through their word; 21 That they all may be one; as thou, Father, art in me, and I in thee, that they also may be one in us: that the world may believe that thou hast sent me. 22 And the glory which thou gavest me I have given them; that they may be one, even as we are one:

I have given you My glory, holy one. I go with you everywhere I send you. I am with you at home and abroad. You need not fear, for I have you under My protective wing. The season is upon us for My glory to shine in all the earth. I guide your thoughts and I speak My thoughts into you, for you are My righteous one. No one can stop what I have planned for you, no power is stronger, for I am in control. You give to Me with all your heart, I know your thoughts, My love. I have given you My beauty and placed it deeply inside of you. The way is prepared, and the path is set for you to walk in My pure love. I do not leave you unattended, I meet your every need. You see the dawn is breaking and change is in the air. Do not fear the change I bring, for I have prepared you for this journey. Rest your love inside of Me and let Me fill you with My plenty. Worship Me, for I bring peace to you with each new step you take. The meadowlarks are singing, My love songs fill the air, for I have My chosen ones who come to obey My every Word.

April 21

Isaiah 55:8-9

8 For my thoughts are not your thoughts, neither are your ways my ways, saith the Lord. 9 For as the heavens are higher than the earth, so are my ways higher than your ways, and my thoughts than your thoughts.

I walk among My flowers in the garden of My love and tend to each with all My love sent down from up above. I water those who wither from the dryness of their soul. I send you out to water them from My garden filled with love. Tend to them with My tender touch and speak gently as they grow, My precious ones I have transplanted, in My garden filled with love. Oh holy one, you know the seasons that I bring. Stretch forth your arms around them and give them of My rain. I come to you and fill you with My fullness all day long – I give you what you need, My love, and strengthen you in Me. The darkness tries to take away the ones I love so. But I Am God and there is no other who comes to replenish the ones I love. I stand among My frightened ones and I speak in My gentleness of tone. My love is kind and gentle, yet My fight for them is strong. I show no gentle mercy to the ones who kill My song, from the lips of those who love Me and serve Me all day long. Take heart, My beloved, for you are Mine, and I give you back your song. Ring out in Me, My harmony, I love you tender one. Lift your head unto Me, Your Lord who brings the rain, to wash away your sorrows and give you My new day.

April 22

John 15:12-14, 17

¹² This is my commandment, That ye love one another, as I have loved you. ¹³ Greater love hath no man than this, that a man lay down his life for his friends. ¹⁴ Ye are my friends, if ye do whatsoever I command you...
¹⁷ These things I command you, that ye love one another.

You have entered into Me, you see the world through My eyes. I live in you – you live in Me and I sustain you in these times. I have control of all of you, My faithful holy one. I take you in My chambers and I speak to you, My love. I speak to you of holy things, the things that matter most. The earth must be replenished from the dryness of their souls. I come to you in tenderness and reveal Myself to you. I tell you what to tell them and they will soften to My Words. I unveil the eyes of those you see and soften each hard heart. I take you to the uttermost and give you of My love. The tender touch I have given you, with gentleness of tone, will bring them back to Me, My love, you please Me, holy one. It is not stern commands I bring of legal rights and wrongs. It is compassion and mercy too – My love will bring them home. I yearn for them and cry My tears for every lost one I hold so dear. Bring them back to Me, My love, with compassion from your suffering. I held each tear inside of Me and wept with you, My love. You are My special, precious one I hold so dear inside My heart.

April 23

Luke 2:34-35

[34] And Simeon blessed them, and said unto Mary his mother, Behold, this child is set for the fall and rising again of many in Israel; and for a sign which shall be spoken against; [35] (Yea, a sword shall pierce through thy own soul also,) that the thoughts of many hearts may be revealed.

The price I paid will not be silenced for My blood cries out for more. Bring My children home to Me – I cover them in My blood. I have My ways, My chosen one, to move upon each heart. My Holy Spirit is in you and works in every heart. I will give you every soul, My love, you ask of Me in prayer. I will shine My light upon them and help them come to Me. I live in you, I reign in you and I keep you close to Me. Feel My warm embrace, My love, and let Me speak through you. The door has opened wide for you by My mighty hand. No one can shut what I have opened, for I Am The Great I AM, My love, who holds your trembling hand. Shine out in Me, My beloved one, for I have come to you. My glory rests upon you and I give you of My favor, a greater love cannot be found, for I Am Yours, My love. My heart is yours, your heart is Mine – we are one, My precious love. My abundance is upon you – it is My latter rain. I bring to you My power in My everlasting love. My smile is safe upon your face.

April 24

Matthew 16:11-12

[11] How is it that ye do not understand that I spake it not to you concerning bread, that ye should beware of the leaven of the Pharisees and of the Sadducees? [12] Then understood they how that he bade them not beware of the leaven of bread, but of the doctrine of the Pharisees and of the Sadducees.

I fill your heart to overflow, that is My great design. My passion lives inside of you, oh holy love of Mine. I keep them at a distance, for I protect you from the fall. You walk in Me and live in Me for I Am Your All In All. There is no other power as great as Me, My love. I protect you from the evil that schemes to destroy your very soul. Keep your hope inside of Me and keep your eyes on Me. I hear your prayer for every soul you bring before My Throne. I hear you in My chambers and I speak to you alone, inside My secret place of love. I have you close inside My heart, I show you how I love you so in the darkest of your days. You feel My touch, My holy breath fills you with My peace, and gives you all the joy you need to walk in strength in Me. I want your love, I want more of you, I hunger for your love. I give you My desire to love Me more and more. I Am Your Great Companion, I call you friend, I love to show you more of Me and hold you deep within. My peace flows through your inmost being like a river that runs deep and heals each one in your path on their way to eternity.

April 25

Ezekiel 17:24

24 And all the trees of the field shall know that I the Lord have brought down the high tree, have exalted the low tree, have dried up the green tree, and have made the dry tree to flourish: I the Lordhave spoken and have done it.

You see My hand upon you and the detail of My touch. I never leave one thing out, My ways are higher than you can imagine. Only I can soften hearts, only I can do all things, and it is Me, Your One and Only, who has come to your rescue. I kept you close while the storms raged on and strengthened you in Me. You held on tightly, you did not let go, and you came through it with peace of mind. I take you through My process until you love Me most. I do not share this place for Me – I designed you for My love. I give to you so willingly from the storehouse of My love. I watch you grow inside of Me, your beauty for Me to behold. Your radiance surrounds Me as I give you more of Me. I Am Your Beauty to behold – come walk deeper in Me still. I use your tender vessel to show the world My love. I take you to them tenderly and give you My great love. Love them in My holiness as I open their hearts to listen. Tell them they are precious, a sacrifice was paid that brought them back to Me, My love, in My holiest of ways. I have prepared the way for every soul you meet. You are My feet and hands, My love – love them back to Me. I give to you the tools you need I do not leave you unattended. Bless each one I give to you.

April 26

Ezekiel 47:11-12

¹¹ But the miry places thereof and the marishes thereof shall not be healed; they shall be given to salt. ¹² And by the river upon the bank thereof, on this side and on that side, shall grow all trees for meat, whose leaf shall not fade, neither shall the fruit thereof be consumed: it shall bring forth new fruit according to his months, because their waters they issued out of the sanctuary: and the fruit thereof shall be for meat, and the leaf thereof for medicine.

Sing as it rages, your voice will calm the sea of tumult all around you, sing your songs unto Me. Let My Name ring out in you from the deepest of your places. My heavens split open wide for you. I send out My chosen ones to come to meet your every need from My storehouse, holy one. I have restored your shattered soul, My love, and restored you unto Me. You are complete inside of Me and I meet your every need. Each shattered piece was mended in My furnace with My heat. I purified and sanctified each piece you gave to Me. I kept My eye close on you so you would not burn beyond repair. Then I cast My love upon you and I cleansed you in My love. The tarnished places from the world had stained you from My love. My light reflects upon you now in My purest holy frame. You are restored completely from My storehouse filled with love. I send you to them, holy one, for I can trust you with My touch. You know My voice, My strong hand too and My peace floods your soul.

April 27

1 Samuel 30:24-26

²⁴ For who will hearken unto you in this matter? but as his part is that goeth down to the battle, so shall his part be that tarrieth by the stuff: they shall part alike. ²⁵ And it was so from that day forward, that he made it a statute and an ordinance for Israel unto this day. ²⁶ And when David came to Ziklag, he sent of the spoil unto the elders of Judah, even to his friends, saying, Behold a present for you of the spoil of the enemies of the Lord;

I have ordained every detail in your life, My holy one. My instructions come so clear to you, for you know My voice, My love. I walk among you in My radiance for all the world to see. My chosen one, My holy one, I have come to you. I say "Yes" to all you ask of Me and I am pleased with your request. You know I Am Your Mighty One who can give without restraint. I show you more of Me, My love, each day you see Me clearer. That is by My design, My love, for I Am Your Revealer Of All Things. I delight you in My holy place and satisfy your need. I have shown you of My mystery, and how to use your keys to unlock the door to victory for each and every need. The door has swung wide open and you walk inside with joy. Oh teach them how to walk in Me and live in all My joy. My Word is alive in you, refreshing the weary soul, some may run away from Me – oh but some run straight to Me. Bring them to Me in My Holy Throne that is open unto you. I listen to you speak to Me with My smile upon My face. Oh how I love to hear your heart, what a beautiful creation I have made! I love you, tender one.

April 28

Psalm 46:4-5

⁴ There is a river, the streams whereof shall make glad the city of God, the holy place of the tabernacles of the most High. ⁵ God is in the midst of her; she shall not be moved: God shall help her, and that right early.

It seems so large to you, My love, this problem that you see. Oh holy one, I meet each need, it is a small thing for Me. Remember Me, in times before, I helped you, precious one. I am here to help again – I am at the door. Walk in this door I open, smell the richness of My plan. I come to you in this hour, My time is full at hand. You do as I command, My love, and follow Me in all My ways. It is time for Me to come to you and bless you in your wait. Behold the face of Me, My love, everywhere you see. I am in every detail, I am in every thing. Lift your head, My royal one, who has chosen Me your King. I give you all My treasures, from My heart I give to you. Your heart beats one inside of Mine, feel the passion of My love. No one can touch the plan I have, it unfolds before you now. The dawn breaks forth around you, you see My mighty hand. Hold tightly to Me and Only Me, do not look around. I am in the midst of you, My love, and I call you holy unto Me. I left My world in heaven and I came to live in you. I needed to be closer, deep inside of you. You are My love, My greatest love, and I keep you safe in Me. Do not worry, precious one, I am here with you forever. I will not leave you, ever, I am doing things for you. I love you, precious treasure, and I smile when I call you Mine.

April 29

1 Thessalonians 5:11-12

[11] Wherefore comfort yourselves together, and edify one another, even as also ye do. [12] And we beseech you, brethren, to know them which labour among you, and are over you in the Lord, and admonish you;

My healing has come to My land with My touch of sorrow and laughter, and depths of My love. I do not turn away from any who come to Me for their love, My holy one. Tell them I am in their midst all the time. They may call on My Name and I will call them to Me. They are Mine, holy one, and I want them to know of My love, and come to My Throne Room of mercy and love. I have given each one a gift from My heart, to love Me the most and bring Me the lost. Give My love to another all the days of your life, and I will give to you My joy with eternal life. Let My rivers of peace flow from you to another, and heal My parched land from My glory above. My glory surrounds you as you walk in My ways with a thankful heart that gives Me much praise. I live in your heart, so thankful and true, and I forgive you, My love, when you ask Me to. I know you are wrapped in the shell of the man that is mortal and constantly fighting My plan. I watch you fight for the strength of your spirit, and I bless you with more of Me to see you through. I look at your heart and I know its intent, you love Me the most and I bless you within. I strengthen your spirit to stand firm for Me, and I help you, My love, for you cannot do this without Me.

April 30

John 12:23-24

[23] And Jesus answered them, saying, The hour is come, that the Son of man should be glorified. [24] Verily, verily, I say unto you, Except a corn of wheat fall into the ground

and die, it abideth alone: but if it die, it bringeth forth much fruit.

The mighty ones are here and surround you day and night. They do not rest or slumber, My angelic host on high. I put My hedge of protection around you, holy one, for I Am God, The God Most High, who protects My holy ones. The songs I sing are upon you, the dawn has broken through the skies. Praise My Holy Name on high for I Am The King of All The Times. Reach out your hands and worship Me, Your Savior and Your Friend, I welcome your arms embracing Me reaching up into My heavens. Lift your head high unto Me and let Me see your sweet embrace, your smile of love, your songs so sweet coming forth from you today. I join you in your love songs and I dance upon My Throne, for My time has come upon you – you are washed in My own blood. I give you power from on high with tender, gentle ways. I give you tones of sweetness to comfort those in need. My words have come upon you, speak My words of love in them. I have the journey paved for you with gemstones by the plenty. They sparkle for Me most of all – the treasures on your path. I made the way for you, My love, the beauty that surrounds you – sparkle with them, holy one, for you are My hidden treasure.

May 1

Jeremiah 51:15-16

¹⁵ He hath made the earth by his power, he hath established the world by his wisdom, and hath stretched out the heaven by his understanding. ¹⁶ When he uttereth his voice, there is a multitude of waters in the heavens; and he causeth the vapours to ascend from the ends of the earth: he maketh lightnings with rain, and bringeth forth the wind out of his treasures.

I Am The God of All That Is And Was And Is To Be. I Am The Holy One Of Israel, and I have taken you by the hand and captured your heart. The passion of Me lives inside of you, there is no turning back, for I have prepared you for Me. You hunger for more, for you belong to Me, your mind and your soul have surrendered to Me. I show you My love as you represent Me and you weep in response from the joy you receive. Delight yourself in Your One And Only, I am here to beseech you, come deeper, My love. Dance on My mountain of all that I AM and sing out Hosanna for I Am Your King. You have wrapped yourself around Me and clung to My Word, you held on so tightly, you know My anchor holds. Your roots run deeply in My richest of soil and intertwine in My vine for we have become one. Your eyes look to Me in every situation, for I Am Your Great King who oversees every thing. I have stretched you beyond what you thought you could do and I have come to your rescue when you thought you were through. I lifted you higher and showed you My strength from above, and you smiled and you said, we made it through one more day.

May 2

Jeremiah 38:12-13

¹² And Ebedmelech the Ethiopian said unto Jeremiah, Put now these old cast clouts and rotten rags under thine armholes under the cords. And Jeremiah did so. ¹³ So they drew up Jeremiah with cords, and took him up out of the dungeon: and Jeremiah remained in the court of the prison.

My passion has come upon you, My time has arrived to bring in My lost, for it is harvest time. My process unfolds before you today and I smile on your heart so tender and true. My love does not fail you, precious one in My heart. My faithfulness comes to you each step of the way. You glorify Me and bring honor to My Name, I bless you in every step you take. My honor is true and I place it on you for My world to behold My love for you. I give you My strength when persecution comes knocking, and I hold you even closer while I take you much higher. My power is in you, holy one I have called, My Name will protect you and I never leave your side. Drink from My waters that are available to you, every night and every day, to keep you full. Breathe deeply in Me for I am here for you, every breath you take is coming from Me. I give you My fullness and love beyond measure to give to My hurting ones who are wounded and suffering. I rush to their side and bring comfort to them, through your holy vessel, I come to them. Tell them I love them with all of My heart and I will give them their health back, in every part.

May 3

Revelation 3:7-8

[7] And to the angel of the church in Philadelphia write; These things saith he that is holy, he that is true, he that hath the key of David, he that openeth, and no man shutteth; and shutteth, and no man openeth; [8] I know thy works: behold, I have set before thee an open door, and no man can shut it: for thou hast a little strength, and hast kept my word, and hast not denied my name.

I put a love, a special love, into the hearts for you. They do not understand the love they feel inside for you. They do not know I bless them for the kindness that they show. I use them, precious treasure, and they do not really know. Do not fret when I give to you from those who do not know, it is for them to give to you, for I bless them, holy one. You are My righteous one who comes to Me with all your love. I give you all of Me, My love, My holy righteous one. I take you to My secret place, designed for you alone, and tell you how I love you, My holy righteous one. I have split the skies of heaven to reach out to you, My love. You hear the roar from heaven, booming out for your relief! I have come to your rescue, My love, My holy righteous one. You bow your head before Me and weep with deep emotion, for you have seen My hand, My love, and you have felt My holy touch. My hand has come without a limit to rest on you, My love. The favor of My mercy and the favor of My grace are walking side by side with you, behold My holy face.

May 4

1 Kings 3 NLT

[10]The Lord was pleased that Solomon had asked for wisdom. [11]So God replied, "Because you have asked for wisdom in governing my people with justice and have not asked for a long life or wealth or the death of your enemies—[12]I will give you what you asked for! I will give you a wise and understanding heart such as no one else has had or ever will have! [13]And I will also give you what you did not ask for—riches and fame!

Blessed are you who comes in the Name of The LORD. Blessed are you, for I have come to you in all of My splendor to restore you back to Me. Blessed are you for I call you holy and righteous in Me. I direct your paths, I control all things, I Am Your God who hears you and I Am Your God who answers you – always. Give Me all the praise and honor, for I Am Your God who rests My glory on you. I Am Your God who sings over you. I rejoice over you for I have created your heart for Me. I love you, tender one, and I keep you in all your ways. I humble you and exalt you. I prepare you, I do not destroy. I build up, I do not tear down what I have built. I Am Your Solid Rock and you have come to Me, Your Holy One of Israel, to meet your every need. I meet your every need from the holiness of My Throne, and I send to you My vast army to surround you. The battle is won by Me and only Me, for you have given Me your life. I take your life into My bosom and I hold you in My mighty arms as I speak My Word into you.

May 5

Psalm 78:52-55 NLT

⁵² But he led his own people like a flock of sheep, guiding them safely through the wilderness. ⁵³ He kept them safe so they were not afraid; but the sea covered their enemies. ⁵⁴ He brought them to the border of his holy land, to this land of hills he had won for them. ⁵⁵ He drove out the nations before them; he gave them their inheritance by lot. He settled the tribes of Israel into their homes.

Look to the north, My precious one, as far as you can see, I bless each face before you, speak to them and love them tenderly. Look to the east, My holy one, as far as you can see, I touch each heart that listens to My Word I speak to you. Look to the south, My treasure, for I have come to you, to bless each one before you, from the goodness inside Me. Look to the west, My chosen one, for I have called you out by name to speak to all My hurting ones who have come to hear of My great love. I do not leave you ever, remember things I've done, and hold on tightly to Me, My love, My holy chosen one. I am in every heart you see, for I am bringing back My chosen ones to live with Me forever. There is no in-between with Me, no compromise can be. I want their full devotion and I will give them what they need. Come forth My bright light shining, and let My warmth emit from you. My tender ones are hurting and they need Me, precious one. I hold you closely, each step you take, I fill you with My love, and give you what you need in Me each day, My holy one.

May 6

Jeremiah 33 NLT

⁸ I will cleanse them of their sins against me and forgive all their sins of rebellion. ⁹ Then this city will bring me joy, glory, and honor before all the nations of the earth! The people of the world will see all the good I do for my people, and they will tremble with awe at the peace and prosperity I provide for them.

My face is upon you in this holy day, My love. I smile in your presence and I receive all your love. I know your heart, My precious one, for I have prepared you for this day. You clung to Me, Your Solid Rock, and I Am Your Firm Foundation. The rivers flow from deep within your holy precious soul. I send My rains to pour on them – every precious one I've chosen. Keep your eyes on only Me, My love, for I guide your path today. I bless you in this day I bring and call it holy unto Me. My waters flow in peace and love and heal with My own touch. Reach forth your hand upon them and give them of My love. I Am Your Holy God who has called you out from all you know and love. I give you all you need in Me, My precious holy love. I will not share you with another for you are Mine and Mine alone. Lift up your head high unto Me and let Me breathe My love on you. I embrace you in My holy love, there is no better place, rest your love in Me and return My sweet embrace. I love our time, our holy time of communion, precious love. Let your heart sing unto Me and bless Me, precious one.

May 7

Psalm 131 NLT

[1]LORD, my heart is not proud; my eyes are not haughty. I don't concern myself with matters too great or too awesome for me to grasp. [2]Instead, I have calmed and quieted myself, like a weaned child who no longer cries for its mother's milk. Yes, like a weaned child is my soul within me. [3]O Israel, put your hope in the LORD—now and always.

You have come to the place of My center, My love, to dance in the light with Your Holy Love. My light shines in you and sheds light on another, oh fill them My love, with My holy splendor. The way is pre-planned and the tests come and go to keep you inside My center of love. Precious you are to Me, holy one, I call you My friend and enjoy your sweet songs. I live in your midst and satisfy you with My peace and contentment when you go by My rules. Love one another, let no one be unforgiving, for therein lies the evil to take away your harmony. Protect your sweet song you sing unto Me and walk in My fullness and My victory. I am not a hard taskmaster, you will see, it is for your own good to live in oneness with Me. I sing to your heart and dance with your soul and give you the strength in times to endure. There is no other way, precious one I love, to live in My fullness and live in My love. Let no man offend you, forgive everyone, for you cannot do this without Me, precious one.

May 8

Romans 9 NLT

[21]When a potter makes jars out of clay, doesn't he have a right to use the same lump of clay to make one jar for decoration and another to throw garbage into? [22]In the same way, even though God has the right to show his anger and his power, he is very patient with those on whom his anger falls, who were made for destruction. [23]He does this to make the riches of his glory shine even brighter on those to whom he shows mercy, who were prepared in advance for glory.

These are the decisions that must be made to walk in My perfect will. If it does not flow, My holy one, it is not Me. Jealousy and envy have no part in My great plan. My holy ones cry out to Me from the anguish in their heart. I send you to them precious one, and speak to them through you. There is no greater sorrow than the piercing of the heart. Speak kindly to their brokenness and let My healing flow. The storms rage all about them and shatter all their dreams. Tell them I am here and I listen to their hearts. I bring to them My comfort and I help them overcome the rage the tide has brought to them, in this season, holy one. Extend your hand to each, My love, and help them see the love in Me. They cannot overcome the waves without their trust in Me. I oversee each detail, every thing that causes an uproar, and I bring it forth for good, My love, to destroy the plot for harm.

May 9

Ephesians 6 NLT

¹⁰Finally, my brethren, be strong in the Lord and in the power of His might. ¹¹Put on the whole armor of God, that you may be able to stand against the wiles of the devil. ¹²For we do not wrestle against flesh and blood, but against principalities, against powers, against the rulers of the darkness of this age, against spiritual *hosts* of wickedness in the heavenly *places.*

Do not be sad, precious one, I am here and I am all you need. There is none but Me and I Am Holy. I call you holy and I call you unto Me. I require much from you, I want more of your time. I will shut you down if you do not obey. You cannot do this without all of Me for I Am Your Strength. My people need Me, holy one, and I send you to them. You have been separated from the world, you do not belong to it. You belong to only Me – forever and ever. Let no one come in and try to control what I have ordained for you. I am in control of you – always. I keep you in My holy place and I feed you from My table. I give you all you want, My love, and talk with you continually. The love we share is not to be compromised – ever. My time has come upon you, I separate you even more, for you are My tender one who comes to Me for all your love. I give you words, My Words to speak in every situation. You look upon their faces and you see My touch upon their lives. You see the hurt within each heart and you hate the evil one.

May 10

Numbers 11 NLT

²⁹But Moses replied, "Are you jealous for my sake? I wish that all the LORD's people were prophets and that the LORD would put his Spirit upon them all!" ³⁰Then Moses returned to the camp with the elders of Israel.

The One you call Holy is in your presence, precious one. I leave My Great and Holy Throne and come to you, My love. I sit among your holiness for I have separated you to come and dine in My embrace and love Me. Your heart is open to Me; I enter with much ease, for your worship is so pure and acceptable by Me. I show you who I Am, My love, from My tenderness of you, and I tell you I have come to you and meet your every need. There is no greater love on earth than My love for you. I give you all of Me, My love, each minute in each day. I tend to you continually for that is My great delight. I honor you with all of Me from morning through each night. The places that you enter, inside of Me alone, are for My great refreshing from My storehouse filled with love. I do not leave you, ever, for My love for you is strong and I never tire of you. I Am Your God and you are Mine. Seasons come and seasons go with hearts that break and shatter. I send you out to heal the wounds of things that really matter. The things that matter are of the heart and love is above all. When love exists inside the heart, all other things are covered. My love breaks through and triumphs in the beauty of My song, the sweetest song I sing to you, of My love all day long.

May 11

Jeremiah 51:15-16 NLT

15The LORD made the earth by his power, and he preserves it by his wisdom. With his own understanding he stretched out the heavens. 16When he speaks in the thunder, the heavens are filled with water. He causes the clouds to rise over the earth. He sends the lightning with the rain and releases the wind from his storehouses.

The fighters must fight, the lovers must love, all for My Kingdom to each has his gift. Stretch forth your great hand, for I have strengthened you to uphold all My hurting ones and see them through. I come swiftly, My love, and then it is over, have kindness and mercy for those who must perish. Not all will be chosen and destruction is near for those who do not choose the love that I give. Have pity, My friend, for wailing and sorrow for them will never end. Let your heart beat one with Mine, holy one, and live in My compassion and mercy, My love. My time is at hand to draw My chosen ones in, keep your eyes on Me to keep My peace deep within. Flow out from Me, and only Me, for you cannot do this without all of Me, My love. Look deeper in My heart, you know Me, My love, and walk in My holiness and live in My love. No one will escape My righteous right hand and no one is forgotten and left alone in this fight. I summon forth My best to protect the ones I love, and I speak to each heart I send to you, My love. My call is great upon you, My friend, for you walk in My fullness and come to Me for your needs.

May 12

2 Corinthians 12 NLT

[8]Three different times I begged the Lord to take it away. [9]Each time he said, "My grace is all you need. My power works best in weakness." So now I am glad to boast about my weaknesses, so that the power of Christ can work through me. [10]That's why I take pleasure in my weaknesses, and in the insults, hardships, persecutions, and troubles that I suffer for Christ. For when I am weak, then I am strong.

The healing comes from within, then without. The soul is My goal, My chosen one. My process tears down and My process builds up and I strengthen and teach the ones I love. There is abundance in Me, that is true, precious one, to give to the hurting, and come to their rescue. Preach the Good News to the hurting ones and encourage the ones who are healing, My love. Some wounds are much deeper than others, My love, and time in My love heals each one from above. I have poured out My love on your tender heart and I give you My power to give of My love. My wisdom is rich and I bestow it on you for you have asked Me to give you this gift, holy one. You please Me each day and I smile upon you and I give you My "Yes" with My holiness too. I direct you, My love, in your path I have chosen and live in you fully with all My delight. I come to you tenderly and sing you My songs – they are sweet and gentle, and peaceful and strong. I pour into you extra kindness and love, for you need it to walk in My perfect love.

May 13

Romans 15 NLT

⁵May God, who gives this patience and encouragement, help you live in complete harmony with each other, as is fitting for followers of Christ Jesus. ⁶Then all of you can join together with one voice, giving praise and glory to God, the Father of our Lord Jesus Christ.

Oh the beauty of the "Yes" from My lips to you, My precious holy one. I resound the "Yes" in harmony with all of My creation. Our union is sacred and precious to Me, My love, and I enjoy giving you the desires of your heart. My passion rages, and My strength breaks forth from the love in My heart for My creation, My delight. I give you My power and I fill you with Me for every situation and every need. Let the earth ring out her pleasure in Me for I have come to receive her unto Me. Blessed is My Name and Holy I Am, filled with love and compassion, and honor and fame. Every knee will bow and every tongue will confess that I Am The LORD and there is no other. Lovely one, so pure before Me, I show you the ones who bow before Me with willing hearts and humble adoration. They speak to Me in reverence and holiness, for they know I Am Their Father and they know I really care. I have blessed you to see the hearts that love Me, they are wonderful and so precious to Me. Think on these who love only Me and praise Me, Your Father, for giving them to you. Holiness runs through your veins, precious one, for you are My treasure, My royal one. Keep your head lifted high and your eyes on Me with that beautiful smile.

May 14

Proverbs 27 NLT

¹⁷As iron sharpens iron, so a friend sharpens a friend. ¹⁸As workers who tend a fig tree are allowed to eat the fruit, so workers who protect their employer's interests will be rewarded. ¹⁹As a face is reflected in water, so the heart reflects the real person.

The war rages on as My end is near, the last days are upon you with fighting sincere. The anger is real and the hurts are many, with pain from within lashing about. I take you in Me and I show you some things, and I tell you to warn them and listen to Me. I speak to My creation, every ear can hear, if they cry out to Me for their listening ear. I want them to know Me, from youngest to oldest, and follow My footsteps to life everlasting. No one is unheard when they cry out to Me. I take every tear, every frustration and pain, and use it for all things in My eternal realm. No one is exempt from My tender touch of love and mercy, and gifts from above. I strengthen and train you in this holy war and mend every wound from the battle that leaves scars. You will not regret every step you take when you choose to release all into Me. The battle is won and the victory rings out from the heart of the ones who have completely sold out. There is no in-between in this holy war that is unseen by mortality. Let your spirit soar high on My eagle' wings and let Me continue to show you some things. My Kingdom Plan is marching on, for the goal is eternal, I want your heart in Mine. I am all around you, I never leave you, My fullest attention is set upon you.

May 15

Leviticus 26 NLT

3"If you follow my decrees and are careful to obey my commands, 4I will send you the seasonal rains. The land will then yield its crops, and the trees of the field will produce their fruit. 5Your threshing season will overlap with the grape harvest, and your grape harvest will overlap with the season of planting grain. You will eat your fill and live securely in your own land.

The winds are blowing the rains from the east. They are coming in the clouds as whirlwinds with the power of Almighty God. No one can stop it, no one can delay it – no one. I have prepared your heart, I have poured My strength in you to the point of no return. You will not look back and you will go forth in the glory of My favor, for I have come to you. I have rested My hand of tenderness upon your face. I have rested My hand of mercy upon you and I have given you My grace. I have come to you in My holiness and you have received Me with your open heart. You have obeyed Me in My timing and you have trusted Me completely. Now is the time for My power, for I have given you My wisdom and My ever flowing river runs strong in you. Do not worry, you are safe, you are protected in Me, and I Am Your Friend. There is no roar louder than My roar! There is no power greater than My power! Rejoice, for I Am The Reason For Your Rejoicing. My song comes forth, hold your head up high and receive all of Me from My mighty right hand.

May 16

2 Samuel 7 NLT

And I will give you rest from all your enemies. "'Furthermore, the LORD declares that he will make a house for you—a dynasty of kings! [12]For when you die and are buried with your ancestors, I will raise up one of your descendants, your own offspring, and I will make his kingdom strong.

My Kingdom has come to live inside you. My holiness has taken and saturated you. Every beat inside you is in harmony with Me. I bless you, My love, in My holiness. Enjoy all My gifts as I honor you. Our walk is complete inside one another, for we are united in our holy love. I join you, My love, and I live inside you and hover and guide you to see you through. My plan is perfect and under control, for My holy hand holds the balance, My love. My creation is yearning for My return, yet it rings out in love in My harmony. The strength of its song is diminished some from the day of creation, My holy one. But My songs will be sung unto Me, until My return when I gather them up and bless each one. You are My song, holy one, My creation of beauty, made in My image, adorned with My heart. I gave you My holiest gift from My heart, in My precious Son, I gave you My heart. My body was broken so you could receive the beauty of Me from the seed of creation. My Word is inside you, My Spirit is Truth, and He lives and He breathes inside of you. It is My great gift to strengthen you, for the times are too great for only you.

May 17

Isaiah 26 NLT

⁷But for those who are righteous, the way is not steep and rough. You are a God who does what is right, and you smooth out the path ahead of them. ⁸LORD, we show our trust in you by obeying your laws; our heart's desire is to glorify your name. ⁹All night long I search for you; in the morning I earnestly seek for God.

The demonstration of My power comes from the heart who loves Me. Oh the welcome I receive from the heart who loves Me. I enter into your praises and hover over you. I settle Myself among the songs of your heart and I breathe My love into you. Even the storm has a song for Me as it crashes and tosses the waves in the sea. My mighty hand is upon all things and I hold everything in the palm of My hand. But you are My tender one, special to Me, for you are My very own possession, made in the image of Me. I have given you My armor, and gifts inside Me, that sustain you and keep you in My harmony. Reach up to the sky and take each blessing I give, with thanksgiving of heart and joy from Me. I gather you up and breathe upon you, abundance from Me I give to you, My love and My power are united in Me and I give you My passion upon that old tree. No man can harm you, fear only Me, for I Am Your God who has passion for you. I do not forsake you, I walk by your side and give you the strength to walk in the tide. The ebb and the flow are part of creation, the process is growth from the dawning of time. All of creation is part of you for I made it in love to complement you. Every star, every ocean, every mountain, every breeze, the songs of creation bring comfort to you.

May 18

Ephesians 4 NLT

²Always be humble and gentle. Be patient with each other, making allowance for each other's faults because of your love. ³Make every effort to keep yourselves united in the Spirit, binding yourselves together with peace. ⁴For there is

one body and one Spirit, just as you have been called to one glorious hope for the future.

Because of your love, I will heal. Because of your heart, I will restore. The power is in the love, the unity of our love is the passion of My heart. The peace I bring is perfect when you walk in My ways. My Spirit is at rest when you obey My commands. I will not let you rest when you disobey, for you will suffer without Me. You need Me, precious one, obey Me, for it is for your own good. The work is great and I have called you out by name. Let My gentle touch be upon you, mighty one. The power is in My love, My tender precious one. My ways are much higher than you could ever know, and all My ways are good for you, holy one. Take Me in your quiet place and draw deeply from Me, for I am here inside of you, living in our love. I soothe your heart and take you to My secret place in Me. Let My waters cleanse you and refresh yourself in Me. I Am Your God and I have chosen you, and comfort you in My Holy Spirit. Drink from Me, Your Mighty King, for I have called you friend. Dine with Me, My holy one, for I have My table set for you. Take from all you see in Me, My gifts are yours to have. I help you on your path, for you live in My blessings. All the things you need, My love, are here inside of Me.

May 19

Colossians 1 NLT

[15]Christ is the visible image of the invisible God. He existed before anything was created and is supreme over all creation, [16]for through him God created everything in the heavenly realms and on earth. He made the things we can see and the things we can't see—such as thrones, kingdoms, rulers, and authorities in the unseen world. Everything was created through him and for him.

I Am A God of Mystery and I Am A God of Promise. Trust Me in all things, for I Am A God of Faithfulness. Not one thing is overlooked, My love, and not one thing goes unnoticed. I work My plan, My Kingdom Plan, for My people will perish without Me, precious one. I do not fail you – ever. I am among you bringing about My good and perfect will. My love for you is beyond what you can know or see. That is why I came, My love, to live inside of you. My plan is for eternity, with your heart one with Mine, live inside My love for you, one minute at a time. There is no hope without Me, Your Savior and Your King, I am here among you with My hand on everything. Lift your head and praise Me in the sadness of the hour, sacrifice your praise to Me in this holy hour. Sing your song of love to Me and let Me drink of your great praise, for I am close inside of you in your sacrifice of praise. There is no greater power, no strength can be as strong, as the strength I give to you, My love, in this needy hour. I Am Love, My holy one, and My love is sure and true.

May 20

Psalm 40 NLT

[1]I waited patiently for the LORD; And He inclined to me, And heard my cry. [2]He also brought me up out of a horrible pit, Out of the miry clay, And set my feet upon a rock, *And* established my steps. [3]He has put a new song in my mouth—Praise to our God; Many will see *it* and fear, And will trust in the LORD.

Precious is your name upon My lips. I speak over you with much tenderness and passion. I long to give you more of Me, I intend to give you more of Me, for I Am Your God who loves you so. No man can take away what I have given you. No man can come between us, for I Am Your Love, Your Great and Awesome Creator who created you for Me. I bless you, My creation, all the days of your life, and I take you into Me and fill you with My delight. I Am Your Every Need and I Am All Things Wonderful And Good. My eyes are fixed upon your face and My smile rests on you. Oh the beauty I behold as I look upon you and receive your love into Me. I take you in My arms and I nurture you. Oh give to My world what I give to you. I give to you, more and more every day, and I strengthen you for even more today. I Am Holy and I take you into Me and keep your heart in the center of Me. The blessings I give, you pour into Me, and fill Me with all I have given you. How pleasing you are, My holy one, I call you precious, My tender one. My glory fills you and I shine out in you, from My holiest love, I give to you. Drink deeply of Me, every place I do fill, come saturate yourself in My holy will.

May 21

Isaiah 51 NLT

[14]Soon all you captives will be released! Imprisonment, starvation, and death will not be your fate! [15]For I am the LORD your God, who stirs up the sea, causing its waves to roar. My name is the LORD of Heaven's Armies. [16]And I have put my words in your mouth and hidden you safely in my hand. I stretched out the sky like a canopy and laid the foundations of the earth. I am the one who says to Israel, 'You are my people!'"

Let My Spirit pour down on you like rain, My love. Lift up high your head unto Me and receive Me with your smile. I fill every place I have created in you with My holiness and love – I saturate you. I fill you completely for this new day as you walk in My favor, I bless you today. The strength I give you, one day at a time, is all you need – one step at a time. My mercy has fallen on you, My love, and I have captured your heart for only Me. I have a great work for you to do and I give you My promise, you will follow through. I have strengthened your heart with My holy protection, and I show you what to do as you prepare for My glory. Let no man deceive you, keep your eyes on only Me, and I will show you some things that no man has ever seen. You have captured My heart, and I devote it to you, with all of My pleasure, I commune with you. I rest My eyes on you, My faithful heart, and I give you the tools you need to minister to Me. My holiness surrounds you, My glory fills My universe, I am always with you, giving you My power.

May 22

1 John 4 NLT

[18]Dear children, let's not merely say that we love each other; let us show the truth by our actions. [19]Our actions will show that we belong to the truth, so we will be confident when we stand before God. [20]Even if we feel guilty, God is greater than our feelings, and he knows everything.

My light has dawned on your heart, holy one. I have shown you the importance of repentance, My love. There is no one perfect, no one indeed; all must bow low their heads unto Me. It is My great plan for the humble and needy to come into My fullness of love that is plenty. My love is the greatest of all things, holy one. It cures and it heals every wound. The bitterness binds and holds one so tightly, they cannot love, for it blinds and it darkens. The anger and resentment tear at the soul and cause even the sweetest to sour, My love. Repentance brings healing and washes the wounds and opens the sores and deep cleanses the root. The life that is broken comes running to Me for relief from the pain that only My love can heal. I Am Righteous and True, Holy and Pure, there is no other who can open the door for loving your enemy and forgiveness, My love. There is no other way to walk in My fullness – forgive one another as I forgive you. Let no one deceive you. All love comes from Me, all holiness too, every righteous one you see comes only from Me. I protect you from harm when I speak directly to you, do not compare what I have given you. Your portion is set from the beginning of time to serve only Me in My love and devotion.

May 23

John 21 NLT

¹⁵After breakfast Jesus asked Simon Peter, "Simon son of John, do you love me more than these?" "Yes, Lord," Peter replied, "you know I love you." "Then feed my lambs," Jesus told him. ¹⁶Jesus repeated the question: "Simon son of John, do you love me?" "Yes, Lord," Peter said, "you know I love you." "Then take care of my sheep," Jesus said. ¹⁷A third time he asked him, "Simon son of John, do you love me?"

To walk in My fullness, My price you must pay. Die to yourself and walk in My ways. Nothing can harm you or take you from Me when you walk in My fullness, I live among you. Everything you need is provided by Me, for I Am Every Thing and I Am Every Need. I give you My power, the sword is His Name, My Word sustains you when you live in My ways. No one can destroy you, or steal your peace and your joy, when you follow My footsteps and walk in My love. My Holy Spirit guides and directs, and comforts and lives in your holy temple. Let no man deceive you, My Word is true, never to change one promise to you. Live in My ways and walk in My Word. I strengthen and mend each heart I send, for you are My faithful one. Repent every day for the evil that lurks to steal and to kill My holiest ways. My Spirit gives power in every situation to bring about change in the heart of the repentant. My fire walks through you and cleanses your soul in the deepest of places, I purify you. Go out in My power and cry out to Me for all of the hurting ones you must see.

May 24

Joshua 3 NLT

⁵Then Joshua told the people, "Purify yourselves, for tomorrow the LORD will do great wonders among you."
¹¹Look, the Ark of the Covenant, which belongs to the Lord of the whole earth, will lead you across the Jordan River!
¹³The priests will carry the Ark of the LORD, the Lord of all the earth. As soon as their feet touch the water, the flow of water will be cut off upstream, and the river will stand up like a wall."

I give you what you need, My love, inside My perfect will. Today I give you strength and courage to fulfill the call upon your life, and My love to do My perfect will. Each day I guide you in My great and awesome ways always ever present in My holiness each day. I Am Your Sovereign King, My love, and give you My heart. Our communion is so special, My heart I give to you, and draw you that much closer to dwell inside of you. I fill you so completely with Me, My holy love, go tell of My great love. My power is inside you, take courage and have strength, for I always go before you and prepare the way, My love. There is no greater power – it is Me, My holy one, do not fear the unknown, for it is known to Me, Your Great And Awesome Love. I have a plan, a holy plan, and I walk in victory, for I Am God Almighty and I have called you out from Me. My rivers run so deeply inside your holy vessel, your roots grow deeply inside My love, and you are sustained by Me.

May 25

Isaiah 49 NLT

[24]Who can snatch the plunder of war from the hands of a warrior? Who can demand that a tyrant let his captives go? [25]But the LORD says, "The captives of warriors will be released, and the plunder of tyrants will be retrieved. For I will fight those who fight you, and I will save your children.

Let it be known in all the world, My salvation is near. I have My chosen ones who proclaim My love to My hurting ones. Glory to My Name on high for there is none like Me. I Am The Great And Mighty God who loves My great creation. Ring out amid My orchestra of love and full devotion, for I am here among you protecting you, My love. My power is upon you, My holiness abounds, for you are chosen for Me, I take you by the hand. My hand is tender, yet so strong, that holds your hand in Mine. I feel the tremble of your hand and hold it even tighter. You are safe inside My gentleness, My eye is keen on you, do not doubt or fret, My love, you are safe inside of Me. The world and all its splendor is created just for you – by My own hand, I created – all of it for you. There is no greater love than Me and I steady you, My love, for there is much I ask of you, My holy precious love. I breathe your "Yes" deeply in Me and smile upon your face, for you have come to Me, My love, and welcomed My embrace. I have My mighty warriors surrounding you, My love, for I have come to give you more of Me, My mighty one. I give you strength and courage as you walk in each new day, for I am in control of you each step along the way. I lead you and guide you inside My perfect will.

May 26

Acts 8 NLT

[4]But the believers who were scattered preached the Good News about Jesus wherever they went. [5]Philip, for example, went to the city of Samaria and told the people there about the Messiah. [6]Crowds listened intently to Philip because they were eager to hear his message and see the miraculous signs he did.

I have heard the cries of My hurting ones and I have come to their side to rescue them. I give you My heart, your feet and your hands will go to the hurting ones and give them My love. My Holy Spirit beats one in My love, and I have deposited Him inside of you. He is the power and comfort from Me to give to My hurting ones and set them free. My rubies adorn you, every drop of My blood glistens upon you, My holy one. I give you a crown from Me to you that gives you authority to carry them through. My Name is holy and you have come to My Throne and asked for My favor upon you, My love. My "Yes" is inside you, for you received My great love and entered My holiest place in My love. My power is great and fills inside you for every need and every place I send you. I replenish you each day in My presence, My love, and give you My plenty that never runs dry. The depths of My wells are endless, My love. Reach deep into Me and take all you want. I give you freely, for you love Me so, and walk in My presence and live in My love. I drink from your praises and live in your love and fill you completely in My holy love. My harvest awaits you, I watch you, My love, go out in My harvest and give them My love.

May 27

Isaiah 46 NLT

[9]Remember the things I have done in the past. For I alone am God! I am God, and there is none like me. [10]Only I can tell you the future before it even happens. Everything I plan will come to pass, for I do whatever I wish. …
[13]For I am ready to set things right, not in the distant future, but right now! I am ready to save Jerusalem and show my glory to Israel.

Peace I give you that the world does not see, for I Am Your Holy One who has come to you. No king ever reigned higher than Me, for I Am The Holy King who has come to honor you. You sit in My presence and drink of My love. I fill you completely and live in your love. No power is greater, for I Am All Powerful, The Great Creator, Your Holy King. I set before you life and death, you chose the path of life everlasting. I give you a hunger for more of Me, come into My presence and I will feed you. Eat from My feast set before you and I will give you My gift of devotion. I meet every need from My Great Holy Throne when you come to Me and present them, My love. I give you authority from Me, The Holy One, and My power to do what pleases Me, My love. Your heart is My heart, beating one with another and living and breathing in life everlasting. Let no man deceive you, LOVE is My Name and I come to replenish all that has been taken from Me. I bring you My love from My tender heart and I show you I love you through the blood of My Son. No love is found outside of Me, for I Am LOVE and I have come to you. I flow in your love and give you much more than you ever asked, for I Am Your Love.

May 28

Isaiah 9:6-7 NLT

[6]For a child is born to us, a son is given to us. The government will rest on his shoulders. And he will be called: Wonderful Counselor, Mighty God, Everlasting Father, Prince of Peace. [7]His government and its peace will never end. He will rule with fairness and justice from the throne of his ancestor David for all eternity. The passionate commitment of the LORD of Heaven's Armies will make this happen!

My mountains are rumbling and crashing down for you have spoken My Name in authority with your crown. Look out from among you and see My ones – My chosen ones who are wearing My crown. My ring I have given to My precious few who accept all of Me and My orders too. They go forth in love and steady the trembling of hearts, filled with pain, and thoughts that are wavering. Hold fast to My promises, every one, for My mountains are trembling and falling down. My time has come to those who persevere, for the times are now and will be greater still. My earth has its time, let no man deceive you, for I have My set plan from before its foundation. I teach you, My holy, tender vessel, and I pour out My love for all to see. I fill you with praises to Me, and I give you My tender reception. I bask in your sweetness; I bask in your love. Pour out from My holiest place inside Me, for many are hurting I send to you. My love is full inside of you, and pours out among the weary of heart. I give you My strength and love everlasting and I wash you in Me and I smile upon you. I give you the love to bestow on My hurting ones.

May 29

Micah 4 NLT

¹In the last days, the mountain of the LORD's house will be the highest of all—the most important place on earth. It will be raised above the other hills, and people from all over the world will stream there to worship. ²People from many nations will come and say, "Come, let us go up to the mountain of the LORD, to the house of Jacob's God.

I fill you with My holiness, for I Am The Holy One and I Am Your Great Father who has called you by name. You listen to Me with all of your heart and I give you a spirit that is teachable, My love. I tell you many things inside of My love and I show you My holiness and you receive My love. I have strengthened you this day to behold more of Me and I send you My gifts to serve only Me. I love you, My treasure, I look upon you with all of My love and devotion too. I remember your "Yes," I breathe in your "Yes," and your love, how you minister to Me! I Am Your Holy King who has come to you and I take you into My holiest place. You have entered into My sacred place where there is no other but our tender heartbeat. I flow through your veins, every beat of your heart is Mine. I take you and lead you, all the words you speak belong to Me, inside our heartbeat. I honor your words you speak to Me inside of My holiest place, I answer you. My "Yes" is with passion, from My heart to yours, and I call you deeper in Me, for I love you so. My power is upon you, My holy one, I call you My beloved, My tender one. There is no one greater inside of Me, your love and devotion belongs to Me.

May 30

Deuteronomy 30 NKJV

⁷"Also the LORD your God will put all these curses on your enemies and on those who hate you, who persecuted you. ⁸And you will again obey the voice of the LORD and do all His commandments which I command you today. ⁹The LORD your God will make you abound in all the work of your hand, in the fruit of your body, in the increase of your livestock, and in the produce of your land for good.

I will not allow harm to come to you as you work in My field, My love. I have My sincere ones who have a pure heart before Me. I have My teachable ones and I train them in My love. My ways are not your ways, My ways are higher and I sit upon My Throne and direct your paths. My Word sits in you and holds you tightly. You know Me, My love, you know My voice when I call. Your "Yes" comes so quickly to My ears when I call, and I smile in your quickness of "Yes" to My call. You please Me, My love, so tender and true, I give you a loyal heart, from My heart to yours. Sometimes I must wake you in the night to whisper I love you for you are My delight. My passion surrounds you and fills you with Me, for My Holy Spirit lives inside you. My universe explodes with My Holy Presence and I live all around you and show you My love. I move and I shake all of heaven and earth to come to your rescue, My holy love. Your vessel is full of My love and embrace, pour out on My hurting ones My mercy and grace. You have given to Me your feet and your hands to service My people in foreign lands. My power is in you, My strength is upon you – go to My children and love them.

May 31

Hebrews 10:35-37 NLT

[35]So do not throw away this confident trust in the Lord. Remember the great reward it brings you! [36]Patient endurance is what you need now, so that you will continue to do God's will. Then you will receive all that he has promised. [37]"For in just a little while, the Coming One will come and not delay.

My blood runs through your veins, for I have made you holy and you carry My Name. I gave you birth inside of Me to live in My presence eternally. I Am All Consuming and I have consumed you, and purified you to live in My presence, My power and grace. I fill you with more of Me every day as you enter My extra I bestow upon you. I call you holy, for you have run to Me for all of your pleasures and all of your needs. I Am All You Want, you seek Me, My love, and I have come running to give you My love. My passion burns within Me for you, and I have burned you in My flames and purified you. I have cleansed all your parts to service Me and washed you in My blood and holy water too. You come forth radiant, your face upon Me, and smiling your smile that has captured My heart. I never take My eyes off you. I Am Ever Present, never doubt for one minute, I Am Your Great Love, I Am Ever Present. I take you in Me to our secret place of love and devotion, you feel My embrace. Look upon Me, My beautiful one, and live in My fullness, for we have become one. No earthly thing can harm you, My love. I cast away all your fears in My love. Come, holy one, let Me show you much more, for I Am Your Pleasure and I Am Your Love.

June 1

Colossians 2 NLT

[2]I want them to be encouraged and knit together by strong ties of love. I want them to have complete confidence that they understand God's mysterious plan, which is Christ himself. [3]In him lie hidden all the treasures of wisdom and knowledge.

I quench the thirst, I satisfy the hunger, for I feed you My Word and you drink from My wells that never run dry. My mystery is rich and full of things that satisfy the desires that I give you. There is none but Me, and I Am The Creator of All Things, great and small – forever and ever. My holiness and My Throne sits high above all that is and was and is to be. My glory fills the universe and My power permeates the hearts who love only Me. My desire is great for My precious people. I Am All Things and I Am Their Great Desire. Show them who I Am. Shine out among the captives and let My freedom show My great release. I Am The One And Only and there is none but Me. I reign for all to see, I remove the veil from their eyes when you cry out to Me, and I send My Holy Spirit to them. I send you to them and I bring them to you, fill their mind with the things that matter. I Am All That Matters, I Am The Ruler Of All Things, and I Am Their Every Need. My justice reigns, filled with mercy and grace, as I teach My chosen ones in My loving embrace. My goodness is present when I lift the veil from the eyes that have been blinded by the tempter's snare. I untangle the hearts that have been caught in the web and I return them to Me by My holiness. Nothing can stop their return unto Me when you cry out for those I have sent to you.

June 2

1 Kings 19 NLT

After the wind there was an earthquake, but the LORD was not in the earthquake. [12]And after the earthquake there was a fire, but the LORD was not in the fire. And after the fire there was the sound of a gentle whisper. [13]When Elijah heard it, he wrapped his face in his cloak and went out and stood at the entrance of the cave.

There is no God but Me and I Am Holy and Righteous and sit upon My Throne. All glory and honor and power are Mine and Mine alone. My eyes search for the heart that is pure before Me. I have My people, I have My chosen ones who walk in the pureness of My love. The world is My footstool and My mighty right hand rests on My beloved creation It is My good and perfect will, holy one, that you bring Me much fruit. I watch you and smile upon you, I give you the strength to endure with every good and perfect gift to gather My people back to Me. I Am Your Almighty King who rules and reigns and establishes all authority in heaven and earth. I Am All Powerful, precious one, and I have opened My windows upon you and blessed you from My goodness and abundance. My mighty river runs through you with a strong current no man can stop. You are My righteous one who calls upon My Name. I Am Your Authority and I have entrusted My precious people to you. Come to Me for their needs and watch Me release Myself on your behalf.

June 3

Amos 9 NLT

[11]"In that day I will restore the fallen house of David. I will repair its damaged walls. From the ruins I will rebuild it and restore its former glory. [12]And Israel will possess what is left of Edom and all the nations I have called to be mine." The LORD has spoken, and he will do these things. [13]"The time will come," says the LORD, "when the grain and grapes will grow faster than they can be harvested.

I have a chosen people, My love. You see only in part, for that is by My design. Trust in Me, for I Am The One Who Sees and Knows from beginning until the end. I work among My chosen ones and I cleanse and separate you to walk inside My love that abounds in every part of you. My people struggle with this and that, and I watch them from My Throne. I send you to My ones who struggle, and send you in My love. Let My love flow from you, so they may stop and see, the mighty power inside My love I share with them in need. There is no explanation of why My mercy falls, it is My love that lives and breathes inside My holiness. I have restored your ruins and built you a strong city. Dance inside My holiness and live

118

in My awe and wonder. I have come and healed your wounds, and filled you in My love. Reach out your hands to those in need of a tender loving touch. I strengthen you to go to them and show them of My love. No man can tear apart My work, no man can stop My plan.

June 4

Acts 1 NLT

7He replied, "The Father alone has the authority to set those dates and times, and they are not for you to know. 8But you will receive power when the Holy Spirit comes upon you. And you will be my witnesses, telling people about me everywhere—in Jerusalem, throughout Judea, in Samaria, and to the ends of the earth."

Go out from Me, My holy one and speak of My great love and show them power from on high who saves their very soul. My glory is about you, I fill the universe with all of Me, I reign on high and fill My universe. There is no greater power than My holy love. Holy is My Name on high and fills My universe. I grant you all authority inside My Holy Name. Go about My world, My love, and use My Holy Name. Set the captives free, My love, and show them who I Am. There is no greater love on earth known by mortal man. Shout out your praises to Me, as you live inside My glory. I Am Your Holy King on high who controls with My great power. All things are controlled by My mighty hand, and submit to My great power. Shine, My bright one burning, inside My holy love. Live among My hurting ones and show them My great love. I breathe My breath upon you, and fill you in My Spirit, and speak to you of unknown things and guide you in My will. All of My creation sings of My great love. You live inside My beauty, My beauty of holiness. I watch you with My loving eye and see you, holy one.

June 5

Philippians 2 NLT

6Though he was God, he did not think of equality with God as something to cling to. **7**Instead, he gave up his divine privileges; he took the humble position of a slave and was born as a human being. When he appeared in human form, [8]he humbled himself in obedience to God and died a criminal's death on a cross.

There is no other name above My Name. Let My Name rest upon your heart, your thankful heart, and love Me all the time. I take your tender heartbeat and wrap it inside Mine to bring you My relief. I open all of heaven and pour down on you, My love. Let My essence fill you in all My holy love. I fill you full, My vessel, for you have emptied out for Me, now I may live and breathe and dwell deep inside of you. Come out from all among you and worship Me alone, for I bring you through this season to love you, holy one. I take you to My tender place of love in My embrace and whisper how I love you in My mercy and My grace. I Am Your Precious Shepherd who takes good care of you, you need not ever worry, I know just what to do. I look upon your tender heart that serves Me in your love. I will show you what to do, for there are things you do not know. I Am Your Great Protector and I know what I am doing. My peace is all around you. My good and perfect will, prevails in every aspect of your life, holy one. I Am Your Great Teacher and I teach you things. When My timing is upon you, My Word will always flow. My ways are not your ways, for My Kingdom plan is among you. I unfold in part, My love, and take your trembling hand. Keep your trust in Me, My love, for I have chosen you for more.

June 6

John 18 NLT

[36]Jesus answered, "My Kingdom is not an earthly kingdom. If it were, my followers would fight to keep me from being handed over to the Jewish leaders. But my Kingdom is not of this world." [37]Pilate said, "So you are a king?" Jesus responded, "You say I am a king. Actually, I was born and came into the world to testify to the truth. All who love the truth recognize that what I say is true."

This is a day for rejoicing, for you have heard My holy voice, and you are dancing in delight of Me, My holy one. Let all the angels sing with you, My mighty hand has come to heal the sick and dieing and heal the dry, parched land. Rejoice in Me and drink your fill and let Me wash you in My love, for I Am Holy and so strong inside My perfect love. The doubt has gone with trembling fear for I have cast it out, there is no other God but Me and My Glory fills My universe. There is none that is holy outside My precious Son's holy blood. Holy, holy, holy, is sung around My Throne, for there is none like Me, not one, no not one. My heart comes forth with passion for My people, My creation. I love them, precious treasure, I love them, holy one. I come forth from times ago and times present and evermore, for there is none like Me inside My Holy Word. I speak and all creation listens to My call, for I Am God Of All Creation.

June 7

John 15 NLT

¹⁴You are my friends if you do what I command. ¹⁵I no longer call you slaves, because a master doesn't confide in his slaves. Now you are my friends, since I have told you everything the Father told me. ¹⁶You didn't choose me. I chose you. I appointed you to go and produce lasting fruit, so that the Father will give you whatever you ask for, using my name. ¹⁷This is my command: Love each other.

There is only One and One alone and I Am He. My Name rings out above all that is and was and is to be. Proclaim today that My salvation is here, for time is short and I will not tarry My Kingdom plan. My time has been set and My Spirit is upon you. Go out in the streets and bring them to Me. Cry out for the lost and seek Me for their souls, for I am coming soon and I do not tarry, My love. Reach deep in your heart with a fervent prayer for those who are lost and those who are idle. Keep your face upon Me, do not look to another, for I am here searching your heart for love to another. My Spirit is grieved by the hearts that have turned, for love for the lost and the urgency of My return. The world takes its hold and keeps them from Me. I weep as I search for those who will serve Me. It is all about Me, My Spirit is grieved, for many have forgotten, it is all about Me. I Am The

Glory Of My Universe, The Creator Of All That Is, Was, and Will Be, and I am in the midst of all you see. Never question or doubt, it is all about Me. My power is sent to the ones who know Me, and turn not to another, for it is all about Me.

June 8

Matthew 9 NLT

¹²When Jesus heard this, he said, "Healthy people don't need a doctor—sick people do." ¹³Then he added, "Now go and learn the meaning of this Scripture: 'I want you to show mercy, not offer sacrifices.' For I have come to call not those who think they are righteous, but those who know they are sinners."

My Kingdom has come to you and settled within, for you are My vessel, you are My friend. Your love is in Me and I have reached out to you and received you into Me. My power runs through you in My holy love and My love is pure that runs through your blood. I created you from times before and formed you and placed you inside the womb. This is your time to serve Me, Your LORD and Your Savior, Your Holy King. The fullness of time has come to you for I have given you the thing you have asked of Me. I send you out with My pleasure and My smile, and I touch you completely with My holiness. I pour My blessings into all those you love, for you are My treasure, you are My love. Let the earth be aware that My time has come to heal and to free all My hurting ones. There is no great power that is greater than Me, I have all the power to release them and set them all free. You need never worry for I am with you, My love, and My full protection covers you, holy one. My glory reigns and it shines inside you, for you walk in My fullness and you walk in My truth. The way is prepared, My fire has fallen, and you will see mighty things from the touch of My finger.

June 9

Deuteronomy 33 NLT

²⁴Moses said this about the tribe of Asher: "May Asher be blessed above other sons; may he be esteemed by his brothers; may he bathe his feet in olive oil. ²⁵May the bolts of your gates be of iron and bronze; may you be secure all your days." ²⁶"There is no one like the God of Israel.

Your obedience is My refreshing and My great reward. I come forth strong on your behalf, for you have come to Me, Your Refuge And Your Strength. There is no other name but Mine and I Am The One Who Can, I Am The One Who Wants To, oh yes, My love, I Am The Great I Am. No fear comes near your tent, My love, no worry will you see, for you have put your trust in Me and I have come to bring relief. The power that is Mine, My love, lives in your heart and soul, My Spirit lives inside of you and I Am The Greatest One! Let no one deceive you, stand firm upon My Word. There is no lie within Me, there is none, My holy one. My Word is Truth, for I Am Truth, let no one take My place. Live inside My Holy Word and breathe life into the dead. There is no one greater, there is no one but Me, rejoice in Me, My precious one, for I have come to you. All sickness must leave, when you command the thing to go, for in My Holy Name, My love, all sickness must go. My Name rests upon your lips and you know Me, tender one. The battle is not yours, My love, the battle is Mine! I go forth before you as you praise Me, holy one. Grab My Words of promises and cling to every one, for I Am God Almighty, I Am The Only One. I Am Truth, there is no lie, drink deeply from My Word, for it is life to you.

June 10

Ephesians 1 NLT

¹⁵Ever since I first heard of your strong faith in the Lord Jesus and your love for God's people everywhere, ¹⁶I have not stopped thanking God for you. I pray for you constantly, ¹⁷asking God, the glorious Father of our Lord Jesus Christ, to give you spiritual wisdom and insight so that you might grow in your knowledge of God.

My heart heard your heart. My heart felt your heart. I beat one with you in our perfect love. I have sent forth My power to deliver each one into My holiness, in My perfect love. I know your heart, there are many more you have not named but you love them so. I take each one you love and I hold them so closely inside My great love and I keep them in Me. There is a place you have reached inside Me that gives Me much pleasure to say "Yes" to you. Let the wind and the rain come to you, My power and blessings I bestow upon you. Rejoice in My love and love one another, for I am in your midst, I am in your love. The love that we share is set aside and holy, no one has this place inside our holy love. I speak to you gently and prepare you for more, hold tightly to My Word and live in My love. I Am Tender And Strong, I surge and I ebb, and strengthen and weaken, and correct you, My love. I keep you in Me each step of the way and guide you to greater things hidden in Me. I walk by your side and speak to you gently, go here, now go there, now come back for refreshing. Observe as you go and cry out to Me, for all the lost souls I have shown you, My love.

June 11

Luke 11 NLT

[41]So clean the inside by giving gifts to the poor, and you will be clean all over. [42]"What sorrow awaits you Pharisees! For you are careful to tithe even the tiniest income from your herb gardens, but you ignore justice and the love of God. You should tithe, yes, but do not neglect the more important things.

Keep your eyes on only Me, Your Heavenly Father, for you will wither and die without Me, My love. Our time and our place are united in love, for we are one in our spirit, one in our love. The evil one tries to distract you from Me, keep all My commands and serve only Me. You have been bought with a price that is holy. You belong to Me only in the blood of My Son. Cover yourself in My Son's holy blood and walk in My goodness and walk in My love. My shadow is on you everywhere you go, walk in My fullness, walk in My love. Lay hands on the sick and watch them recover, for the cost has been paid in the blood of The Lamb. Obey Me completely, for that is My will, it is for your own good to obey Me, My love. Breathe deeply in My glory, for it fills My universe. I Am GOD Almighty and I Am Holy. My power comes forth from My love and My grace. My mercy is with you and My favor too, come out from among them and follow My lead. The dance I have given you is precious to Me, dance in My joy and let Me honor you. My love sways and lives in My harmony, the dance of the ages, come, dance with Me.

June 12

Psalm 9 NLT

¹I will praise you, LORD, with all my heart; I will tell of all the marvelous things you have done. ²I will be filled with joy because of you. I will sing praises to your name, O Most High. ³My enemies retreated; they staggered and died when you appeared. ⁴For you have judged in my favor; from your throne you have judged with fairness.

The ways of sin – oh the death that it brings. My people, My precious people, do not obey Me, holy one. Oh pray for them, My love, for they are lost and are dying. They need Me, holy one, they do not know, they need Me so. Oh the sin, the sin that so easily besets them, they cannot let go, they cannot move forward, help them, My love. Cry out from your soul, let your fervency penetrate Me, I will move – I will move. You walk in My love, walk in My wisdom. As I show you a need, cry out to Me. I Am God, Your God, and I send them to you. Every need, bring them to Me. I do not place you by accident, I send you, I send them to you. Observe all you see, cry out for their relief, for I make you aware, do not let one go unattended by your prayer. You are on assignment, this is not your home. You belong to Me and I sent you to help My hurting ones. They are hurting, holy one. Cry out to Me, I will ease their pain. Let My obedient ones cry out to Me. The evil takes, the evil destroys, the evil kills. Live in My fullness, walk in My ways, seek Me, you will find Me and I will answer you. My "Yes and Amen" are upon My lips for you. Do not let one go unattended, pray for one another, My love, for I heal, I mend, I restore and I bless.

June 13

Luke 5 NLT

²He noticed two empty boats at the water's edge, for the fishermen had left them and were washing their nets. ³Stepping into one of the boats, Jesus asked Simon, its owner, to push it out into the water. So he sat in the boat and taught the crowds from there. ⁴When he had finished speaking, he said to Simon, "Now go out where it is deeper, and let down your nets to catch some fish."

My Word is revealed, My Name is honored, for you have found My heart and you have obeyed Me, My love. You know My plans for you are good, I allow you no harm, for you walk in My love and forgive everyone. My blessings flow down like My sweet gentle rain and refreshing comes down upon your face. Lift high your smile unto Me and let Me behold your face, precious one. My heart overflows when you honor Me, and I swoop down like an eagle and pick you up. Rise higher in Me, for I have much to show you, come into this place of more in My love. When revelation comes upon you and repentance comes next, My process is working and you grow in My love. I sing over you, for the victory is won, when you walk in My precepts and follow My plan. My dance is upon you, My joy overflows and bursts from your heart – enjoy Me, My love. The rivers run deeply inside your great love, for you have My great love that flows freely in you. You have lengthened your days for you honor your parents. You walk in forgiveness, and love all your neighbors, and bless all your enemies.

June 14

Jeremiah 31 NLT

³³But this *is* the covenant that I will make with the house of Israel after those days, says the LORD: I will put My law in their minds, and write it on their hearts; and I will be their God, and they shall be My people. …
³⁵It is the LORD who provides the sun to light the day and the moon and stars to light the night, and who stirs the sea into roaring waves.

Is there a mountain in your way? Oh, what mountain do you say? The one that keeps you far from Me and blocks your view of all of Me. See beyond the eyes of the mortal inside your mind of reason and logic. Come into My world of holy divine favor and walk in My light and live in My glory. You limit yourself by the mountain view, come climb up higher, let Me show you My view. Breathe deeply in Me and believe every Word I have given to you by My Son's Holy Blood. The mountains you see crumble in Me when you look to My Word to teach you of Me. The more you behold My holy pure love, the more the great mountains diminish, My love. The power in Me comes from My great love, filled with passion and determination to make you see Me. I set before you choices to make, some can destroy you and some can restore you. Do you prefer the view of the mountains, or do you prefer the view of My holiness? The choice has been set before you, My love. Do you want to honor Me, Your Holiest Love? Come, seek My great face, for I have turned My face to look upon you. My banquet is set for you and for Me, come dine in My presence and let Me speak to your heart. Reach deeply inside Me and ask what you will, for I answer you in love.

June 15

Luke 13:6-9 NLT

[6]Then Jesus told this story: "A man planted a fig tree in his garden and came again and again to see if there was any fruit on it, but he was always disappointed. [7]Finally, he said to his gardener, 'I've waited three years, and there hasn't been a single fig! Cut it down. It's just taking up space in the garden.' [8]"The gardener answered, 'Sir, give it one more chance. Leave it another year, and I'll give it special attention and plenty of fertilizer. [9]If we get figs next year, fine. If not, then you can cut it down.'"

Do not be too busy to hear My voice, for I Am Your Great Love and I always come first. You yearn for more of Me because I long for more of you. Live in My love, drink from My fountains, eat at My table and commune with Me. Walk in My love, let it flow out from you, for you have been in My presence and taken from Me. I give you much more, just ask of Me, I fill you completely with all of Me. Go when I tell you, come back when I tell you, rest when I tell you, dine when I tell you. Live in Me fully and delight in My Word, obey Me completely, for you are not your own. Ask Me for much to serve Me well, for I Am Your Fullness and My well never runs dry. I stand by your side as you feed all My needy, with holiness about you, I protect you in Me. I go before you and touch the hearts of My people to receive Me in love. My heart overflows into your tender heart and I take every tear and count it as holy.

June 16

Matthew 25 NLT

[34]Then the King will say to those on His right hand, 'Come, you blessed of My Father, inherit the kingdom prepared for you from the foundation of the world: [35]for I was hungry and you gave Me food; I was thirsty and you gave Me drink; I was a stranger and you took Me in; [36]I *was* naked and you clothed Me; I was sick and you visited Me; I was in prison and you came to Me.'

The winds are now blowing in every direction. Take heed as I show you which direction to take. I prepare you for much and I have watered you in Me and now is the time to flourish for Me. Hold tightly to the things I have told you, My love, for now is the time to receive more of Me. Let no one deceive you, My Spirit has come to separate you, My holy one. Stand tall in this time, do not let fear come upon you, for that is not Me, and you must trust Me only. I take you inside My secret place, let no one disturb your time in My presence. You cannot survive, not one breath can you take, without Me, My love, without My great grace. The evil watches and waits without resting, to tear you apart if you give it an opening. Keep My full armor on and remember My Words, for you have My promises and you have My assurance. My blessings flow down upon you, My love, for you are My obedient one who walks in My Word. My rivers run deeply inside you, My love. Keep your thoughts on Me only, and lift high your head, as you sing in My presence that surrounds you, My love.

June 17

Jeremiah 8 NLT

[20]"The harvest is finished, and the summer is gone," the people cry, "yet we are not saved!" [21]I hurt with the hurt of my people. I mourn and am overcome with grief. [22]Is there no medicine in Gilead? Is there no physician there? Why is there no healing for the wounds of my people?

Ah, yes, the balm of Gilead still flows today. My nations spread forth from the balm I have sent, to heal and restore. Let My blessings flow, for I have heard you, holy one. The cries and the sorrows are heard by Me, and I have come forth for such a time as this. The mighty finger of God has moved – no evil can move – no evil can stand – all evil must flee when I lift My holy hand! I lift My hand and I wave My Spirit and I hover and I see, and I redeem and restore. I live in My people, I stir up My people, and I work mighty things through My holy ones. Come forth, My holy ones, rise up in My glory and let Me show you My mighty works among My people. I rain down on the just and the unjust, for I Am Your Merciful God and I Am Your Savior. I Am Your Redeemer and I Am Your King. Bring Me My lost, bring Me My precious creation, let My will be known in all the lands! It is not My will that any should suffer! It is not My will any should perish! Hell has been assigned to the evil one and the demons – not My precious people! Know My Word – hear My Word – live in My Word – for it is not flesh and blood you fight! It is Me, Your Holy One Of Israel, who fights these battles!

June 18

Isaiah 9 NLT

[6]For a child is born to us, a son is given to us. The government will rest on his shoulders. And he will be called: Wonderful Counselor, Mighty God, Everlasting Father, Prince of Peace. [7]His government and its peace will never end. He will rule with fairness and justice from the throne of his ancestor David for all eternity. The passionate

commitment of the LORD of Heaven's Armies will make this happen!

The times are now to assemble yourselves together, encouraging one another, for the times are evil. The snares are set and the one who pounces is ready. Oh, but I Am God, The Almighty One, do not forget your benefits in Me. I never leave you unattended, I never leave you without My instructions, I never leave you – ever. You are not alone, precious one – I have My people, My chosen people, My generation of royal priests, I have you, My beloved, and you have My powerful Holy Spirit. Let not your heart be troubled, look to Me and only Me, for I Am Your Every Need and I Am The One who can meet your every need. There is no need too small for Me, precious one. There is no need too great for Me, My holy one. I Am The Detail in you and I watch over every detail, for you are My heart, My love, My desire. Draw closer to Me for I want to show you My great love, My power is in My love and My glory radiates when you walk in My love. They are drawn out of darkness by My love. I Am The All Powerful One and I Am Love.

June 19

Philippians 4 NLT

⁸And now, dear brothers and sisters, one final thing. Fix your thoughts on what is true, and honorable, and right, and pure, and lovely, and admirable. Think about things that are excellent and worthy of praise. ⁹Keep putting into practice all you learned and received from me—everything you heard from me and saw me doing. Then the God of peace will be with you.

Oh the land of plenty you have found, for in My heart you stay. I relish every word you speak and capture them – to hold and treasure in My deepest place, the center of My heart. My "Yes" and My "Amen" come forth so mightily for you, My precious priceless treasure, I am in love with you. Your arms raised high unto Me are smiled upon by Me. You fill My heart with pleasure as I look upon your praise. The harmony of Me in you rings out its truest tones – oh the healing that flows out from you, inside My storehouse filled with love. My gates have opened wide for you, oh let the rivers flow – I have strengthened you for more of Me inside My perfect love. Glory to My Name on high for I have come to you. My chosen one, My precious one, I am so pleased with you. I protect you and I sing My songs of love from Me to you. Oh how mighty is My song I sing over you, My holy one. Enjoy My presence always, for I am ever at your side. I never leave you – ever – I enjoy being at your side.

June 20

Isaiah 55 NLT

[11]It is the same with my word. I send it out, and it always produces fruit. It will accomplish all I want it to, and it will prosper everywhere I send it. [12]You will live in joy and peace. The mountains and hills will burst into song, and the trees of the field will clap their hands!

I honor your requests this day for I have received your sincere heart. I listen to your fervent prayers, I listen, holy one. The day is here for healing, restoration is beginning, My mighty hand reaches out to all the lost and dying. I say "Yes" to you, My love. I send you to the hurting, I show you of My tenderness and touch their hearts, My love. The hour is upon you, I bless you, precious one. I have My hidden treasures, I know them, holy one. Don't look back, My holy one, don't look back forever more. I take you into more of Me – so high above the storms. I welcome you inside My place of so much more of Me. Come dance inside My holiness and watch Me closely. The honor and the glory you will give Me, holy one. I trust you with the more in Me and protect you from the fall. I keep you humble and so pure inside My perfect love. You were created for My love, My power comes forth for you. You are My treasure, My precious one. I love to show you more, for I have given you of Me, the love that burns within, for My people, precious one. Bring them to Me one by one and give them of My love. Let no one go unnoticed, I'll show you, holy one. Cry out for them and comfort Me as you bring Me more and more, My priceless, hidden treasures, I love them, precious one.

June 21

2 Chronicles 30 NLT

For Hezekiah said, "May the LORD, who is good, pardon those [19]who decide to follow the LORD, the God of their ancestors, even though they are not properly cleansed for the ceremony." [20]And the LORD listened to Hezekiah's prayer and healed the people.

[27]Then the priests and Levites stood and blessed the people, and God heard their prayer from his holy dwelling in heaven.

There is room for you, My holy one. My power runs through you and I have given you My "Yes" and "Amen." I hear your prayers for My people. I know your sincere heart. You know the power of My forgiveness and you know My tender heart. You refresh Me in your love and I am pleased that I have given you My Name. The power flows from My great love, the sacrifice was given. My Holy Spirit lives in you and fills you with My power. I Am Your Love, Your Greatest Love, and I meet you where you are. I have never left you – ever. I am always at your side. My Kingdom comes and My will is done on earth as it is in heaven. I Am Almighty and All Strong to meet your every need. I want to come forth for you, for I love to show you who I Am. I Am Your Blessing and Your Love, I Am Your Great I AM. Never doubt My love for you, I Am Strong on your behalf. I call you holy and righteous, for you obey Me, precious one. I sanctify and purify your soul in My great love. I know your heart, I know your mind, I work inside your faith and love, and show you who I am.

June 22

Romans 15 NLT

[7]Therefore, accept each other just as Christ has accepted you so that God will be given glory. [8]Remember that Christ came as a servant to the Jews to show that God is true to the promises he made to their ancestors. [9]He also came so that the Gentiles might give glory to God for his mercies to

them. That is what the psalmist meant when he wrote: "For this, I will praise you among the Gentiles; I will sing praises to your name."

Oh the praises of My people! My precious, holy vessels, how they pour out themselves to obey My precious Word. How they honor Me, holy one! My heart sings out upon them and I comfort My ones, My chosen ones, who sacrifice for Me. How I honor the hearts of My people! I look deeply inside the heart of man and I see the unseen things. I see the heart, the tender heart, in the captive and the free. I send forth My people, so precious in My heart, to help My poor and hurting ones, so dear to My own heart. I put desires into those who work My perfect will, and send them to the ones I choose to bring My people back to Me. I strengthen and encourage and meet your every need, do not worry, chosen one, I am here to take you deeper into Me. Oh the love I have for you cannot be measured by your finite mind, for I Am Infinity. You cannot know all things I do, for your mind cannot comprehend the ways of Me, Your Almighty God, who sees what you cannot.

June 23

Matthew 7 NLT

24"Anyone who listens to my teaching and follows it is wise, like a person who builds a house on solid rock. 25Though the rain comes in torrents and the floodwaters rise and the winds beat against that house, it won't collapse because it is built on bedrock.

Mighty warrior, I love you so. I see your heart, I see your sacrifice, and oh how I see your obedience. You are My great delight, My smile, My pleasure. I bless the day of your creation and I rest My smile on you. The days of few are over and I give you of My more. You enter into My holiness with My favor and My grace. I listen oh so carefully to your requests both great and small. With all My heart and tenderness, I give you of My all. I surround you, precious love of Mine, in holiness and truth. I come to you so gently and comfort you in Me. I know your fears, I know your thoughts, as I hold you deep inside My love. I give you My assurance, you are not alone, My love. I live in you and breathe in you and surround you, holy one. I have a great work for you, for I trust you with My power. I prepare the hearts of those I chose for you, bring them to Me, precious one, for they are precious in My sight. I Am Your God, My sweet creation, I call you blessed, holy one. I strengthen you for more of Me and heal your deepest wounds – for you have come to Me, Your Creator, for your every need. I straighten all the crooked paths and take you by the hand and lead you down the paths I make for you and you alone. Enjoy My pleasures and My rest when you walk in My harmony. I strengthen and encourage you for each new path you take.

June 24

Matthew 28 NLT

[18]Jesus came and told his disciples, "I have been given all authority in heaven and on earth. [19]Therefore, go and make disciples of all the nations, baptizing them in the name of the Father and the Son and the Holy Spirit. [20]Teach these new disciples to obey all the commands I have given you. And be sure of this: I am with you always, even to the end of the age."

You see My hand about you. My signs are all about, I fulfill My promise to you – every Word is not left out. I give you this, I give you that, and allow you time to heal. Then I take, and take some more, and tell you to trust Me in your wait. You pray and trust Me only, you fast and pray some more. You study and bow down to Me and go when I tell you go. I speak My gentle Words to you and send you those for confirmation. It is My will to strengthen you until your cup is over filled. The time of revelation has come to you. The strings that could have pulled you back are now snapped and thrown away. Hidden things I show you and cleanse you in My blood. When repentance comes, I wash you deeply inside My Word. Your sword is sharpened by My Word, the sharpest sword of all. You may wield it now and cut the cords of those that are so bound. The love of Me is in you, so powerful and mighty. I give you love for another, go help them, precious one. The prophets have all spoken, each thing has been foretold. You know the time is short, My love.

June 25

Ephesians 2 NLT

[4]But God is so rich in mercy, and he loved us so much, [5]that even though we were dead because of our sins, he gave us life when he raised Christ from the dead. (It is only by God's grace that you have been saved!) [6]For he raised us from the dead along with Christ and seated us with him in the heavenly realms because we are united with Christ Jesus.

My tenderness waits, very close by, waiting to hold you after you cry. I live inside you, I never will go, keep your eyes on Me only and live in My love. You do not understand what you see all about, but I know what to allow and I know what to stop. My power is in you for you gave Me your life with all of your heart and all of your mind. I teach you about dominion and respect. I show you My love, and reveal to you My great tender touch. The effective door that is open to you comes with adversity and suffering too. Lean on Me and only Me, and hear Me when I speak. I will not mislead you, I will not remain silent. My love conquers all, do not ever doubt, the resources of Me never run out. The way is before you, the gifts are upon you, My power is in you and I lead you on. The tender reed breaks when the winds start to blow, I have strengthened your frame and rooted you deeply in My love. Go deeper into My waters that flow, and fasten your roots deeply in My love. The pulling and tugging will not take you from Me, for I have prepared you for more of Me.

June 26

Psalm 46 NLT

[4]A river brings joy to the city of our God, the sacred home of the Most High. [5]God dwells in that city; it cannot be destroyed. From the very break of day, God will protect it.

Psalm 47 NLT

[2]For the LORD Most High is awesome. He is the great King of all the earth. [3]He subdues the nations before us, putting our enemies beneath our feet. [4]He chose the Promised

Land as our inheritance, the proud possession of Jacob's descendants, whom he loves.

Oh the praises of My people! The sacrifice of praise is holy in My sight. I sing to you in times like these and nurture you in Me. The mountains crumble in the sea, both great and small they crumble, when you worship Me in the assembly and you worship Me alone. I honor you from your sacrifice and obedience to My wishes. Nothing goes unnoticed for I watch over you tenderly and carefully and meet your every need. I speak to you from times before and remind you of My love. Think of all the times before and refresh yourself in My Great Word to strengthen you this day. I have fortified you in My power, My great and awesome love flows through you like a river that strengthens as it goes. No one can stop the things I do, no one can slow it down. I have My ways, My perfect ways, and My timing is on schedule. I Am Your Mighty King and I rule above all the earth. Nothing goes unnoticed, nothing small or great.

June 27

Psalm 46 NLT

[1]God is our refuge and strength, always ready to help in times of trouble. [2]So we will not fear when earthquakes come and the mountains crumble into the sea. [3]Let the oceans roar and foam. Let the mountains tremble as the waters surge! *Interlude* …
[7]The LORD of Heaven's Armies is here among us; the God of Israel is our fortress.

The fish carry coins when commanded by Me and the ravens feed My chosen one when ordered by Me. The leprosy leaves by a thought of Mine and withered hands are restored when I command. The blind see when I speak, whether it is by this way or that, and the thousands are fed by a boy's little lunch. The disobedient can live in the fish for three days and the one who denied Me three times was forgiven. I Am Merciful And Just and I love My people so. I forgive and restore and protect in My love. I see the destroyer among My great people and I send you to tell them – My love is the key. I give and I take and I restore you to Me, for you are My treasure, hidden – oh, but I see! The Words I speak are powerful and true. If you obey Me and follow My rules, I heal you inside My greatest love. I sing over you and I restore your precious soul. The protection is great and surpasses all evil, when you turn to My Son for He shed His blood. The sacrifice was given; the price has been paid, by the blood of The Lamb, The Holy One Of Israel is His Name. Live in My fullest, surrender to Me, and watch Me take over, for goodness to bring. I give you a choice, whether life or death, you chose Me, My love, I bless you and your children all the days.

June 28

Mark 9 NLT

49"For everyone will be tested with fire. 50Salt is good for seasoning. But if it loses its flavor, how do you make it salty again? You must have the qualities of salt among yourselves and live in peace with each other."

I have My ways, My higher ways, which you cannot imagine, for I Am God and I Am The Keeper Of All Things. Oh the touch, the tender touch, of every detail I give. Nothing is left to chance and nothing is wasted in My precious tender ways. I make all things good the evil intended for harm. Live in My love, rejoice in My promises, sing in the times of waiting and uncertainty, for I am certain of all things, I have no uncertainty in Me. Rejoice, precious one, for I Am Your Savior! I do not come and then leave you. I have many attendants who attend to every thing in all of heaven and earth. Rejoice, My one who waits, for you will always hear from Me. When you seek Me, you will always find Me. I am not hard to find and I am not silent on your behalf. My voice booms, and the earth trembles, and I command the things I have for you. With no delay and not half-way, I command the promises set for this day. Receive My blessings and rejoice, My precious love. I Am Your God who tends to you in My very careful ways, My higher ways, not your ways, My higher understanding, not your understanding. Oh the power inside My love, My great and awesome mercy flows from Me to you in such a mighty way. Oh the glory that is Mine to give to each and every vessel. I love you, chosen vessel, I love you, precious one.

June 29

Luke 3 NLT

⁴Isaiah had spoken of John when he said, "He is a voice shouting in the wilderness, 'Prepare the way for the LORD's coming! Clear the road for him! ⁵The valleys will be filled, and the mountains and hills made level. The curves will be straightened, and the rough places made smooth. ⁶And then all people will see the salvation sent from God.'"

Oh the rivers of joy, how it strengthens the current and flows in My mightiest power! Oh the joy of the humble soul, the one who loves and adores Me and appreciates My love. My touch is sacred, My will is holy, and I do not release My power to those who condemn! I Am The Keeper Of The Seas and My tempest roars! I open and close and I give and take. I Am The Revealer Of Things, I soften the hearts and open eyes to see Me. I harden the hearts and veil the eyes of those who do not see, I Am Power and Might and I waiver not. I Am Love and I Am Tender, I Am Kind and I Am Gentle. I Am Merciful And Forgiving, and I am intolerant of things. You find Me mysterious and loving in you. My revelation is upon you as I have taken you through a mighty open door that is effective for Me. I have set you upon My eagles' wings and taken you higher than the insignificant things. Soar high on My lift and sing unto Me, Your Precious Redeemer, Your Great And Mighty King. Let Me take you higher and higher and watch you, My love, come fly on My heights of infinity, holy one. Breathe in My presence and swim in My love, and live in My holiness and walk in My love. The hand of My mercy has come to you.

June 30

1 Kings 8 NLT

"O LORD, God of Israel, there is no God like you in all of heaven above or on the earth below. You keep your covenant and show unfailing love to all who walk before you in wholehearted devotion. ²⁴You have kept your promise to your servant David, my father. You made that promise with your own mouth, and with your own hands you have fulfilled it today.

138

Oh the wisdom I bring when you call upon Me and I send you My chosen ones to bring you relief. My Comforter is in you, hearing your cries, and bringing to Me your needs and desires. He has searched My mind and knows you so well. He knows what you need and He brings you relief. Let My Holy Spirit speak through you, My love, for He has the answers for the hurting ones who come to you. My power is in you, all bondage is gone, you fly with My eagles, oh holy one. I come to My hurting ones and bring them relief. I Am The Good Shepherd and I tend to My sheep who are living each day in burdens, My love. I send you to them and I send them to you, the times are full of evil and My children need My attending. I Am Ever Present and I never look away, My ear is always open to hear you when you pray. My response is immediate; My answer is "Yes," for I have captured your heart in My holiness. My thoughts live in you, so easily received by your willing mind to please Me, Your King. I delight in your love and I smile upon you, for you have been through the valley and repented to Me. My forgiveness is rich and so free to all who want to serve only Me and live in My love.

July 1

Psalm 52 NLT

8But I am like an olive tree, thriving in the house of God. I will always trust in God's unfailing love. 9I will praise you forever, O God, for what you have done. I will trust in your good name in the presence of your faithful people.

I set you apart for times inside Me to saturate you with My peace and harmony. I give you this day, rest in My love, for times are now changing, My holy one. My "Yes" has come sweetly and tenderly, for I honor your love for My precious holy people. The ones I give you to bring to Me are of My greatest of value, My hidden most treasures. I give you times of refreshing after the anointing. Remember the prayers you have cried out to Me, and reflect on each one as I have answered you. I have never deserted you, not for any part of time, I have always been close and I have always heard your cry. In your darkest of places, I have comforted you and I have given you My needed touch. I come forth mightily for you, and I take you even further on this new path. Do not worry, My love, for you have given Me your every desire and your every need. I take each one and breathe My tender "Yes" and "Amen" inside you, My love. My mightiest ones are sent out to you, enjoy Me, My love, enjoy all My gifts. Oceans do roar and crash about but are nothing compared to My little finger. The sun shines its brightest set in its place, but nothing is as bright as My holy face. My face is upon you, My glory is here, My people are precious, bring them to Me. Tell them I love them and I want their soul to live in My love for eternity. My never ending song is sung over you as you walk in My love and follow My rules.

July 2

Genesis 49 NLT

25May the God of your father help you; May the Almighty bless you with the blessings of the heavens above, and blessings of the watery depths below, and blessings of the breasts and womb. 26May the blessings of your father surpass the blessings of the ancient mountains, reaching to the heights of the eternal hills. May these blessings rest on the head of Joseph, who is a prince among his brothers.

Let this new day shine brightly for you, My beloved, My treasure, My holy one. My smile is so sweet when I look upon you and I behold the beauty I have created in you. Let My Name be praised in all of heaven and earth, for I created your beauty from before the creation of the world. My song over you is loud and is strong to shatter the windows of heaven, My love. Let My blessings break forth from each shattered place, and sing to Your Holy One and behold My sweet face. Oh the glory of Me I give to you, ring out, precious one, in My harmony. Let your heart rejoice and be glad, for this is the day I created for you to celebrate My love. Tremble oh mountains and fall into the seas, for My chosen one comes and speaks to you. My Name is used boldly for you trust Me so. Oh come holy one, enjoy My great song. Dance on the heights of forever, My love, for My yoke is easy when you walk in My love. Oh the sound of My victorious ones who live in My praises and sing My love songs. I inhabit your praise in My mighty way, for I Am Your King who rules in great display!

July 3

Joshua 1 NLT

[5]No one will be able to stand against you as long as you live. For I will be with you as I was with Moses. I will not fail you or abandon you. ...
[8]Study this Book of Instruction continually. Meditate on it day and night so you will be sure to obey everything written in it. Only then will you prosper and succeed in all you do. [9]This is my command—be strong and courageous! Do not be afraid or discouraged. For the LORD your God is with you wherever you go."

Hold tightly to My promises, hold tightly, precious one, for I have given much to you inside My perfect love. Let My bright light shine upon the much I have given, for My hurting ones are many and they need My tender touch. My love flows abundantly into your willing heart, for you obey Me quickly and never doubt My love. Your love has been established inside My perfect will, for I have taken you in Me and kept you close inside My

141

heart. I speak to you in tenderness and guide you in My ways. I give to you My greater things for you walk in victory. My mighty right hand is upon you and My smile is in your soul. You know I love you, mighty one, you know I love you so. The evil tried to take you, oh, but I created you for Me. Before I formed the world for you, I created you for Me. My love rests deeply within your heart, the center of your soul. Your desires are for Me, My love, you hunger for much more. I desire more of you, oh come, My hungry one. My glory rests upon you for you flow inside My love.

July 4

Isaiah 12 NLT

¹In that day you will sing: "I will praise you, O LORD! You were angry with me, but not any more. Now you comfort me. ²See, God has come to save me. I will trust in him and not be afraid. The LORD GOD is my strength and my song; he has given me victory." ³With joy you will drink deeply from the fountain of salvation!

Flower, precious flower, you bloom so rich and free, oh the colors of your love, I behold them just for Me. Oh the sweet scent wafting into Me as you pray, for salvation to My hurting ones you meet along the way. I breathe My deepest "Yes" to you and bring them great relief, for I take them in My fertile soil and teach them about Me. Glory, glory to My Name, The One Who Sits Much Higher, I Am God Almighty and this is My finest hour. Gather My great harvest, for I have come to you. Behold the beauty of My love, the freedom found in Me. Flower, precious flower, who blooms so rich and free, My soil is good beneath you, your roots grow deep in Me. My water rains down on you, so refreshing from the heat. Let My cool and gentle breezes bring you joy inside of Me. Lift your head, My beautiful one, stand up tall for Me, for you are My refreshing and you bring Me much relief. I name My precious flowers and I put them in My fields and watch them grow and live for Me inside My perfect love. Oh My fields of plenty stretching up to Me, stand tall beloved flowers, stand up tall for Me. Sway and sing and clap your hands and smile your sweetest smile, for I am looking on My lands and tending all My soil. I separate the weeds, My love, and give you of My touch.

July 5

2 Corinthians 9 NLT

[9]As the Scriptures say, "They share freely and give generously to the poor. Their good deeds will be remembered forever." [10]For God is the one who provides seed for the farmer and then bread to eat. In the same way, he will provide and increase your resources and then produce a great harvest of generosity in you. [11]Yes, you will be enriched in every way so that you can always be generous.

The roar of Me, the oceans crash, the waves, the billows, the doors and the latches. I open, I shut, I heal, and I destroy the evil that knocks at your door. No one can touch My anointed ones for their appointed seasons and their loved ones. My mighty right hand rests on you, and none can stop what I have for you. Hear My roar, feel My winds, let the earth tremble and quake! Then listen, My love, for My soft gentle whisper. Come, precious one – come this way. I am right beside you holding you close, lean on Me, My beloved, I am devoted to you. Trust Me completely, for I Am Yours – forever. I died in your stead on that glorious day. Let My third day ring out, My victory stands strong, you are My beloved, you are My very own. Look to Me only, I Am Your Relief, I Am Your Savior, Your Holy King. I assure you, I remind you, I never tire of keeping you. I answer you patiently and show you My way. You are My precious treasure, I have set you in Me, you adorn Me in beauty when you obey Me. I lavish you in love and I sing over you, for you are My holy one, appointed by Me.

July 6

Psalm 16 NLT

[8]I know the LORD is always with me. I will not be shaken, for he is right beside me.

Psalm 37 NLT

[23]The LORD directs the steps of the godly. He delights in every detail of their lives.

Lamentations 3 NLT

25The LORD is good to those who depend on him, to those who search for him.

The forks at the crossroads, the bumps on the way, the blind curves and the ditches are on each path. I Am The Great Guide who directs the new path and I Am The Teacher And Protector, The Straight And The Narrow. The more you want, the more I want, I desire more of you, then you yearn for more of Me. Dig deeper in My Word to see what you can see. I reveal Myself in mighty ways and I thrill your soul with My amazing love and grace. Lean on Me only, trust Me completely, for the blind curves are there and I know how to prepare you. Some bumps are small and some bumps are bigger – some bumps can throw you off course if you let them. Hold tightly to Me and the bumps will not harm you, stay on My right path where My protection is about you. Stay in the center of My perfect will – far from the ditches that are close to the edge. I know the way, holy one, for I Am The Way. Live in My fullness and enjoy the paths I have chosen. Each mile that you walk takes you closer and closer into My holiness and into My knowledge. The road signs are clear, the warnings are many, I give you My map and My chosen ones to help you.

July 7

Acts 2 NLT

25King David said this about him: 'I see that the LORD is always with me. I will not be shaken, for he is right beside me. 26No wonder my heart is glad, and my tongue shouts his praises! My body rests in hope. 27For you will not leave my soul among the dead or allow your Holy One to rot in the grave. 28You have shown me the way of life, and you will fill me with the joy of your presence.'

I let the world see who I Am through My obedient ones. I show My great mercy to My precious people, for they stumble and fall and I lift them up. I Am The Great Healer And Restorer Of Things. My mercy and goodness follow you wherever you go. I set you apart to cry out to Me for those I have chosen for you to give Me. My pleasure is you and giving My "Yes" and "Amen" to all you ask in My Great Name. All heaven opens up when you call on Me and I stop and I listen and I record every thing. Oh pleasure of Mine, how I richly bless you in every area and season, My love. My wisdom is here to guide you. Listen closely, My love, and remain on alert, for I am here and I am restoring. Rejoice, holy one, rejoice, blessed one, for I Am Your Savior and I Am Your Love. Protection surrounds you whirling My might and My wisdom to assist you, My love. Oh the power of Me – I release unto you! Go forth, My beloved, and let them see Me bless you. The favor of Me, The Mightiest One, rests on you, My love, for you are My own. Oh blessed day of the cross, when I bought you back – how I long to return and take you home with Me!

July 8

Psalm 19 NLT
[1]The heavens proclaim the glory of God. The skies display his craftsmanship.

Psalm 67 NLT
[5]May the nations praise you, O God. Yes, may all the nations praise you. [6]Then the earth will yield its harvests, and God, our God, will richly bless us.

Psalm 118 NLT
[24]This is the day the LORD has made. We will rejoice and be glad in it.

I have heard your prayer and declared My glory to rise upon you in this day. This is the day that I have made, rejoice and be glad in it! Let all complaining cease, and worship Me, for I Am God and I Am Holy and I Am The Keeper Of All Things. I hear you, mighty warrior, and I come to you, for you seek Me and you find Me. My army is assembled and is strong, holy one. I have My people, I have My positions and I have My strategic plans set forth before the foundations of the earth. Line up, blessed one, and take your stand, mighty watchman on the walls. Pray for My people and cry out to Me on their behalf! I am listening to you and oh how I hear you and come to your side. I fight for you with My armies – they are fully armed and ready at My command. Worship Me and praise Me and watch Me fight for you. You are My beloved and I cover you, My love. Hear the shouts of victory, oh join in this great shout, for I Am God

Almighty and I command on your behalf. The winds are blowing strong for you, breathe deeply in My great power, for holy is My Name!

July 9

Isaiah 49 NLT

23Kings and queens will serve you and care for all your needs. They will bow to the earth before you and lick the dust from your feet. Then you will know that I am the LORD. Those who trust in me will never be put to shame."

Psalm 147 NLT

13For He has strengthened the bars of your gates; He has blessed your children within you.

I command and it is done. I hear you, I see you, and I am not silent on your behalf. It is done. Let all of heaven and earth rejoice, for My will is done and My chosen ones call out to Me. I hear you, My treasure, My gifted one. I Am Your Portion and I have come. No evil can take you from My grasp and I have My firm grasp upon you, My beloved. You call on Me and I protect you and your loved ones. I hear your heart; I know your heart, for I have placed My music into your heart. You walk with Me and you know My voice. I come forth for you in My mighty roar, and I do not hesitate when evil comes knocking at your door! My love reaches deeply into all that you are and all those you love are safe in My arms. My wings' cover you and My will is done, for you are My chosen one, My beloved one. My ear hears, My eye sees, all you love are protected by Me. There is no other name you call on but Mine, for I Am The Holy One and you are Mine. I give you My blessings, every promise is true and that covers your children for a thousand generations too! Never doubt, My precious one, I am here keeping all those you love. I send you to those who need Me so and you cry out to Me and I heal their soul.

July 10

2 Chronicles 20 NLT

[17]But you will not even need to fight. Take your positions; then stand still and watch the LORD's victory. He is with you, O people of Judah and Jerusalem. Do not be afraid or discouraged. Go out against them tomorrow, for the LORD is with you!" Believe in the LORD your God, and you will be able to stand firm. Believe in his prophets, and you will succeed."

I watch you in the night and My protection hovers, let no one touch My holy one, I command it, My love. I protect you with My whirlwind, for I Am God and I Alone Am Mighty. Apple of My Eye, I call you blessed and I call you holy, for My blood shed upon you that day at Calvary. There is no thing on earth that is not Mine. There is no force that can take away My chosen ones. I have My beloved and they are Mine. Bring them to Me, holy one, for it is time for My deliverance. Let My dawn break forth upon My appointed ones and let the harvest be reaped. I have My reapers, and I have My times appointed unto man, for I have My plan. My Kingdom plan is here and it is at work among My people. Separate yourself unto Me and call Me holy, for I Am Your God and I Am The Holy One Of Israel. I Am Your Shelter and I Am Your Safety. Let no man deceive you, let no man speak against My people – vengeance is Mine and I have come. My breath is upon you, My beloved, My power runs through your veins, for I have sent My Holy Spirit, and He lives and reigns, and hovers and controls the forces that come against you.

July 11

Nehemiah 7 NLT

[1]After the wall was finished and I had set up the doors in the gates, the gatekeepers, singers, and Levites were appointed. [2]I gave the responsibility of governing Jerusalem to my brother Hanani, along with Hananiah, the commander of the fortress, for he was a faithful man who feared God more than most.

As you take authority over what I have given you, I give you more. Let Me teach you My great and awesome ways, learn from Me, for I Am Your Master, The Teacher Of You. I anoint My people and I send them to My hurting ones. Go when I send you and tell them I love them so. Keep the watch and stay on alert and command the things I tell you. My power is upon you and My "Yes" and "Amen" rest upon your head. Let My will be done you say, oh beloved, I say "Yes!" My will is good and perfect and none can stand against it! I hear My people cry out to Me and I reach out across the nations, for I hear My precious people and I come to their rescue. Beloved, My beloved, I have sent you to My people, for they are in My mighty hand as I send you to My people. My love flows through you, My mighty river flows, bringing home My precious ones – oh how I love them so. Glory to My Name on high, for I Am Your Beloved and you walk beside Me shining in My glory. I declare and decree the world will know Me, precious one, for I have My chosen vessels who obey Me, holy one. I work among My people, My precious great creation, and My redemption is upon the names you call out to Me, My love. I bless you in My perfect ways of delight and mystery. Enjoy My pleasure, holy one, enjoy My sweet embrace.

July 12

Philippians 4 NLT

⁴Always be full of joy in the Lord. I say it again—rejoice! ⁵Let everyone see that you are considerate in all you do. Remember, the Lord is coming soon. ⁶Don't worry about anything; instead, pray about everything. Tell God what you need, and thank him for all he has done. ⁷Then you will experience God's peace, which exceeds anything we can understand. His peace will guard your hearts and minds as you live in Christ Jesus.

Oh how pleasant are the words I hear as you cry out to Me for those I love. My breath is here, My power is among you and I call you Mine. You have brought Me the ones, My precious ones, and held them up to Me. I take each one and wrap them in My great and awesome covering. The evil is cast out and I come with the balm of Gilead and bring My healing to My precious people. I will soothe their wounds, and mend them, and call them forth for My Kingdom plan. I honor you, My beloved, for you have heard My call, and you walk in My ways. The morning comes and brings her dawn to rest upon your head. Feel the kiss of My day bless you and tenderly take you into My presence – Your Most High God. I call forth My blessings upon you, My obedient one, and I rejoice over you with gladness. Let My song fill you and complete you in this blessed day I have set for you. My Kingdom has come to you and My will is done on earth as it is in heaven, My faithful one.

July 13

John 15 NLT

[9]"I have loved you even as the Father has loved me. Remain in my love. [10]When you obey my commandments, you remain in my love, just as I obey my Father's commandments and remain in his love. [11]I have told you these things so that you will be filled with my joy. Yes, your joy will overflow! [12]This is my commandment: Love each other in the same way I have loved you.

I remember the day you gave your heart to Me, oh how sweet was your hungry face and your heart so yearned for Mine. I took you that day, My beloved, and sealed you to Me forever. I smile on that day and My heart fills again with joy when I tenderly took you in My arms and held you while you wept your sins away. I dropped My blood upon you with tender mercy and grace while all of heaven stood still for that sacred moment so holy and precious to Me. I received your love so tenderly as I gently touched your face, so beautiful in its love for Me. I drank deeply from your praises on that holy day and gave you all of Me forever and ever, My holy one. I separated you for Me, for I could not share you, My love. I wanted you for only Me – I sealed you with My promise that day. I will never leave you and I will never forsake you. I will give you My abundance and I will meet your every need. These are the things I whispered to you on that holy sacred day. I am still here, beloved, I have not left you. You do not know what the minutes hold – but I do. I have you securely in My secret place and I do not allow any harm to come to you. My mightiest angels surround you at all times and no evil can touch you.

July 14

2 Kings 11 NLT

¹¹The palace guards stationed themselves around the king, with their weapons ready. They formed a line from the south side of the Temple around to the north side and all around the altar. ¹²Then Jehoiada brought out Joash, the king's son, placed the crown on his head, and presented him with a copy of God's laws. They anointed him and proclaimed him king, and everyone clapped their hands and shouted, "Long live the king!"

The dawn rises upon you, My beloved, and I give you My warmth, My new day to meet you where you are. I smile upon you and bless you as I whisper all My love into your ear. Come forth, My beloved, and shine for Me, for I have let My glory shine on you. The war rages on, yes this is so, I strategically place you and tell you which way to go. Today comes with rejoicing in her wings as you celebrate this day that I do bring. Let the distraught hear the sounds of rejoicing and praise, and come to see how they may have this great peace. Peace I give to you, and joy comes too, when you worship Me in My fullness and honor My Truth. Obedience is the key to freedom in Me, and sing for your joy that renews your strength. My Kingdom plan unfolds to you, for you have been faithful and sought Me, holy one. My power is great and lives in you to fight for your loved ones and your neighbor too. The battle rages on, yes this is so, oh but I have My chosen ones who live in My holy love. Shake mighty mountains and crumble into the sea, for I hear the shout of My mighty ones indeed!

July 15

Psalm 18 NLT

¹I love you, LORD; you are my strength. ²The LORD is my rock, my fortress, and my savior; my God is my rock, in whom I find protection. He is my shield, the power that saves me, and my place of safety. ³I called on the LORD, who is worthy of praise, and he saved me from my enemies.

I speak calmness to the sea. Peace, be still, for My beloved needs to rest. I come forth on your behalf, My holy one, and I stand before you with My shield! The enemy flees at My command, mighty warrior, for My authority has been given. I rule and reign above all and I have My times and seasons. Walk in My freedom, live in My love, seek the deeper truths in Me, for My time has come. I straighten the path beneath your feet and show you the way. Walk in My glory and live in My love. The gifts have been given to help you, My love. My mighty right hand has extended to you – give to My hurting ones the gifts you have been given. Secure them in Me and cry out for their souls, for My time is short, My holy one. Bring Me much fruit and honor Me, for I Am Your Beloved and I Am Your Great King. Step out in My peace that only I can give, and walk in My joy and bring them to Me. Teach them, My love, for they will perish without knowledge. Train them for My spiritual battles. I stand tall beside you, My love, go forth in My strength and live in My love. I open your eyes to the evil that abounds and teach you to help My chosen ones. Praise Me continually – let your worship ring out, and cast out the darkness that looms all about.

July 16

John 17 NLT

[17]Make them holy by your truth; teach them your word, which is truth. [18]Just as you sent me into the world, I am sending them into the world. [19]And I give myself as a holy sacrifice for them so they can be made holy by your truth. [20]"I am praying not only for these disciples but also for all who will ever believe in me through their message. [21]I pray that they will all be one, just as you and I are one—as you are in me, Father, and I am in you. And may they be in us so that the world will believe you sent me.

You cannot know the depths of My love, for I Am Deeper than that. You cannot know the height of My love, for I Am Higher than that. You cannot know the width of My love, for I Am Wider than that. Oh mortal man, so pleasant to Me, I Am Your Great GOD who created you. I love you beyond measure and I give you My love to give to My hurting ones – oh share My great love. No darkness prevails over My light, holy one.

Shine out in the darkness and diminish its terrors. The light of My love brings warmth and peace, and floods through your soul with a welcome relief. Keep your eyes on Me, Your One and Only, and praise Me continually and worship Me only. The doors that I open are calling to you – go forth, holy one, I am with you. Remember My promises, I am always with you. I never leave your side. I am closer than a breath and mightiest of all, you need not fear, for I am at your side.

July 17

Isaiah 63 NLT
Judgment against the LORD's Enemies

[1] Who is this who comes from Edom, from the city of Bozrah, with his clothing stained red? Who is this in royal robes, marching in his great strength? "It is I, the LORD, announcing your salvation! It is I, the LORD, who has the power to save!"... [4] For the time has come for me to avenge my people, to ransom them from their oppressors.

I bless those who bless you and I curse those who curse you. I show Myself mighty on your behalf, for you are Mine and I love you so. I command the days to come forth and produce My blessings upon My lands and on all those you love. I command the terrors of the night to flee and I let you rest. My seasons are appointed and My watchful eye never leaves you. I will not put more on you than you can stand, My chosen one. It is Me, Your Savior and Your Friend, and I strengthen you in the battle. It is Me, Your First Love, and Your Joy, and I give you times of refreshing. Drink from My fountains and fill your soul with the pleasures of Me, Your Nourishment And Your Drink. Oh the days I have blessed for you – bring Me My children and I will meet their needs. Tell them I love them and I created them for more. Tell them to come through this open door. My doors have been opened and My arms are reaching for their souls, tell them I want them eternally with Me. I anoint you to serve Me, My precious one, go forth in My favor, go forth in My love.

July 18

Mark 1 NLT

35 Before daybreak the next morning, Jesus got up and went out to an isolated place to pray. 36 Later Simon and the others went out to find him. 37 When they found him, they said, "Everyone is looking for you." 38 But Jesus replied, "We must go on to other towns as well, and I will preach to them, too. That is why I came." 39 So he traveled throughout the region of Galilee, preaching in the synagogues and casting out demons.

My love is not too short for you, My love is not too narrow. I have widened your path and lengthened your days, for you have chosen life not death. My mighty touch rests upon your head and I come forth boldly on your behalf. I Am Your God who comes forth for you, My precious one. I show Myself tender to you. I show you My compassion and I teach you My ways. My process is at work among you as I bring My people home. The days are numbered and My return is soon – gather My harvest I have assigned to you. Obey only Me all the days of your life and walk in My victory and glorious delight. Train up your children in the ways of The LORD, for I Am Your GOD and I Am Your LORD. Let no man deceive you, it is all about Me, never forget, it is all about Me. You flourish in Me and I feed you My plenty, for you hunger for more and I honor your love. I have your steps ordered, and your path straight and narrow, and widened at times to prepare you, My love.

July 19

Daniel 9 NLT

17 "O our God, hear your servant's prayer! Listen as I plead. For your own sake, Lord, smile again on your desolate sanctuary. 18 "O my God, lean down and listen to me. Open your eyes and see our despair. See how your city—the city that bears your name—lies in ruins. We make this plea, not because we deserve help, but because of your mercy.

153

I come this day to speak to My people. See Me, Your Jehovah; hear Me, Your Provider, Your Protector, and Your King. I see your heart. I hear your cries and I know you do not understand. I have you in the palm of My hand and I will not let you fall. Though you may stumble, I lift you up, for I know your heart and I know your mind. My mercy and grace are upon you. My will is for you to flourish in the call of My design, My Kingdom comes to earth. Keep your eyes upon My face and seek Me more and more. I have you, holy one of Mine, inside My perfect will. Live inside My greatest peace, of knowing you are Mine and you are My great, great pleasure, designed by My own hand. Crumble mighty mountains, My breath has been sent forth, My beautiful creation suffers My return. Come quickly to My resting place, so safe and so secure, I have you in My mighty hand, rest inside My perfect love.

July 20

Romans 15 NLT

7 Therefore, accept each other just as Christ has accepted you so that God will be given glory. 8 Remember that Christ came as a servant to the Jews to show that God is true to the promises he made to their ancestors. 9 He also came so that the Gentiles might give glory to God for his mercies to them.

My love is deep, My salvation is here, I heard your prayer and I bring them in. The pain will come and the pain will go, but I give you My peace to weather the storms. My love is stronger than you know, and I have reached down to help them, My love. I sent you there to show you, My love, the hurting hearts and the needs in their lives. You have cried out to Me and I listened to you and I have said "Yes" – I will follow through. Oh My salvation, how near it is, even at the door of My needy ones. The precious heart in My creation, oh the depths of its sorrows, oh the depths of its joy! I created it to love and worship Me. I fill it with love and supply it in Me, no other can satisfy the depths of its love. I pour My great love into the depths of your heart and beat one with you, My precious love.

Keep your mind on Me only, consider My ways, walk in My love and enjoy your days. The precious mind in My creation, oh the depths of its thoughts and the power it brings. My love will amaze you when you ponder My ways and think of My lovely things I give you. I fill it with love from Me to you, dwell in Me and think on these things.

July 21

2 Kings 23 NLT

3 The king took his place of authority beside the pillar and renewed the covenant in the LORD's presence. He pledged to obey the LORD by keeping all his commands, laws, and decrees with all his heart and soul. In this way, he confirmed all the terms of the covenant that were written in the scroll, and all the people pledged themselves to the covenant.

Everything you do, you do for Me, for I Am Your Creator and I Am Your King. Your kind touch to a hurting one represents Me, for you are My feet and My hands, precious one. Look about you, My love, and see what I have done. I surround you with those I have chosen. Go about your day helping and serving, for that is My will and that is My way. Worry not for tomorrow, for I have My plan, and you are not forsaken, you are My great love. I do not let another take My place, for I Am Your Jealous God who keeps you safe. Let the winds roar and the storms toss about, lift up your head with a victory shout! The paths have been paid with a price that is higher than anything else, there is no greater value. Do not compromise what I give you, that would not please Me, holy one. Listen only to Me and not another, for I have prepared you for this new level. I see the end from the beginning, My love, and I have chosen you from My heart filled with love.

July 22

Isaiah 10 NLT

[20] In that day the remnant left in Israel, the survivors in the house of Jacob, will no longer depend on allies who seek to destroy them. But they will faithfully trust the LORD, the Holy One of Israel. [21] A remnant will return; yes, the remnant of Jacob will return to the Mighty God.

Some blessings I give are obvious, My love, oh but some blessings are hidden, it is for your own good I do not reveal it all. You walk each day in My mighty grasp and are strengthened as you go. My way is a process, My way is filled with love. I see your need and give to you each day, My holy one. Do not doubt, My mighty strength comes forth for you, My love. Breathe deeply, holy treasure, into My truth and love, for I am in your everything and I am in your mind. My heart has captured you for Me, there is no going back, for you are devoted to My truth, My holy one. Enjoy the moments I bring, of great things and of small. I Am Your Glory And Delight, I Am Your All And All. Lavish Me, oh holy one, in praises to My Name, for I Am Great and I Am Strong and I Am Your Great Anointing. Blessed are you, priceless one, for I have My stamp on you – sealed to Me forever, I have My claim on you. The heavy cloud above you cannot hold another drop, saturated is My cloud and drops have now begun. This drop came from that one, this one came from over there, and this one comes from far away and the rains have burst wide open. Lift your head and receive My rains, for they pour out and bring the floods.

July 23

Isaiah 12 NLT

[3] With joy you will drink deeply from the fountain of salvation! [4] In that wonderful day you will sing: "Thank the LORD! Praise his name! Tell the nations what he has done. Let them know how mighty he is! [5] Sing to the LORD, for he has done wonderful things. Make known his praise around the world. [6] Let all the people of Jerusalem shout his praise with joy! For great is the Holy One of Israel who lives among you."

I fill your dry and thirsty land with blessings from above, and walk with you on paths I design for you and Me, My love. I talk with you and listen as you speak so tenderly, and tell Me how you love Me – I listen as you speak. My tender love is in you – your heart is My design. I give you gifts, My precious one, designed by My own hand. Fill yourself inside My love each day I give to you. I meet you in our secret place of devotion and adoration. Walk among My people and serve Me in My places where I send you. I live in you, My precious one, and guide you all your days. I put My hope inside your heart and give you strength for each new day. The beauty is about you, I see the ending, holy one, I answer all your prayers, My love, each and every one. Rejoice My precious treasure, for you have called them out by name and I have said My "Yes" to you with My holiest Amen. So be it – it is done, My love, those are the words I speak.

July 24

Psalm 99 NLT

They cried to the LORD for help, and he answered them. [7] He spoke to Israel from the pillar of cloud, and they followed the laws and decrees he gave them. [8] O LORD our God, you answered them. You were a forgiving God to them, but you punished them when they went wrong. 9 Exalt the LORD our God, and worship at his holy mountain in Jerusalem, for the LORD our God is holy!

Prayer is the key to success, My love, for I bring about the changes, whether they are painful or fruitful, holy one. Pray in earnest and seek My face, for prayer is what I want – talk to Me, My precious one. I want your conversation to be to Me, My love, and let your other conversations be about Me, holy one. My hand comes down so swiftly to punish or preserve, prayer is the key, My love, to persevere in these last days. Come to Me and only Me to replenish yourself. I Am Your Refreshing and I Am Your Deepest Drink. Let My waters fill you and wake you from your sleep. Come, praise My Holy Name, My love, for I want you to live deeply inside My great relief. The world is watching, holy one, that is by My design. Let them watch and behold My touch upon My faithful ones. I come forth from My silent time when I hear the prayers ring out! I come

157

upon My clouds, My love, hidden – oh but there. I burst through shining like My glorious dawn. Behold the beauty of My approach for My precious holy ones.

July 25

1 Kings 11 NLT

[4] In Solomon's old age, they turned his heart to worship other gods instead of being completely faithful to the LORD his God, as his father, David, had been. [5] Solomon worshiped Ashtoreth, the goddess of the Sidonians, and Molech,[a] the detestable god of the Ammonites. [6] In this way, Solomon did what was evil in the LORD's sight; he refused to follow the LORD completely, as his father, David, had done.

It was disobedience that caused Solomon's fall, My love. It was fear that overtook Jeroboam and he began to disobey Me too - do not fear what man can do, fear only who I Am. I Am The One and Only that changes things around. Listen to My guidance from My Holy Word. Obey Me only, holy one, and you will not fail. Love Me most and seek Me all your days. Then love your neighbor as yourself and respect My precious people, they are My great creation. Cry out to Me for lost souls and seek Me for your instructions. I give you wisdom and discernment when I send you to them, holy one. Never let another tell you something different – keep your eyes on only Me and listen to My voice. Test the spirits as I have shown you. Ask them if I came and died upon the cross for My creation. One I have chosen, study and seek to do My will and watch the revelations unfold, My love. I delight you and I thrill you with things you do not know, for I love you, holy vessel, oh how I love you so! Do not worry, do not fret, I am here at your side.

July 26

Mark 13 NLT

26 Then everyone will see the Son of Man[a] coming on the clouds with great power and glory. 27 And he will send out his angels to gather his chosen ones from all over the world—from the farthest ends of the earth and heaven.

Ah, the overflow, the overflow! I send to My ones who obey Me completely and live in My love. It is My pleasure, My great delight, to give you My overflow, prayer warrior of Mine. Let your heart be encouraged as you look all about for My Hand has come down and shows mightily on your behalf. Laugh in the joy of My Mighty Right Hand and weep in the ache of the sorrow all around. I show you My sorrow for My hurting ones, for the evil is much, My holy one. Go forth strong and courageous with the tools I give, and fight the great fight for My chosen ones. Walk in My fullness – the overflow. My love is inside of you doing My great work. Follow My footsteps for I have gone before you, preparing the hearts of My chosen ones, My love. Live in My love, the fullness of Me, and give, holy one, to meet the needs of the poor. The women, My women, are hurting, My love, and so are My children who are beaten and tortured. I hear the cries of the lesser ones and reach out to you to help them, My love. The men live in rage and anger and terror, and fight all the ones who try to help them, My love.

July 27

Revelation 3 NLT

11 I am coming soon. Hold on to what you have, so that no one will take away your crown. 12 All who are victorious will become pillars in the Temple of my God, and they will never have to leave it. And I will write on them the name of my God, and they will be citizens in the city of my God— the new Jerusalem that comes down from heaven from my God. And I will also write on them my new name.

time is now, the figs are on the tree and you are close enough to see and touch them, My love. There is no doubt, you have experienced Me and now you are ready for My more. The process of Me is not quick or easy. My process consists of faithful and steady – growth from the roots that have been watered well, and grounded in rich soil that stands the test of time. I have watered you from the depths of My well and nourished your soil from My Holy Word. I have taught you some things, and more is to come, but you are now ready to reach farther, My love. I Am Your Tender Father, your Abba, for I Am Your Tender Caretaker who takes good care of your soul. Your mortal man cannot understand the ways of Your Keeper, Your Sovereign LORD. Oh, but your spirit knows Me, My love, for you are one with Me in our holy love. I give you My strength, your strength will not do, for the work I have assigned to you. Do not worry or fret, I am here by your side, listen closely to Me and obey Me quickly. Remember My Words I have spoken to you and cling to each one steadfastly and true.

July 28

Matthew 11 NLT

²⁸Come to Me, all *you* who labor and are heavy laden, and I will give you rest. ²⁹Take My yoke upon you and learn from Me, for I am gentle and lowly in heart, and you will find rest for your souls. ³⁰For My yoke *is* easy and My burden is light."

My precious Holy Spirit prays in you and guides you in My perfect will. I watch you closely, more than you know, and wash you clean in My Holy Word. My blood is upon you, for you have chosen Me, and I umbrella you with My covering. The evil that attacks bounces off like rubber, for My full armor is in place and you live in My safety. Glorify Me all the days of your life, for I direct your steps, I direct your life. Your children are rich in the blessings from Me – watch, holy one, and you will see. Praise Me continually, for I have given you life – life in abundance filled with blessings not curses. I call you blessed, all heaven rejoices, they know how I love you, how I love you so! I keep you, My love, close in My center and lead you to places where My people hunger. Feed them, My love, feed them with My love overflowing, and watch Me saturate them in My Holy Ghost power. The days are full and abounding, My love. I honor My chosen ones. I am worth it, you say, and I smile in My knowing – oh yes, holy one, I am worth it, My love. Give of yourself all the day long, for you are giving them Me and My precious song. Laugh with the joyful and mourn with the mourning, and speak of My ways all throughout your journey. I Am Exciting and Strong and I come through for you, My precious one.

July 29

Matthew 5 NLT

[21]"You have heard that our ancestors were told, 'You must not murder. If you commit murder, you are subject to judgment.' [22]But I say, if you are even angry with someone, you are subject to judgment! If you call someone an idiot, you are in danger of being brought before the court. And if you curse someone, you are in danger of the fires of hell. [23]"So if you are presenting a sacrifice at the altar in the Temple and you suddenly remember that someone has something against you, [24]leave your sacrifice there at the altar. Go and be reconciled to that person. Then come and offer your sacrifice to God.

Has your spirit settled for less? Do you give up so soon? Do you want to be My friend, or do you choose society's ways? To get all of Me, you must give Me all of you. There is no in-between with Me, for I Am Creator and I Am King. Do you choose your own flesh and blood, or do you choose My Holy Spirit's ways? Do you choose to honor Me, or do you let another take My place? Decide this day which life you choose, for I will call another forth who will do My perfect will. Heaven waits in anticipation. Do you choose My power, or do you choose another? I paid the price for abundant life, but I Am A Gentleman and I will not force you to surrender. Is it about you and the things that you want, this way or that, without regard to My timing? Is it about Me from the depths of your heart? Is it Me you want to please all the days of your life?

July 30

Nehemiah 6 NLT

[1]Sanballat, Tobiah, Geshem the Arab, and the rest of our enemies found out that I had finished rebuilding the wall and that no gaps remained—though we had not yet set up the doors in the gates. [2]So Sanballat and Geshem sent a message asking me to meet them at one of the villages in the plain of Ono. But I realized they were plotting to harm me, [3]so I replied by sending this message to them: "I am engaged in a great work, so I can't come. Why should I stop working to come and meet with you?"

The Master of the sea is here, My love. See the billows rise at My command. Water My dry and thirsty land, I decree, the time is now. Break forth, oh mighty rains and bring relief, for I have spoken. The touch of Me is seen by all – let no man go unnoticed. I Am Your King and I decree and declare the things that can be. I have called you forth and spoken to you with questions from Me, I have asked of you. I took your "Yes" with pleasure and delight, and sent forth My mighty ones to be at your side. Your protection is much in this fight for My people and victory is won on every level. Pierce through the darkness, My holy one, and rescue My dying in their domain. My bright light shining, I have given you more, the brightness of Me comes forth, holy one. The places are darker and darker, My love, My light shines out brighter and brighter to lift it, My love. My steady right hand does not falter or fail, it is holding you up, you will not fall.

July 31

Hebrews 4 NLT

[1]God's promise of entering his rest still stands, so we ought to tremble with fear that some of you might fail to experience it. [2]For this good news—that God has prepared this rest—has been announced to us just as it was to them. But it did them no good because they didn't share the faith

of those who listened to God. [3]For only we who believe can enter his rest.

I flow through you so easily, precious one. I prompt you so gently and then you go. My tender one, your heart beats one with Mine and you know My peace and you know My will. I protect you in the flow and watch you carefully during your assignment. No harm can come to you, for I have My protection all around. I have shown you the need and I send you to them. I bless you, My love, and I go with you to them. I guide every word, and I penetrate hearts with My Holy Spirit, for I work from the heart. My Word goes deeply to the center, into the innermost thoughts and desires. Keep My full armor on wherever you go, for the evil is lurking around every corner. My children are burdened and weighted down with cares, whether earthly or spiritual, the weight is still there. Bring them relief from the storms that batter and bash. My ways are higher and above all things, I am in control and I send you the rains. Flow mighty river from the depths of Me, out to My hurting ones and wash them in Me. I cleanse with My Word and I yoke you to Me, to work in My field I have chosen for you.

August 1

Deuteronomy 33 NLT

³Indeed, he loves his people; all his holy ones are in his hands. They follow in his steps and accept his teaching. ⁴Moses gave us the LORD's instruction, the special possession of the people of Israel. ⁵The LORD became king in Israel—when the leaders of the people assembled, when the tribes of Israel gathered as one."

I have My warriors, My mighty ones, who go about working in the fields I assign. Do not be overwhelmed at the many who suffer. Be encouraged that you serve Me, Your God, The One And Only who can meet each need. I send you to them and require you to pray – give them relief on their life's journey, My love. Fill them with My Words that are tender and true, so gentle and kind to see them through. My strength is enough to meet every need, and I come forth strong for each heart that seeks Me. I guide and direct, and send forth My encouragers, who bring aid to the fallen, who are on the front lines. My victory rings out in each field, holy one, for I have heard the cries of My people, and I answer each one. My power was given on that holy day and rings out forever – don't give up, holy one. I strengthen your heart and My grace does abound, I fill you with mercy and teach you to stand. I never give up and I never leave your side. Ask Me for more, I am here, holy one. My strength is sufficient for this great fight, keep your eyes on Me only, I will show you what to do. My arm is not short and extends to you, for you are My obedient one – I can rest My head on you.

August 2

Matthew 13 NLT

²²The seed that fell among the thorns represents those who hear God's word, but all too quickly the message is crowded out by the worries of this life and the lure of wealth, so no fruit is produced. ²³The seed that fell on good soil represents those who truly hear and understand God's

word and produce a harvest of thirty, sixty, or even a hundred times as much as had been planted!"

I will teach you, I will show you, for you have called on My Name. Listen to Me and only Me, for I Am The Creator Of All that you see and all that you do not see. Lean on Me, not your own understanding, and trust Me, My love, for I Am Yours and you are Mine. Do not be offended, for I am at work, and I teach and I train, and I guide and rebuke. No one is perfect, no not one – ask Me, precious one, I will show you the way. Rest in My love and enter into Me, deeper, come into My innermost chambers, My love. Adore Me and praise Me and visit Me there and chat with Me, beloved, for I listen and I care. My attentive eye and ear is on you – make no decision without coming to Me. I Am Your God, Your Savior And King, and I have called you forth to come to Me. Let no man deceive you, it is all about Me, forever in eternity I want you to be with Me. Tell My precious people how I love them so – all else is vanity and pride that deceives the soul. Come out from among them and set your eyes on Me only, for I Am The Redeemer and I am at your side. Assemble yourself with My holy ones and not with another for the evil is much.

August 3

Luke 12 NLT

[47]"And a servant who knows what the master wants, but isn't prepared and doesn't carry out those instructions, will be severely punished. [48]But someone who does not know, and then does something wrong, will be punished only lightly. When someone has been given much, much will be required in return; and when someone has been entrusted with much, even more will be required.

Let not your heart be troubled, for I have come to you to give you My "Yes" and "Amen," precious love. I lean down and pick you up, and bring you much closer to My heart, precious one. I fill you full to overflowing in Me and set you back on the path to work for Me. I give you My blessings and confirmations too, you are My chosen one to do this, My love. I flourish in you every step of the way, and delight in your obedience as I honor you today. Let My rains fall upon you more and more – every day, for you have been faithful all along the way. My peace is the key to the doors I open, and you walk through them in My holy splendor and bring glory to Me. Let the mountains shake and tremble as you approach each one, for My beloved one enters and My will is done! Glorify Me all the days of your life and rest in My presence with much delight. Come forth, holy one, for your feet have been shod with the preparation of Me in our holy times.

August 4

Psalm 96 NLT

[9]Worship the LORD in all his holy splendor. Let all the earth tremble before him. [10]Tell all the nations, "The LORD reigns!" The world stands firm and cannot be shaken. He will judge all peoples fairly. [11]Let the heavens be glad, and the earth rejoice! Let the sea and everything in it shout his praise! [12]Let the fields and their crops burst out with joy! Let the trees of the forest rustle with praise [13]before the LORD, for he is coming!

The works that I do are seen by all. The knees, every one, will some day bow. I Am GOD and there is no other, My Kingdom plan is at work among My people. The space inside you cannot be filled with another, for it was created by Me and for Me – worship Me only. I do not compromise or share this space designed for Me only – seek My face. The kings and the queens are placed on their thrones for My holy purpose, My Kingdom plan. Your days are numbered and so are your hairs, each sparrow that falls is recorded and kept. The records are there, each one for their time. The seasons come and the seasons go, and I strengthen you for the times ahead, holy one. I called you forth for this time in My season, the harvest is here and the reapers are gathering. Keep your eyes on eternity for that is what matters, the souls for My Kingdom and not for the other. This matters to Me the most, precious one, or I would not have paid the great price, My love. Gather them up, then go gather some more, the times are now short and My coming is soon.

August 5

Psalm 52 NLT

[8]But I am like an olive tree, thriving in the house of God. I will always trust in God's unfailing love. [9]I will praise you forever, O God, for what you have done. I will trust in your good name in the presence of your faithful people.

2 Kings 19 NLT

[25]"But have you not heard? I decided this long ago. Long ago I planned it, and now I am making it happen. I planned for you to crush fortified cities into heaps of rubble.

I have searched your heart and I have judged your faithfulness. I decree and declare – your petition is granted. Your children are Mine and I bless them, for you are Mine and I bless you. Rejoice in the land that I give you, My love, for I give you My joy and My peace everlasting. The seasons and times have been set over you from before the world, I set them in place. My hand placed your heart into you on that day, with My breath upon you – I vowed My love would stay. My love shines out from your heart I made holy, to serve only Me and love Me completely. I give you My love I pledged long ago, and I watch you learn to receive Me more and more every day. My heart sings to you and My smile rests upon you, for you are My love and I honor you, holy one. I was with you each day that you waited and prayed, and searched in My Word and hoped in that day. You will not be put to shame, holy one who has waited, for you have My Word and it is holy, and will not be defiled. Rejoice in this day that I have given, for you are My treasure that has been hidden.

August 6

Psalm 139 NLT

[1]O LORD, you have examined my heart and know everything about me. [2]You know when I sit down or stand up. You know my thoughts even when I'm far away. [3]You see me when I travel and when I rest at home. You know everything I do. [4]You know what I am going to say even before I say it, LORD.

I Am Your Righteousness, there is none good but Me. The good in you is Me. I give and I take away. I produce the good in you and I uproot what must be taken away. I guide and I lead, I direct each step, for I ordained you long ago and I brought you forth for this new day. Praise Me in this day I give, for I am the one who ordered it. No one can stop what I design, no one can stop My plans. I created the entire universe and hung each star in its place. I set the sun and moon to shine in its perfect place. How much more than this I do, much more, oh holy one, but you cannot comprehend it all, for you are My mortal man. I created every aspect of you and watched your form develop. I have cared for you most tenderly and kept My hand on you. I have My plan, My chosen ones, My settings and My times, go forth as I command, My love, for I Am Your Righteousness. My blood is worthy to proclaim your pureness at My Throne.

August 7

Isaiah 11 NLT
²And the Spirit of the LORD will rest on him—the Spirit of wisdom and understanding, the Spirit of counsel and might, the Spirit of knowledge and the fear of the LORD. ³He will delight in obeying the LORD. He will not judge by appearance nor make a decision based on hearsay. ⁴He will give justice to the poor and make fair decisions for the exploited. The earth will shake at the force of his word, and one breath from his mouth will destroy the wicked. ⁵He will wear righteousness like a belt and truth like an undergarment.

Stand tall, My mighty warrior, for I am at your side. I control this battle, I have the victory. You have chosen sides, My holy one, you have chosen Me, Your King. Therefore I give you victory over each and every thing. My ways are so much higher than your ways, holy one. Do not fret this battle for the victory is won. My blood, My Name, My Word is here standing tall with you, My love, and My Holy Spirit rises in you, holy one. The power I bestow upon you is My power. There is no other power greater than Me, My holy one. I sent you here to bring My precious people back to Me. My creation, My beloved ones, they need Me so, tell them I am here,

My love, tell them I want to draw them near. The price was not a token of My love to take so lightly. The sacrifice was power I gave to them that day. All other power deceives them, it is not greater, not at all. Tell them to come back to Me and fight under My blood, holy one.

August 8

Jeremiah 18 NLT

As the clay is in the potter's hand, so are you in my hand. [7]If I announce that a certain nation or kingdom is to be uprooted, torn down, and destroyed, [8]but then that nation renounces its evil ways, I will not destroy it as I had planned. [9]And if I announce that I will plant and build up a certain nation or kingdom, [10]but then that nation turns to evil and refuses to obey me, I will not bless it as I said I would.

I have filled you with Me, now pour out to another, for that is My plan – love one another. My love is patient and oh so kind, do not underestimate the power in My kindness. I Am Love and there is no other – love one another, and serve Me only. My breath has entered your soul and your spirit, the depths of you belong to Me. My blood is upon you and My power is in it, stay covered, My love, for the times are beginning. The evil is much, fight in My power – My love and My kindness wins every fight. I Am Love and there is no other, be kind and considerate of those that are in bondage. The thief has come to destroy their souls – be kind and be gentle and show them My love. The ones who attack have much to lose, pity their souls, and be kind at all times. I Am Love, and there is no other, all of your love comes from Me only. My presence is with you, My love draws you near, and softens your heart to the angry and lonely. Keep yourself in the depths of Me, and pray in My love continually. Pray in your solitude and pray corporately, pray for My fruit to reveal inside you.

August 9

Jeremiah 30 NLT

¹⁸This is what the LORD says: "When I bring Israel home again from captivity and restore their fortunes, Jerusalem will be rebuilt on its ruins, and the palace reconstructed as before. ¹⁹There will be joy and songs of thanksgiving, and I will multiply my people, not diminish them; I will honor them, not despise them. ²⁰Their children will prosper as they did long ago. I will establish them as a nation before me, and I will punish anyone who hurts them.

I have ordained you to represent Me and I have given you My gifts. Go forth in My joy, and live in My strength, for My mighty right hand is upon you. I hear you, I listen intently, and I search your heart. I know your heart, it beats one with Mine. My love comes forth as you pray for another, for your desires are My desires and that is My will. My "Yes" comes tenderly with all of My passion, for you are My chosen one to represent Me. The cost has been paid for the damage was done against My beautiful creation, each and every one. My love has stretched forth through My chosen ones who represent Me to spread My Word. The good news comes forth out of My tender love and heals all the hurting ones and restores them to Me. My power is stronger, never forget, and never give up, holy one. I give you My peace in the storms that are raging, and I give you My peace in the calm of the day. I do not leave you unattended, My love. Praise Me and love Me all the day long.

August 10

1 Corinthians 3 NLT

⁵After all, who is Apollos? Who is Paul? We are only God's servants through whom you believed the Good News. Each of us did the work the Lord gave us. ⁶I planted the seed in your hearts, and Apollos watered it, but it was God who made it grow. ⁷It's not important who does the planting, or who does the watering. What's important is that God makes the seed grow.

You have seen My touch, you have heard My voice, you have obeyed My Word and you have honored Me. You have come to Me and you have asked Me for things, I have given to you from the depths of Me. Much is required of you in My more, but I give you strength and I help you endure. I Am The God Of All and I control all things. My laws have been set and My decrees have been given. The blood of My Son cannot be crossed by the evil that lurks to destroy My holy ones. I paid the price with the power of Me, more precious than rubies, every drop is for you. My Word is established, My power rings out and teaches you how to fight, holy one. Seek Me first, consider the cost, then go forth in My glory and gather the lost. My heart listens in the beat of yours and hears the love in your heart for My hurting and lost. I come forth mighty on your behalf, for you love Me the most and you love another as yourself. That is the law I came to fulfill, love is the key to the victory in Me. I Am Love and I give to you, more of Me as you ask and seek My will. My will is perfect and is for good, it is freedom from bondage with truth in My Spirit.

August 11

Psalm 139 NLT

[5]You go before me and follow me. You place your hand of blessing on my head. [6]Such knowledge is too wonderful for me, too great for me to understand! …
[17]How precious are your thoughts about me, O God. They cannot be numbered! [18]I can't even count them; they outnumber the grains of sand! And when I wake up, you are still with me!

The wages of sin is death but the repentant shall live. The heart that rejects Me is hardened, but the heart that accepts Me is softened. The wicked are crushed but the righteous are disciplined. My fruit is produced through trials and pain, and My beauty comes forth like the dawn and fresh rain. I strengthen the ones who obey Me, My love, and I anoint them to walk in My glory and love. Beautiful one who unfolds before Me, I have given you My richness of color and strength. You have saturated yourself in the fullness of Me, and your roots have grown deeper and

171

deeper in Me. Reach to Me, My holy one, and receive all of Me, for I give and I give, and I give more to you. My plenty is much and never runs dry, receive all you want, My holy bride. There is no limit to Me, precious one. I Am Higher than all you see or imagine. My river runs deeply inside of you for you obey Me and love Me and seek to please Me. Rest in My presence and replenish your soul, and live in My glory and enjoy My great love. I heal and I mend broken lives that are shattered when I hear you cry out for the ones I send you.

August 12

Isaiah 50 NLT

⁴The Sovereign LORD has given me his words of wisdom, so that I know how to comfort the weary. Morning by morning he wakens me and opens my understanding to his will. ⁵The Sovereign LORD has spoken to me, and I have listened. I have not rebelled or turned away.

Look around you, pay close attention, I am bringing them into your life. My will is perfect and My ways are higher than anything you know, pay close attention. Nothing is random when you serve only Me, I bring you the ones who have need of Me. Uphold them to Me, and counsel and teach, for I fill your mouth with My Words to speak. The glory is Mine, shining out in the darkness, draw them into Me, let My light shine out. The evil is much and hearts fill with fear, tell them I Am The Prince Of Peace to all who draw near. My power is greater and meets every need. Tell them, My love, they can trust Me completely. Oh light that shines out for Me in your love, you please Me so, My precious love. I have you in Me and I am in you – we are one, holy treasure, you are united in Me. I do not forsake you, I never reject you, I stand by your side and guide you completely. The love in My heart reaches deeper in you and beats one with you, My delight, My friend. I smile when I hear you cry out for the hurting, the ones I call friend. Encourage My children, let them know My great love, tell of My blessings all the day long. Reach out, holy one, to the ones I send, My peace is inside you, My hand is upon you, My glory surrounds you, My call is upon you, My time is upon you, the harvest is here.

August 13

Isaiah 55 NLT

[10]"The rain and snow come down from the heavens and stay on the ground to water the earth. They cause the grain to grow, producing seed for the farmer and bread for the hungry. [11]It is the same with my word. I send it out, and it always produces fruit. It will accomplish all I want it to, and it will prosper everywhere I send it. [12]You will live in joy and peace. The mountains and hills will burst into song, and the trees of the field will clap their hands!

Time sweetens the fruit on the vine. Perseverance brings rewards. There is no way out of My process, for it is the one that works. My design is better than any you devise, for I Am GOD Almighty and it is I who does decide. I choose who I want, I favor who I choose. I have chosen you, My holy one, to please Me in your love. I gave My heart to you, My love, on the day of your creation, and I promised you My holy things and called you My beloved. I gave you words to speak of My wonders great and small. It is the smallest things I do that pleases you most of all. It is in the smallest things I show you who I Am. I Am Tender And So Kind to those who love Me so. It is My will to bless you and give you all My love. The days advance so quickly and evil oozes everywhere. Oh but My mighty river runs rapidly and deeply. Wash over those I send to you with My refreshing drink. Flow great river running, swifter than the evil one, come to the rescue of My ones who are hurting. I have cleansed you for this fight, My love, I have cleansed you in My Word. Speak of all you know of Me, My children will take heed and listen to your voice.

August 14

Jeremiah 29 NLT

[11]For I know the plans I have for you," says the LORD. "They are plans for good and not for disaster, to give you a future and a hope. [12]In those days when you pray, I will listen. [13]If you look for me wholeheartedly, you will find me. [14]I will be found by you," says the LORD. "I will end

your captivity and restore your fortunes. I will gather you out of the nations where I sent you and will bring you home again to your own land."

I am here and I am listening to you praise My Holy Name. How precious is the sound of your heart! My love pours in and My love pours out to My hurting ones. I have created you for this time and I have anointed you for this time. My presence hovers over you and protects you from all harm. I walk beside you and hold your hand. I do not regret the day My blood spilled out for you. Oh how precious you are to Me! I made you in My image, and it is you I have chosen to represent Me. Oh precious one, how you please Me so! I smile upon you and I enjoy you in this day. I made this day for you, oh let My glory shine, for I Am Your Savior and I Am The Keeper of All Things both great and small. I never let you fall. My love is stronger, My power is greater, and I live in you. Fly high upon My wings, come soar with Me, My holy one, for there is much I want to show you. There is much I want you to see – hold on tightly to My mighty hand, for it is My hand that steadies you in Me.

August 15

Psalm 45 NLT

9Kings' daughters are among your noble women. At your right side stands the queen, wearing jewelry of finest gold from Ophir! 10Listen to me, O royal daughter; take to heart what I say. Forget your people and your family far away. 11For your royal husband delights in your beauty; honor him, for he is your lord.

I have anointed you, My beloved, go forth in My Great Name, for I trust you in the power and the beauty of My Name. I have washed you in My Word, so holy and so pure, your heart is clean before Me, go forth with My great sword. My love is overflowing, give to them, My love, for I have called you forth in the holiness of My love. Your roots are saturated with Me, Your Holy King, and I have steadied you in Me for each and every thing. The purposes of Me unfold and bring you much relief. Praise My Holy Name above and sing your love songs to Me. I delight Myself in you,

174

My love, and sing My great love song. It is for you I died that day and rose on that great dawn. Shout My praises to the world! Rejoice and let your heart be glad, for I have overcome the darkness and brought light upon the land. Changes come and go, My love, with the turning of events, to work My great and holy plans into you, My dear friend. I listen as you speak to Me and I answer you so quickly. I Am GOD Almighty, Your Father and Your Friend. You are in My thoughts continually, I am always at your side. Prepare yourself, My holy one, for the changes that I bring. I come to you in My royalty and My majesty, My queen.

August 16

Psalm 97 NLT

[10]You who love the LORD, hate evil! He protects the lives of his godly people and rescues them from the power of the wicked. [11]Light shines on the godly, and joy on those whose hearts are right. [12]May all who are godly rejoice in the LORD and praise his holy name!

The power is in My love, oh tell them, holy one, without My love they are as sounding brass. I created you out of My love, it is My love I gave so freely that day. My peace is what I bring, this day brings forgiveness and peace. Live in My joy, for I Am Love. Love one another, for I Am Love. Live in Me and work in love, for all else will fail, for I Am Love. Rejoice in this day, for I give it to you. Speak to your mountain and watch it crumble. My Name is given to you, My love, with all of My power, I give to you. Live in My freedom and work in My love and watch Me amaze you and delight in your love. The needs of My people are plenty, My love, I give you much to give them, holy one. I have My assignment just for you, I give each one the tools to do My will. I require much and I strengthen you for it. Praise Me each day and live in My love. The strength is in the joy of Me, let no one deceive you, it is joy in Me. Walk forward in boldness and the peace that I give, encourage each other and assemble in My Name. I give to My body the gifts they need, receive from each other, the gifts I bring. My table is set and unfolds for you, take from My pleasures and share them too. Praise Me and sing your love songs to Me and worship Me only, for I Am Your Great King.

August 17

1 John 5 NLT

[20]And we know that the Son of God has come, and he has given us understanding so that we can know the true God. And now we live in fellowship with the true God because we live in fellowship with his Son, Jesus Christ. He is the only true God, and he is eternal life. [21]Dear children, keep away from anything that might take God's place in your hearts.

There is no peace without Me, there is no peace at all. It is overrated, the peace the world proclaims. My peace is everlasting, no short span does it reign. It lasts forever in the hearts of those who choose My Name. Sing out My praises to My Name with loyalty and power, let your soul go higher, and soar to My great levels. I live inside your loyalty and I come and settle in your praise. Worship Me, Your Only King, and live in My great peace. Everlasting flower, you bloom such beauty to behold, you brighten every field inside My holy love. I place you here and send you there and show you many things. Oh the prayer I hear from you brings rejoicing in the heavens, for I have stamped My "Yes" and "Amen" upon you. My chosen ones are gathered and trained to go much farther, oh praise My Holy Name! I bring loyalty and justice to My ones who need Me so. Watch Me unfold before you in the beauty of My love. My love has wrapped around you, another layer has been added. Feel My warmth and gentle touch flowing forth in this great hour. I have My people, yes I do, positioned for this time. Go forth in all My glory. Live and breathe inside of Me for I have come to give you more. I have My strength within you and great courage in your soul.

August 18

Proverbs 3 NLT

[3]Never let loyalty and kindness leave you! Tie them around your neck as a reminder. Write them deep within your heart. [4]Then you will find favor with both God and people, and you will earn a good reputation. [5]Trust in the LORD with all your heart; do not depend on your own

understanding.   ⁶Seek his will in all you do, and he will show you which path to take.

I release you from some things this day, for I take you through another door. The many are waiting for you to enter at this time. Times ago are not the same, for you go forward in a place some are not allowed to go, hold fast to what you know. I am with you, precious one, always call on Me, for I am here beside you whispering many things. I protect you from the elements that try to hold you back, there is no going back, My love, inside My perfect will. With each lesson learned, My love, then a release must come. Go forward always – always – you may never return to the already known. Step forward with My hand in yours, some things are for you alone. Each calling has a time in Me for direction, holy one. Live inside My holiness and let the worldly worry for its own. You are called to walk in holiness and gather My people home. Some are called and some are not, be wise in Me, My love. I am here beside you directing every step. Keep your steady gaze on Me and enjoy My fruit, My love. I bless you, holy treasure, for you obey Me faithfully.

August 19

Revelation 5 NLT

¹³And then I heard every creature in heaven and on earth and under the earth and in the sea. They sang: "Blessing and honor and glory and power belong to the one sitting on the throne and to the Lamb forever and ever." ¹⁴And the four living beings said, "Amen!" And the twenty-four elders fell down and worshiped the Lamb.

The blowing winds are about you, tossing here and there. I Am The Wind that is blowing, I have a purpose for it. Go forward with your face like flint and stand upon My Word. Take each blessing I give and take My wisdom too. Let them go with you, hand in hand, to do My perfect will. Comfort those who know no love from their fellowman. Let them know I love them and made them with My hand. My hand makes all things beautiful with treasures hidden deeply within. Dig deeply, beautiful treasure, find the beauty at your core and build your life around Me and My love, precious one. So much I want to show you, so much more for you to see, let Me surprise you and amaze you with My delightful things. My

Eye is ever on you keeping you in Me, for I created you for Me and I protect you endlessly. Holy one, My separate one, I take you from the crowd, and teach you of My holy ways and speak to you, and show you who I Am. Your heart has been created from the beginning of the times to honor Me and cherish Me. I Am The Center Of It All, nothing else will do, for you are My creation – created just for Me. The rhythm of My heartbeat is one with yours, My love. My peace has settled in you and My joy is in your soul.

August 20

Exodus 6 NLT

⁶"Therefore, say to the people of Israel: 'I am the LORD. I will free you from your oppression and will rescue you from your slavery in Egypt. I will redeem you with a powerful arm and great acts of judgment. ⁷I will claim you as my own people, and I will be your God. Then you will know that I am the LORD your God who has freed you from your oppression in Egypt. ⁸I will bring you into the land I swore to give to Abraham, Isaac, and Jacob. I will give it to you as your very own possession. I am the LORD!'"

My glorious wings have stretched wide and long, to cover all you love. It is with My great pleasure to protect them, holy one. My love for you will never end and I honor you in My love. The love of Me runs through you and is covered in My blood, My life sustaining blood is over you, precious one. My love overpowers you when I send you on assignment. My strength is given to you as you go to those I love. My favor is upon you with each one I give to you. Water them in My great love and watch them flourish, holy one. I keep My seeds protected until the fullness of their time. I know what I am doing, lean on Me, My holy one. I draw them in My holiness, they cannot resist the power in My love. I created them for Me, and I created them in love. The evil cannot have the ones who are chosen and are called. I come forth mightily to rescue them, and teach them of My love. Let them see the facets of the beauty of My love, and let them know of My great love. Let My sweet aroma settle in their souls and dwell inside their secret place designed for Me alone.

August 21

Luke 8 NLT
¹⁵And the seeds that fell on the good soil represent honest, good-hearted people who hear God's word, cling to it, and patiently produce a huge harvest.

The tempter cannot have you for I have sealed your heart in Mine. I have shown you My great mercy and My faithfulness in your need. I have given you My heart and I suffered for your love. I waited and I waited for your heart to fall in love with Me. My song rings out from the joy in Me, for you have given Me your all, I enjoy our fellowship, and I rejoice in our great love! The world becomes more foreign, to you every day, for you belong to Me, My love, My Kingdom is your home. I long for you each morning to wake you from your sleep, and I whisper My great love to you, I love you, oh how I love you so. You delight Me when you smile your sleepy smile, upon the hearing of My voice, and welcome in My presence with your acceptance, holy one. My song is placed upon your heart and your lips follow your heart's leading – the beauty of your love song to Me and Me alone. I give you this day with much love and rejoicing, for you are Mine and Mine alone – I have captured all of you. I smile as I watch you choose this day to serve Me, holy one. I listen as you pray, I prompt your heart to ask of Me. The words you speak are not your own, I fill you with My Words. Listen closely to My heart and go with My great love. Shadows fall about you, on every side you see, the evil that has fallen, and you cry out to Me. Let My light beam brightly from My Spirit deep within and watch them come to My great light and watch the shadows fall!

August 22

2 Samuel 22 NLT
²⁶"To the faithful you show yourself faithful; to those with integrity you show integrity. ²⁷To the pure you show yourself pure, but to the wicked you show yourself hostile. ²⁸You rescue the humble, but your eyes watch the proud and humiliate them. ²⁹O LORD, you are my lamp. The LORD lights up my darkness.

Heart of My heart, feet that are Mine, go where I send you and live in My love. Do not be overwhelmed, My love, by this thing or by that, be overwhelmed in My great love, for no one is more powerful. My creation responds to Me and I Am Love. No other way is possible, except through the door of love. The power, pride, and arrogance, the world seems so proud to know, come from the inferior one – not the one who loves. Humbleness and kindness are used in My great vessels. The beauty in the love for Me attracts the ones who want to be set free. My ways are good and solid, upon a firm foundation you must stand, or you will fall at every turn the evil one has planned. Hold tightly to every promise and keep your trust in Me. Place your feet on solid ground, My peace brings you great relief. Hold firmly to My Holy Word and seek to know Me more. I never turn My back on those who want the more in Me. I give so freely with delight and teach you many things. My love for you reaches deep in Me. I Am Your Great Creator – I Am Your God of All. I want to shower you with blessings and heal the suffering all around. Love Me first and only, and trust Me in all things. I'll show you things that will amaze you, daily, holy one.

August 23

Jeremiah 31 NLT

33"But this is the new covenant I will make with the people of Israel on that day," says the LORD. "I will put my instructions deep within them, and I will write them on their hearts. I will be their God, and they will be my people.

My healing arm is not too short, holy one. I have heard your plea and I have smiled, and I have moved, and I have touched, and I have restored, for you are My feet and hands. My heart says "Yes" to you. I fill you with My joy, I fill you with My love, and oh how My power works through your love. Your tears are holy, for they are for another, and I count each one priceless and dear to My heart. My blessings abound everywhere you go. Give them My touch and let Me show them Who I Am! My joy is complete when I see you, My love, doing My works for My hurting ones. I rejoice in the day I created you, for you are My great pleasure and you minister to Me. Your love fills My heart and lifts My sorrow as you go to the rescue with My full armor on. My blood is upon you, My power is in you, My smile remains on you all the days of your life. I protect you mightily and go before you. The way is prepared, let My grace and mercy follow you forever and ever, for you are Mine. Rejoice in My love, for I Am Love, and I give you My love as you go forth in My Name. The ones I give you are called for My purpose to gather the many and live in My victory. Rejoice, holy one, for the pleasures I bring on the wings of victory – I bring you many things. I give you the tools to serve Me, My love. Help the ones I give you – you will know the ones.

August 24

Isaiah 54 NLT

[11]"O storm-battered city, troubled and desolate! I will rebuild you with precious jewels and make your foundations from lapis lazuli. [12]I will make your towers of sparkling rubies, your gates of shining gems, and your walls of precious stones. [13]I will teach all your children, and they will enjoy great peace.

My mercy flows today upon the one you touch. I send you to My hurting ones, go forward, holy one. My presence is upon you, My love is in your soul, My power in My Spirit is at work, My holy one. Treasure, My sweet treasure, I found you in the rough, and now you shine so brightly with My holy touch. My glory is about you, dancing in delight, for you are My obedient one who lives in My great love. They see My beauty in you as you speak of My Great Name. I give them comfort in the hope of My great things to come. The seeds are planted and watered by My obedient ones, and the harvest comes forth bountiful into My arms. I give increase to My ones who obey My call, My love. I give and give, and give some more to all who ask of Me. I Am Your Great Provider who gives you increase. I never leave you, this you know, I am ever at your side. Rejoice in Me in this new day, for I have heard you. I meet the needs of those you call upon by name. Rejoice, for I have promised you the desires of your heart. It is with great pleasure I meet the needs of those who hurt. I listen for your heartfelt cry and I bring victory in My wings.

August 25

Jeremiah 50 NLT

23Babylon, the mightiest hammer in all the earth, lies broken and shattered. Babylon is desolate among the nations! 24Listen, Babylon, for I have set a trap for you. You are caught, for you have fought against the LORD. 25The LORD has opened his armory and brought out weapons to vent his fury.

I Am Beauty and I Am Light, I Am the Way to eternal joy. I Am Peace, I Am the touch you place upon the needy. I Am the laughter when laughter is needed. I Am the tears you weep for the lost, and I Am the answer when I hear your cries. I Am the pureness and I Am your hope – I Am Your Redeemer who can save you, My love. I Am All Things, great and small, I Am Wonderful and I Am Your LORD. I Am The One who loves you so, I Am Your Creator – I Am Your Great Love. I created you in the image of Me – every emotion is filled with compassion from Me. Be wise, holy one, in the gifts I give. Let My light be spread throughout My nations from the gifts that I give to My chosen creation. Falter not, and never waver, obey Me completely and live in My glory. Climb up higher, My precious one, and mount upon My eagles' wings. Soar, blessed one, soar high in My love, I fill you with joy and great peace from above. Tremble mighty mountains that stand in the way, for I have My obedient ones who come to destroy you today. Blessed be My Name on high, for I have a people, I have a great people, who live in My Name and reveal My glory.

August 26

Psalm 46 NLT

4A river brings joy to the city of our God, the sacred home of the Most High. 5God dwells in that city; it cannot be destroyed. From the very break of day, God will protect it. 7The LORD of Heaven's Armies is here among us; the God of Israel is our fortress.

The garden of My love is where I walk with you. I commune with you in the garden of My love. Replenish yourself in all of Me, for I am here giving you all you need. Take from Me all you desire, and live in My glory as you serve in love. I withhold no good thing from you, take all you want, I give you in love. I Am Mighty And Strong and I love you so. You want more of Me? Take all you want. My love for you is endless, you see, there is no measure of My love for you. I keep your face before Me, My love, for you bring Me much pleasure in all of your love. I receive your love you give to Me and I give you My love and enjoy your receiving. I go forth mightily on your behalf, with My mighty right hand upon you, My love. You are safe in Me, forever and ever, for I have a great army who protects you, My love. I am at your side everywhere you go, and I whisper My love to you all the day long. Never do I leave you – I could not bear it, My love. I live in your vessel and fill you with love. I guide you continually, and show you My glory and sing you My song. My armor is about you, My love is your power, keep yourself humble in this great hour. Live in My glory and let the world know, I love them and want them in My Kingdom of love. My gifts come with peace and joy, and love without measure.

August 27

Matthew 7 NLT

[7]"Keep on asking, and you will receive what you ask for. Keep on seeking, and you will find. Keep on knocking, and the door will be opened to you. [8]For everyone who asks, receives. Everyone who seeks, finds. And to everyone who knocks, the door will be opened.

Take the road where freedom lives where Truth is at your side. The chains of darkness fall away when you walk in My great light. Oh the joy I give you, My pureness covers you. I call you righteous, holy one, for you put your trust in Me. The blowing of the trumpets, the ringing of the bells, oh let the celebration begin for this new era. I call you blessed treasure, My beloved, I do not regret the price I paid to keep you, holy one. I give you of My eternal things – forever, My love. Rejoice, My precious treasure, rejoice in this new day, for many things I do for you in this new holy day. Live,

My love, in full measure, with peace I give to you. My love lives in your vessel – pour out on those in need. I fill you full, then overflow spills about, refresh My hurting ones, My love, refresh them with relief. I am here among you, you have seen My mighty touch, tell them of My holy ways and show them My great love. I have given you My holiness, I have separated you for Me. Work in My fields of plenty, My harvest is here waiting, I give you what you need, My love, I give you of My plenty. Glory to My Name on high, for I have a chosen people who delight in My great love for them and do My perfect will. My grace is all about you, My abundant rains are here with all of My promises. Come, rejoice!

August 28

John 15 NLT

7But if you remain in me and my words remain in you, you may ask for anything you want, and it will be granted! 8When you produce much fruit, you are my true disciples. This brings great glory to my Father. 9"I have loved you even as the Father has loved me. Remain in my love.

My hand is wide, My hand is strong, yet so tender in My touch, for you are My beloved and I gently cover you. My arm is long and not too short to come to your rescue, and pull you up into Me to give you My relief. I watch you oh so closely, I will not let you burn, I cleanse you and I strengthen you, I love you, holy one. I comfort you in times of need and tell you many things. I do not leave you – ever. My heart is tender and so strong and holds your beat in Mine, what rhythm we carry as we sing our great love song! I Am Your Strength, I Am Your Love, I Am Your Direction in this day. I give you what you need of Me, I bless you in this day. Reach high, My precious flower, stretch as far as you can see, and I will take you even higher, for My arm stretches out to you. Rise into My glory, set your face on only Me, and I will bring you much delight as you strive to please just Me. My desire is inside of you, I send you here and there, and speak with all My confidence from inside your holy vessel. I have watched you empty yourself, My precious holy vessel, and I have prepared you for the filling of all of Me, My holy one. Breathe deeply in

My glory, for it rests on you, My love. Drink from My streams of plenty, and give to the hurting ones.

August 29

Psalm 91 NLT

[9]If you make the LORD your refuge, if you make the Most High your shelter, [10]no evil will conquer you; no plague will come near your home. [11]For he will order his angels to protect you wherever you go. [12]They will hold you up with their hands so you won't even hurt your foot on a stone.

I see your heart, I know you, and I love you, precious one. You are My great creation and I give you all My love. There is no one who can take your love from Me. I chose you, precious treasure, to love Me. My love is strong, I strengthen you in the beauty of My song. I sing over you and replenish you in the beauty of My song. When My hand touches you, you will know. No doubt will be left inside your mind, I Am The Holy One Of Israel, and I Am Your Great King who takes good care of you. Come to Me, I am here, and I listen as you speak. I do not leave you all alone to fight this battle, precious one. Sing to Me your love songs, lift your voice to Me, and feel My mighty right hand come forth for you, My love. I Am Your Great Provider, I Am Your Great Relief. There is no other stronger, come to Me for your relief. I have My chosen vessels who honor My Great Name, and they obey Me when I speak. I am in control, My love. It is Me, Your Savior, coming to you in My plan, My Kingdom plan is unfolding, and you are My chosen one. I give you My assignment, go forth in My great love, for I am here among you working in My love.

August 30

Hebrews 12 NLT

[1]Therefore, since we are surrounded by such a huge crowd of witnesses to the life of faith, let us strip off every weight that slows us down, especially the sin that so easily trips us up. And let us run with endurance the race God has set

before us. ²We do this by keeping our eyes on Jesus, the champion who initiates and perfects our faith.

I teach you My ways, beloved one. Walk in My ways and honor Me, for I Am Your Savior and I have paid the great price for you. Serve Me completely and obey Me only, for I have a great work designed for you. I complete you in Me, for I love you so. I have given you My heart, My love. Walk in My ways as you go through this door, for I have a purpose, I have a great plan. I guide you along this path I have chosen, follow My footsteps for I have gone before you. My hand is upon you, I will not let go, for I love you too much to leave you alone. I have given you shade and cool breezes too, to refresh you until My rains fall on you. You have seen My touch, My mighty right hand, and you praise Me and speak of My blessings to come. I smile when you speak of the things I have promised. I am pleased with your song and those you encourage. Keep your hand in Mine, do not let go, for many things are coming, they are at the door. Open wide your heart to receive more of Me, for I am here giving to you richly. You are My precious treasure, more valuable to Me than all of the things I have set before you. My blood covers you and protects you completely.

August 31

Isaiah 11 NLT
¹⁵The LORD will make a dry path through the gulf of the Red Sea. He will wave his hand over the Euphrates River, sending a mighty wind to divide it into seven streams so it can easily be crossed on foot. ¹⁶He will make a highway for the remnant of his people, the remnant coming from Assyria, just as he did for Israel long ago when they returned from Egypt.

All things must be, all things must come, for My Kingdom has come upon you this day. You may take from My pleasures, or reject Me for another, I give you the choice, you choose – this day. Be not deceived, you have My Word, I do not leave you blinded by My Word. Seek Me, I say, and I will be found. Die to yourself and wear My crown. Bear your cross; I will give you the strength, for the joy I give is beyond anything. Fight this great fight in your love for another. Live in My fullness and live in My glory. Shine out in the darkness that surrounds every corner and walk in My ways and live in My love. The darkness will not overtake you, My love, when you walk in My ways and live in My love. Reach deeply into Me for each new day and I will give you the strength and wisdom you need. Cry out to Me in the uncertain times, I do not leave you confused, I do not leave you blind. Serve only Me, I make My path clear. Climb higher and higher as you go forth in My Name. Depend on Me only for there is no other way. I Am The One who makes the path straight, I go before you and I prepare the way. Trust Me completely, for I Am The Way, the price has been paid, the path has been paved.

September 1

Psalm 99 NLT

¹The LORD is king! Let the nations tremble! He sits on his throne between the cherubim. Let the whole earth quake! ²The LORD sits in majesty in Jerusalem, exalted above all the nations. ³Let them praise your great and awesome name. Your name is holy! ⁴Mighty King, lover of justice, you have established fairness. You have acted with justice and righteousness throughout Israel.

The opportunities are set before you, My love. Take each one and go forth in My love, pour out what I give you to them. Vessel of honor, reach deeply from My well, for many are hurting and many are dying. Revive them in My gifts I bring. Live in My glory and represent Me. No tear falls without My tender love, that reaches out through you to touch them, My love. Be gentle and kind, yet firm in your knowing, I do not compromise, serve Me in total obedience. Separate yourself from the sins of this world and walk in My holiness and live in My Word. Rejoice in My love, for I have taken you to a deeper level of purity in Me. I can send you here and I can send you there, for the chords of this world have been broken, My love. I require of you much in My Name for I give you My plenty in My holy rains. My blessings pour out upon you, My love, pour out on My hurting ones and live in My love. Watch over the ones I give you, and pray diligently for their protection from evil. Keep your eyes on the goal, for eternity is near, the time of judgment will soon be at the door.

September 2

Deuteronomy 32 NLT

32:1"Listen, O heavens, and I will speak! Hear, O earth, the words that I say! ²Let my teaching fall on you like rain; let my speech settle like dew. Let my words fall like rain on tender grass, like gentle showers on young plants. ³I will proclaim the name of the LORD; how glorious is our God! ⁴He is the Rock; his deeds are perfect. Everything he does is just and fair. He is a faithful God who does no wrong; how just and upright he is!

The valley of the shadow of death will not come near you, for I have come forth on your behalf. I place My touch upon your life and I bring life, not death, from My Holy Throne. Let the chatter come and go, I lift you higher than before. I give you My peace, let no man come near you to try to pry you from My hand. I have spoken, and it is so, I give you My plenty with all of My love. My great wing is set over you, I give you My shade and I bring you relief. Look out among the ones I show you, and pray for their souls for they are lost and struggling. Your love for Me will remain steadfast and sure, for I have prepared you, My love, My more is here. Do not be dismayed by the chatter that comes, for I have protected you, My love. My shell is about you, no worldly thing can penetrate you, My holy one. I keep you in Me, let no evil come near, for My fury is fierce upon those who come against My holy ones. I Am GOD and there is no other, I sit on My Throne and prepare you for holiness. You cannot come near Me without My holy blood, do not underestimate the power in My Name.

September 3

2 Corinthians 1 NLT

We were crushed and overwhelmed beyond our ability to endure, and we thought we would never live through it. [9]In fact, we expected to die. But as a result, we stopped relying on ourselves and learned to rely only on God, who raises the dead. [10]And he did rescue us from mortal danger, and he will rescue us again. We have placed our confidence in him, and he will continue to rescue us. [11]And you are helping us by praying for us.

Blow mighty winds from the four corners of the earth! My loved one has spoken and needs My touch! I stretch forth My hand, My mighty right hand and touch you, My love, for you are My very own. I pour out My gifts upon you, My love, go forth in My Name, go forth in My love. Hear My shout! It is done, holy one, for you called upon My Name. I have prepared the way before you from times past, it meets with you now in the present, My love. Pour mighty rains, flood My land with your plenty, restore to Me what the evil has taken. Work in My fields, return to Me what the evil has taken. I give you the tools and rest for the weary, and send forth more workers to relieve the weary. Refresh yourself when I send you relief, and let your vessel receive more of Me. Listen to Me with ears to hear, My ways are greater, for I know what you do not. I allow you to see in part, precious one, but I Am GOD, The Sovereign One. Rejoice in My Name and sing in the days of labor and toil, and strengthen yourself in My holy love.

September 4

Ezekiel 47 NLT

12Fruit trees of all kinds will grow along both sides of the river. The leaves of these trees will never turn brown and fall, and there will always be fruit on their branches. There will be a new crop every month, for they are watered by the river flowing from the Temple. The fruit will be for food and the leaves for healing."

I Am Your Source, flow from Me, let My living waters run its course. My plan is flowing out from Me and into you, and out to them. I Am Your Source, My waters refresh, and cleanse and make whole, let My rivers flow. Stream that begins and deepens in Me, I have planted My trees to drink from you. Love is the depth that flows in My kindness, deeper and deeper does My love flow. Bold and strong are its currents – widening its path as it goes along. Hear the sound, the flowing sound, it is ever moving, it is ever growing. I Am The Source of its great overflowing, making this path and that, for My people are thirsty. Oh land I give you, open wide for My people, and let them rejoice in the drink I bring. Give of yourself to the ones I have chosen, and release My love to this chosen generation. I have opened My windows of heaven, My love, to bring forth My rains to add to your streams. Run river run, deeper and deeper, stronger and bolder to this one and that. Stretch out your great arm and extend it to there, and add another one to flow over there. Run river run, watch My mountains tremble, for I give you the power to destroy the evil. Crush it and sink it deep in My sea, never to return to try to stop you. I Am Your Source, never forget.

September 5

Matthew 20 NLT

¹³"He answered one of them, 'Friend, I haven't been unfair! Didn't you agree to work all day for the usual wage? ¹⁴Take your money and go. I wanted to pay this last worker the same as you. ¹⁵Is it against the law for me to do what I want with my money? Should you be jealous because I am kind to others?' ¹⁶"So those who are last now will be first then, and those who are first will be last."

Be on the alert, for the evil one prowls, seeking those whom he may devour. Pray one for another in every season, for satan never rests and takes when he pleases. Keep My armor about you, My ways that are higher, protect you, My love. Keep your light bright in Me, holy one, for the darkness surrounds and lurks all about. Strengthen yourself in My Holy Word, and stand on My promises, they will help you, My love. Sing to Me your greatest love songs and praise Me continually and let My glory reign. The time is too near, the evil too great, to sit by and wonder about this and that. I come forth as lightening across My skies and judgment comes in the twinkling of an eye. I have given you things from My storehouse above, use them for Me and My Kingdom to come. Rain down holy fire and purify those who want more of Me for My glory to show. Separate yourself from the evil that comes from this way and that, My holy one. Do not forget, it is all about Me and My Kingdom plan I have set forth for you.

September 6

Jeremiah 1 NLT

⁴The LORD gave me this message: ⁵"I knew you before I formed you in your mother's womb. Before you were born I set you apart and appointed you as my prophet to the nations." ⁶"O Sovereign LORD," I said, "I can't speak for you! I'm too young!" ⁷The LORD replied, "Don't say, 'I'm too

young,' for you must go wherever I send you and say whatever I tell you.

The life that you live is designed by Me, Your Holy Creator, I created you, I make no errors, I Am Perfect. I made your flaw, you must depend on Me, for I do not create without leaving a place where you need Me. I want you to depend on Me, for I enjoy helping you as you lean on Me. I created you to be one in Me, not without Me, for you are incomplete. I Am GOD and I create as I please. I am pleased for you to depend on only Me. Come to Me in fervency, and watch Me split heaven wide open for you. I do not lie, My Word is true, believe on Me only and live in My love. I give you the strength to see you through. Life without Me brings death to your soul. I want to show you the glory of Me and I want My glory to rest on you. I created you to represent Me, for we are one and live in harmony when you obey Me completely and live in My love. The power I give you, through My holy blood, is always protecting you from the evil that lurks. These are My Words I speak over you, go forth in My Name and bring My people home to Me.

September 7

Deuteronomy 33 NLT
[13]Moses said this about the tribes of Joseph: "May their land be blessed by the LORD with the precious gift of dew from the heavens and water from beneath the earth; [14]with the rich fruit that grows in the sun, and the rich harvest produced each month; [15]with the finest crops of the ancient mountains, and the abundance from the everlasting hills; [16]with the best gifts of the earth and its bounty, and the favor of the one who appeared in the burning bush.

I Am Generous and I Am Kind. I Am Your Provider and I Am Your Friend. I come to you with a gentle knock, and you stop what you are doing and let Me enter. I enter you, with fullness to bring, and many gifts I deposit in you. I Am Your Tender God who speaks kindly to you. You are My workmanship, My beauty to behold, you obey Me completely for you love Me so. I give you the love to love only Me, for I want more of you, I love you, My friend. My anointed one, I hover over you, and rest My glory upon you. The whisper of Me lives inside you, My breath sustains you, My love is in you. I take you each day into My holiness, and show you some things you will never forget. I hold you closely in the times of weeping, and I help you recover from the things I show you. The power of Me, how it flows through you! I Am The Fire that has purified you, for there is much work to do. My glory is here, how it settles on you! I have My favor resting on you.

September 8

Psalm 93 NLT

[1]The LORD is king! He is robed in majesty. Indeed, the LORD is robed in majesty and armed with strength. The world stands firm and cannot be shaken. [2]Your throne, O LORD, has stood from time immemorial. You yourself are from the everlasting past. [3]The floods have risen up, O LORD. The floods have roared like thunder; the floods have lifted their pounding waves. [4]But mightier than the violent raging of the seas, mightier than the breakers on the shore—the LORD above is mightier than these!

Holy is My Name, powerful is My arm, stretching out to you, My love, in this final hour. No one can take you from Me, the fight is Mine alone, for you have put your trust in Me. I speak and it is done. You are Mine, My tender one, I have strengthened you in Me. Sway in My gentle breezes, you will not break, you have My touch, for I have called you out by name. Refreshing streams surround you giving you My plenty, live in My great love, and pray for those I send you. I will help them, tender one, for you have called upon My Name. My Name is ever higher than any of the things. I will not move you from this place deeply inside of Me. You cannot survive the torrents of what lurks about, My love. I keep you safe inside of Me and I protect you, holy one. I Am Your Personal Savior, I daily take your hand. I guide you through this day, My love, I am ever at your side. My tender love is strong for you, I speak and take My stand.

September 9

Luke 21 NLT

[14]So don't worry in advance about how to answer the charges against you, [15]for I will give you the right words and such wisdom that none of your opponents will be able to reply or refute you! [16]Even those closest to you—your parents, brothers, relatives, and friends—will betray you. They will even kill some of you.

The glory of My Name reigns in you, for you are My vessel, the one I have chosen. I fill you with My love for the unlovable ones and take you to places that fill you with woe. I want you to see these things, holy one, for the evil one steals their hearts from My love. Walk in My beauty and live in My love, and show them My ways and My holy touch. I am here with you as you see the things the evil has taken away from Me. I use you in love to tell them of Me and I draw them to Me as you speak of Me. My Word is alive and active in you, for you obey Me completely and live to please Me. I honor you, for your heart loves Me so. I rain down My blessings from My storehouse above. I teach you My ways and walk by your side, showing you this one and that one, My love. Cry out in your prayers, for their souls need My touch, and I will come rescue them from the pit of destruction. You are My holy one, set aside for Me, I send you to those who need much relief. Care for them, My holy one, for I am in your feet and your hands. I Am The One who strengthens your days, sing from your heart and praise Me, My love. I give you this day, bring encouragement and hope to My lost and My hurting ones for they need Me, My love.

September 10

Mark 9 NLT

[38]John said to Jesus, "Teacher, we saw someone using your name to cast out demons, but we told him to stop because he wasn't in our group." [39]"Don't stop him!" Jesus said. "No one who performs a miracle in my name will soon

be able to speak evil of me. [40]Anyone who is not against us is for us. [41]If anyone gives you even a cup of water because you belong to the Messiah, I tell you the truth, that person will surely be rewarded.

Walk this path with Me, My love, there is joy and there is weeping. The seasons come and go, My love, in this path to eternity. Gather up the ones I give, I help you, holy one. I give you all you need, My love, to help them come to Me. Lean into Me, My holy one, at My great table I set before you. Let Me whisper in your ear the things I have for you. Let Me serve you from My table of many things you need. I give you all My love with every gift I give you. I lavish you, My beautiful one, in My mercy and My grace. My favor rests upon you and all you love, forever, holy one. I have you in the palm of My great hand; I see your face before Me. I listen closely as you speak, I give you what you ask of Me, for your desires are Mine. I show you those who are broken, then I wait for you to speak to Me, I help them, precious one. Leave them at My feet, My love, and I can help them come to Me. I'll speak through you and show them who I Am, My chosen vessel, for I live inside of you. I walk and breathe and live inside the ones who obey Me.

September 11

Isaiah 28 NLT

[23]Listen to me; listen, and pay close attention. [24]Does a farmer always plow and never sow? Is he forever cultivating the soil and never planting? [25]Does he not finally plant his seeds—black cumin, cumin, wheat, barley, and emmer wheat—each in its proper way, and each in its proper place? [26]The farmer knows just what to do, for God has given him understanding.

Come, My beloved, and listen to Me, for I Am Your Deliverer, I Am Your Great King. The way has been paved by My design, and I walk with you and strengthen your frame. My Words speak and do not return void, for it is written in My Holy Word. Opportunities come and go, designed by Me to spread My Holy Word. The wisdom inside man's head without Me, is

195

folly and insignificant, for it is all about Me. I have set eternity in motion, My love, and I have created man in My very own image. Seek the things that belong to Me, and live in My glory and walk in My love. I count it all worthy when in My Name you go. Give them to Me, let Me carry the load. Trust in My Name and give Me the ones I send you, My holy one. Speak of My love and My things of honor. Your vessel is full of the things that matter. The cross that I carried was heavy enough to bind and to break all the evil that lurks. Carry your cross on this path I have chosen. I carry it with you, My mighty right hand helps you along, and carries it for you when it becomes too strong.

September 12

3 John 1 NLT

¹⁰When I come, I will report some of the things he is doing and the evil accusations he is making against us. Not only does he refuse to welcome the traveling teachers, he also tells others not to help them. And when they do help, he puts them out of the church. ¹¹Dear friend, don't let this bad example influence you. Follow only what is good.

There are those who have been fastened, securely fastened, by the serpent of long ago. They are placed in strategic places and assigned to steal your joy. Keep your eyes on only Me and My great ways, My love, or you will stumble and fall down into the great destructive powers. Surround yourself in purity, for the work is great at hand. My Word is rich and full of warnings, know what My Word says. Live in peace and harmony with your fellowman. Mercy is a good thing and needed more and more, but not without My wisdom to steady it, My love. The rivers of My mercy flow throughout My lands. Hate the evil with a passion, not the person, holy one. The flames are hotter than before, for the evil is much closer. Beware of those who come to you in sheep's clothing, holy one. The evil one has planted his people all around. Remain in Me, My meek one, speak only what I say. Protect yourself inside of Me, My holiness will prevail. Separate yourself and give Me more of your time. It is time to show you many things, come deeper in My love.

September 13

Psalm 1 NKJV

[1]Blessed *is* the man Who walks not in the counsel of the ungodly, Nor stands in the path of sinners, Nor sits in the seat of the scornful; [2]But his delight *is* in the law of the LORD, And in His law he meditates day and night. [3]He shall be like a tree Planted by the rivers of water, That brings forth its fruit in its season, Whose leaf also shall not wither; And whatever he does shall prosper.

Oh the sound, the steady sound, of your heartbeat in Mine. I hold you closely, My love. I protect you with My strong hand and go with you always. I Am Your GOD, Your Holy King, Your Savior, and Your Friend. I walk among you daily and teach you of My ways. I give you words to speak, My love, in each and every day. I take you to My mountain and show you many things. Then I set you in a place where you can serve Me on My earth. I send you those to help you meet the needs of those I love. Listen closely when I speak, for I am using you, My love. I Am Tender and Strong, as I come to you in My great power. I will not let you lose Me in this final hour. I have My angels all about to help you live in Me. I do not leave you ever – I am always at your side. I do many things, My love, you do not understand, I am in control of things, I have My holy plan. Trust Me in the things you know and trust Me in the fog. I am ever leading, I know the way, My love. I Am The Way to all the things I promised you. Keep your eyes on only Me, for I Am Enough, oh one I love.

September 14

Hebrews 10 NLT

[16]"This is the new covenant I will make with my people on that day, says the LORD: I will put my laws in their hearts, and I will write them on their minds." [17]Then he says, "I will never again remember their sins and lawless deeds." [18]And when sins have been forgiven, there is no need to offer any more sacrifices. [19]And so, dear brothers and sisters, we

can boldly enter heaven's Most Holy Place because of the blood of Jesus.

Oh flower, beautiful flower, My unfolding one, how your beauty is before Me, how your scent is in the air! I breathe your aroma of loving praise and smile My greatest smile, for you have pleased Me greatly in this final hour. I searched for you and found you, and waited patiently, as I taught you of My love, for all eternity. I opened up your deaf ears so you could speak to Me, the sounds of holy homage, for I Am Your Holy King. I bless you, holy treasure, purified by Me. I give you of My deepest drink from My wells that are so deep. I pour into your holy frame, My portion of My love. I had to stretch your holy frame so you could receive My more. I saw your hunger and your thirst and I came forth to give you more. I Am Your Great Relief, My precious holy one. I Am Faithful to the end, I never abandon nor lie to you. I Am Not Mortal Man, My love, I Am Your Holy One Of Israel. I sing of My great love for you and all of heaven trembles, for they know of My great love for you and the preciousness of surrender.

September 15

Zephaniah 3 NLT

[14]Sing, O daughter of Zion; shout aloud, O Israel! Be glad and rejoice with all your heart, O daughter of Jerusalem! [15]For the LORD will remove his hand of judgment and will disperse the armies of your enemy. And the LORD himself, the King of Israel, will live among you! At last your troubles will be over, and you will never again fear disaster.

Hear the thunder rumbling, the lightening fills the air, the winds are blowing strongly, and My steady arm is here. The clouds are split wide open, and My blessings, how they fall! I am here beside you, helping you, My love. Do this, do that, go here, go there, now rest awhile in Me. Then go again and do again the things that need My great attention. I trust you in My holiness, I trust you in My love. I walk beside you daily, I whisper in your ear. I go before you on this path and make it straight for you. I hold your hand so tightly, I will not let you fall into the pits the evil has designed to snare you from it all. Cling to Me, Your Holy One, Your

Creator, and Your Friend, for that is My great will for you, My precious one, My tender one, My pleasure, My delight. The steady winds are controlled by Me, I do not put more on you than you can stand. I strengthen you and make your roots grow deeper inside of Me. The times are evil and escalating until the day I call My people home. Prepare the hearts I send to you, I show you what to do. I speak through you, My holy one, and give you strength for this new day.

September 16

Malachi 3 NLT

In his presence, a scroll of remembrance was written to record the names of those who feared him and always thought about the honor of his name. [17]"They will be my people," says the LORD of Heaven's Armies. "On the day when I act in judgment, they will be my own special treasure. I will spare them as a father spares an obedient child. [18]Then you will again see the difference between the righteous and the wicked, between those who serve God and those who do not."

The love of Me that pours through you, gives you strength for this great hour. I do not leave you all alone, I am here, right beside you. Do not fear, My precious one, I Am The Mightiest Of All, and victory is Mine alone in this final hour. My glory is among My chosen ones, I give them what they need. I have My mighty right hand upon them, holy one. I show you things and let you weep with those who need My touch. I touch them and keep them safe, I hear you, My great love. Your words go through the center of My heart, My precious one, for My heart beats in unison with your heartbeat, My love. I have you in My center, oh apple of My Eye, I hold you closely, My dear one, My precious love. My power is among you, working for My ones who need My touch, My holy touch. I come forth for them, My love. Do not underestimate the power in My love. I Am The Great Almighty One, Creator Of All Time, I Am The Great I AM, My love, I Am Your Holy One.

September 17

1 Peter 4 NLT

[10]God has given each of you a gift from his great variety of spiritual gifts. Use them well to serve one another. [11]Do you have the gift of speaking? Then speak as though God himself were speaking through you. Do you have the gift of helping others? Do it with all the strength and energy that God supplies. Then everything you do will bring glory to God through Jesus Christ.

The needs are met, each and every one, I hear you cry and weep. My hand comes forth so mightily to bring you much relief. You are Mine, My precious treasure; I speak to you of My great things. I want you to know Me as I Am, and know My love for you. The price was paid on that great day for every day, My love. Today I give you every thing I paid for on that tree. I live in you, My obedient one, I love you with My joy, My heart is full of My great love for you continually. My love does not diminish; it grows deeper in our friendship. The more you come to know Me, the more I show you My great things. I want to show you many things, the wonders of My Name, The Name that overflows in you, holy one. I give to you My precious ones, oh teach them who I Am. I place you in the places, there are no coincidences. I strengthen you and prepare your heart for each new day I bring. I use you for My glory, I love you, precious one. I breathe My breath upon you and give you gifts to use for Me. Bring My children back to Me, I give you the tools you need.

September 18

Hebrews 12 NLT

[11]No discipline is enjoyable while it is happening—it's painful! But afterward there will be a peaceful harvest of right living for those who are trained in this way. [12]So take a new grip with your tired hands and strengthen your weak

knees. ¹³Mark out a straight path for your feet so that those who are weak and lame will not fall but become strong.

Tender one who loves Me so, do not be too busy. Visit those who hurt, My love, visit those who are alone. They need My smile, they need My touch, they need My presence to lift them from their pain. Take the time, the precious time, I give to you, My love, and use it wisely every day, it is not yours, My holy one. Stop in and give My hurting ones a drink from My everlasting well. Refresh the ones along your way, it does not take much time, but in eternity, My love, it gives forever to the one. I will send you to the ones I have assigned for you. I will not let you cast your pearls before the swine, My love. My tender mercy reaches out to the chosen and not chosen. It is a sadness you cannot bear to know the difference, holy one. It is a pain I carry, alone, My holy one, for it would crush you in the knowing of some things, precious one. Lean on Me, and only Me, for I Am The Way to greater things. I have eternity in My hand and I Am in the midst of all the things. I Am The Great Creator of all things large and small, of all the current and the past, and all things yet to come. Seek Me and depend on Me, for I Am The Answer to it all.

September 19

Job 42 NLT

¹⁰When Job prayed for his friends, the LORD restored his fortunes. In fact, the LORD gave him twice as much as before! ¹¹Then all his brothers, sisters, and former friends came and feasted with him in his home. And they consoled him and comforted him because of all the trials the LORD had brought against him. And each of them brought him a gift of money and a gold ring.

Love so tender and so true, I bless you in this day, this day of great awakening, this day that I have made. Blessed are you, holy one, for I have called you out by name. I rest My great hand on you and live inside your frame. My Spirit flows and lives in you, My power is upon you. My holy blood has covered you from the time of My beginning. Go forth in My Great Holy Name, for I bless you, precious treasure. I have prepared your heart, My love, I have strengthened you in Me. I give you gifts you need, My love, for the call I have on you. My wisdom and discernment will not leave you, holy one. The glory of the hour, the honor of My Name, flows upon My flowers who open in Me daily. I water you in My Holy Word and set your feet upon the path, I order every step, My love, I am with you everywhere. I go before you, precious one, no surprises await Me. I Am The One Who Prepared The Way, you can trust Me in My love. I set the things in motion, I can go back, or stay, or go forward, it is controlled by Me, every time frame, it is Mine, I designed it, holy one.

September 20

Ezra 6 NLT

[8]"Moreover, I hereby decree that you are to help these elders of the Jews as they rebuild this Temple of God. You must pay the full construction costs, without delay, from my taxes collected in the province west of the Euphrates River so that the work will not be interrupted. [9]"Give the priests in Jerusalem whatever is needed in the way of young bulls, rams, and male lambs for the burnt offerings presented to the God of heaven. And without fail, provide them with as much wheat, salt, wine, and olive oil as they need each day.

My touch, My hand, My breath, My smile, is on you, holy one, for you are My creation, My beauty to behold! I open you for times of now and seasons yet to come. Behold the beauty of My love, I have My chosen ones. I show you of My mysteries, both great and small, I come to you. I give you My reminders, I am so in love with you. My thoughts are ever on you, My love for you is strong – stronger than the oceans' tides, I pull you into My great love. I Am Your Great Creator and I have chosen you for Me. Do not resist The One who loves you more than these. I capture your heart in Mine, I give you of My love, My power is the strongest, inside My holy love. Love your neighbor as yourself through your love inside of Me. I give you all the love you need to give to those in need. I take you ever deeper, into My greatest love, your submission to Me, is the key to My great love.

September 21

Zechariah 4 NLT

6Then he said to me, "This is what the LORD says to Zerubbabel: It is not by force nor by strength, but by my Spirit, says the LORD of Heaven's Armies. 7Nothing, not even a mighty mountain, will stand in Zerubbabel's way; it will become a level plain before him! And when Zerubbabel sets the final stone of the Temple in place, the people will shout: 'May God bless it! May God bless it!'"

Blessings and curses, peace and terror, are choices given to every generation. My eyes search to and fro to find the heart that loves Me so. I strengthen the ones who come to Me and settle into them, for they call on My Name. The hour at hand fills hearts with terror, for those who do not come to The Author and The Finisher. Seek Me, I plead from My written Word, live in My Kingdom I prepared in My love. The evil deceives the hearts of My many, oh cry out for their souls who are facing their destiny. I come in the quiet and whisper your name, oh pray for My hurting ones, they need Me, My love. Discover the joy of the hurting and lost who finally receive Me, their Savior of All. The path I give you has been widened by Me, for many will come for a touch from Me. I strengthen your vessel to carry the load, for many will not want to let you go. I fill you with mercy, for you need this great gift to represent Me to the masses, My love. You will see those walk away from Me, and sadness will fill your heart for Me. Dwell on the ones who say "Yes" to Me, and gladden your heart by these, holy one.

September 22

Ruth 1 NLT

16But Ruth replied, "Don't ask me to leave you and turn back. Wherever you go, I will go; wherever you live, I will live. Your people will be my people, and your God will be my God. 17Wherever you die, I will die, and there I will be buried. May the LORD punish me severely if I allow anything but death to separate us!"

None can compare to Me, My love, for I Am Your Great Treasure. No price can ever come before the priceless cost of My great love. The suffering in the price I paid was worth it, precious one, for you are My great love of all, you are My priceless treasure. I govern with a mighty hand of jealousy and passion. I will not let the evil one have you, My great friend. My protection is around you, I hear you call on My great Name, I am ever here with you protecting you, My love. My tender mercies flow and flow, I will not lift it from you – ever, for you have captured My heart, the center of My love. I look upon you, precious one, with great love and much emotion. I touch you in your sleep, My love, and I wake you from your slumber, just to hear you whisper, you love Me oh so much. I give you more of Me each day and draw you closer still. The evil is much stronger each day the ending draws nearer. I strengthen you in these last days within My holy love. Cling to Me and listen, closely as I speak, I will not leave you guessing, the things you do for Me. I keep you in My perfect will and guard you ever more, I do not compromise, My love, you know My Holy Word.

September 23

Deuteronomy 30 NLT

[19]"Today I have given you the choice between life and death, between blessings and curses. Now I call on heaven and earth to witness the choice you make. Oh, that you would choose life, so that you and your descendants might live! [20]You can make this choice by loving the LORD your God, obeying him, and committing yourself firmly to him. This is the key to your life.

The valley of decision has come upon you, My creation. Which way will you go in the great valley of decision? I call upon My people, My chosen ones, go forth and spread My good news, I redeem My people back to Me. The time of war, the great war, is here, My holy one. Will you fight the good fight, will you run the race by My Holy Word? Do you see the danger of compromise and ease? Do you know I hold you responsible for your "No" you speak to Me? Listen closely as I speak, for My time has come upon you. Go forth and tell My lost ones about Me, holy one. My lost ones are hurting and hopeless unless they come to Me. I destroy and I restore, oh tell them who I Am. Do not fear the mortal man, fear Me, the giver of your soul, the one who holds eternity and controls it all. I Am Tender and so strong with mercy and with favor, I bless My precious people who walk in My obedience. I bless the children who choose to walk in all My ways, I bless them for 1,000 generations, I have spoken and it is done.

September 24

John 17 NLT

¹After saying all these things, Jesus looked up to heaven and said, "Father, the hour has come. Glorify your Son so he can give glory back to you. ²For you have given him authority over everyone. He gives eternal life to each one you have given him. ³And this is the way to have eternal life—to know you, the only true God, and Jesus Christ, the one you sent to earth. ⁴I brought glory to you here on earth by completing the work you gave me to do. ⁵Now, Father, bring me into the glory we shared before the world began.

The moon reflects My glory, the softness of its glow, gives light to the darkness, and stars that sparkle, to compliment the glow. My plan includes the whole of things, not one thing goes without My touch. I call My great creation, good, My holy one. The flow of Me in man and woman reflect My perfect ways. The glory of Me shining in all of creation – I call good. My rule is set with authority and complimenting ways. It is about My body and unity in creation. One goes with another, hand in hand, they go along, and bring about My glory. My Spirit, oh My Spirit, My breath of life I give, let all of My creation see the gifts I give. The power of My tender touch is greater than all things. I Am Your GOD Of All and touch My precious things. My Eye is as an eagle's, swift to see the things that have need, and I come forth for My creation. I see your needs, My tender one, I hear you call on Me. I take you to My gentle springs and refresh you deeper in Me.

September 25

Jeremiah 29 NLT

[11]"For I know the plans I have for you," says the LORD. "They are plans for good and not for disaster, to give you a future and a hope. [12]In those days when you pray, I will listen. [13]If you look for me wholeheartedly, you will find me. [14]I will be found by you," says the LORD. "I will end your captivity and restore your fortunes. I will gather you out of the nations where I sent you and will bring you home again to your own land."

You wear My Rock, My Solid Rock, well, My holy one. I Am Your Rock Of All The Ages, precious one. You have stood on solid ground, and armed yourself for battle – go forth, My trained one, out to those who need Me so. I have prepared your feet to go with the preparation of My Word. Keep My full armor on you, My holy precious love. I am right beside you, I speak through you, My love. My angels are about you, protecting you, My love. Live inside My holiness and bring Me all My fruit. I have assigned you for many, go forth, My tender one. Mercy is upon you, and My grace is sufficient for each need. I guide you on My holy ground – the path assigned to you. Keep My Name upon your lips, hear Me when I call. Go here, My precious treasure, they need Me there, My love. Walk inside My beauty, behold Me, holy one, for I Am Yours and you are Mine, I love you, tender one. I bless you on My mountaintop, then send you down to gather all My lost and hurting ones – go bring them back to Me.

September 26

2 Timothy 4 NLT

[3]For a time is coming when people will no longer listen to sound and wholesome teaching. They will follow their own desires and will look for teachers who will tell them whatever their itching ears want to hear. [4]They will reject the truth and chase after myths. [5]But you should keep a clear mind in every situation. Don't be afraid of suffering for the Lord. Work at telling others the Good News, and fully carry out the ministry God has given you.

I Am The Master of the sea, bring your troubles to Me. I bring the weary rest, I speak, peace be still. Do not go against the flow of Me, My holy one, for you will not withstand the force against My perfect will. Relax in Me, Your Savior, who has planned the ending and beginning. I Am The One who understands all things, My precious one. Trust in Me, I tell you in My Holy Word, for I am in control of things, I have given you My Word. You are in a battle to the end, until My final hour has come. Keep My full armor on you, it is My plan, My holy one. Fight the good fight with all the rest who have been recorded in My Word. See how I came through for them, for they trusted My great voice. Walk on the raging waters with peace inside your soul, for you can trust Me, precious one, I spoke it long ago. Look upon My righteous face, behold the beauty and the strength, I can take you to My gardens and fill you with My fruit. Walk in Me, and worship Me, and honor Me, My love.

September 27

John 20 NLT

20As he spoke, he showed them the wounds in his hands and his side. They were filled with joy when they saw the Lord! 21Again he said, "Peace be with you. As the Father has sent me, so I am sending you." 22Then he breathed on them and said, "Receive the Holy Spirit. 23If you forgive anyone's sins, they are forgiven. If you do not forgive them, they are not forgiven."

I will teach you how to love Me through this open door. I want you to go forward; it is My will, My love. I will show you many things in the seasons that I bring. Submit yourself to My great ways and trust Me, precious one. I will never hurt you, I will never abandon you, I will always love you, precious one. You have seen My touch before, I will continue to draw you deeper into My great vastness, I Am Your Holy Love. I walk with you continually; I am ever at your side. I Am Your Great Protector; I Am Your Gentle Guide. Take My great and mighty hand and let Me take you through this door. I am right here with you, I will help you, holy one. I love you, precious tender one; My how I love you so! I Am Your Ever Gentle GOD who holds you oh so closely. I never take My

207

eye off you, I watch you continually. You never leave My thoughts, My love, you are ever on My mind. Come to Me in this new way, you will not regret the things I have planned. My laws are set in motion, for your good, holy one. I Am Your Precious Savior, Your Greatest Treasure Of All Times.

September 28

Esther 8 NLT

[10]The decree was written in the name of King Xerxes and sealed with the king's signet ring. Mordecai sent the dispatches by swift messengers, who rode fast horses especially bred for the king's service. [11]The king's decree gave the Jews in every city authority to unite to defend their lives. They were allowed to kill, slaughter, and annihilate anyone of any nationality or province who might attack them or their children and wives, and to take the property of their enemies.

My timing has come to meet you, My love. I place My kiss on this day I have chosen. My tender moments of restoration and joy, fill your heart from My storehouse in love. My heart is full of decisions for you, from My great depths of love, I give to you. I call you My precious one, the one whom I love, I place My tender touch upon you in love. I surprise you with things, both small and great, to show you My power in every thing. Let no one deceive you, tender one with My touch, I am ever giving to you in My love. Peace I give you and joy everlasting, with comfort and assurance that I am with you, My love. I Am The Great King above all that is, and was, and is to be! I planted you in My garden with love, and I come to you and water you well. Drink from My springs and My deepest wells, saturate yourself in the drinks I give. Rest in the moment of laughter, My love, and feast at My table of the good things I bring. I set this table of blessings, My love, in the presence of all who are watching you closely.

September 29

Malachi 3 NLT

[1]"Look! I am sending my messenger, and he will prepare the way before me. Then the Lord you are seeking will suddenly come to his Temple. The messenger of the covenant, whom you look for so eagerly, is surely coming," says the LORD of Heaven's Armies.

The King is coming, The King is coming, oh throw your anger down! Walk among His noble ones and wear His peaceful crown. What is this offering you present to Me? Do you do Me a favor? I Am Who I AM – and there is none but Me! I give, and I take away, and I teach you the way. I prompt your heart, and you obey. My plan is among you at work constantly, I give and I take, for My Kingdom is among you. I seal those to Me and train you for battle. I direct your path in the way you must travel. My plan is here and alive in you, for I have sealed you in Me and you follow My rules. I set before you the way of the cross and I use you continually. I give and I take, then I give you more to use for My glory to honor My Name. My lost ones are hurting, I show you their load, lift them up and help them carry their load. Pray for the souls who walk in destruction, for the evil one deceives and hurts them, My love. Go out from among the ones who do not respond. Go to another and ask them to come into My Kingdom. Pray and weep, and mourn for the lost, until I lift the burden from your tender heart. When I lift you up, and remove the burden, shake the dust off your feet, and go to another. The end is here and My chosen ones must diligently work in the fields where I send them. Honor My Name of long ago and tell of My love wherever you go.

September 30

Acts 2 NLT

[43]A deep sense of awe came over them all, and the apostles performed many miraculous signs and wonders. [44]And all the believers met together in one place and shared everything they had. [45]They sold their property and possessions and shared the money with those in need. [46]They worshiped together at the Temple each day,

209

met in homes for the Lord's Supper, and shared their meals with great joy and generosity—

You speak My Word from your mouth, My precious one, and it comes forth to fulfill My good and perfect will. I set before you the words to speak, to this one and that, for I control the words you speak. I have My set order, let no one denounce it, for useless is he who denounces My Word. The dew of My heavens has blessed your land. The depth of My waters has entered your land. My light shines forth from the brightness of the sun, and the gentle glow of the moon to bless your land. The favor of Me, GOD Almighty Himself, has decreed it, so be it, in love. Let the hills and the mountains crumble to the sea, at your command in My Name, holy one. Glory to My Name, for honor and power are bestowed upon you in this final hour. All things are Mine, every gift I give. All power and honor are Mine to give. Shout out in the triumph of victory in Me, for I Am The Great King who controls eternity. Blessed are you, holy one I named, for I gave you this gift from the beginning, My love. I have set My order of things, holy one, go forth in My blessings, go forth in My love.

October 1

Isaiah 8 NLT

[11]The LORD has given me a strong warning not to think like everyone else does. He said, [12] "Don't call everything a conspiracy, like they do, and don't live in dread of what frightens them. [13] Make the LORD of Heaven's Armies holy in your life. He is the one you should fear. He is the one who should make you tremble. [14] He will keep you safe.

Feed My sheep, My precious sheep, they hunger for My Word. Give them of My deeper Word I give to you, My love. Clothe them from their nakedness that leaves them vulnerable to the attacks, for the evil has much planned for them, oh clothe them, holy one. Let My thirsty ones drink from Me, for they are withered from the drought. Let My living Word fall down and give them of My fountains. Warn My precious people, the evil lurks about to strip them of My holiness and makes them live in doubt. Oh believer of My Word, let My people know, there is no compromise in Me, I speak it in My Word. Love My tender, precious ones, for they need the Shepherd's touch, show mercy and much kindness, show them My great love! I reveal My plans to you in part, go forward as I lead, I have you in My tender hand and calm your shaking knees. Live inside My holiness and reach higher, holy one, for the evil escalates at each new level, precious love. I am here among you, see My great and mighty hand come forth each time for you, My love. I Am Your Great I AM. Glory and honor, and power and might, are Mine, My precious one.

October 2

Psalm 50 NLT

[1]The LORD, the Mighty One, is God, and he has spoken; he has summoned all humanity from where the sun rises to where it sets. [2]From Mount Zion, the perfection of beauty, God shines in glorious radiance. [3]Our God approaches, and he is not silent. Fire devours everything in his way, and a great storm rages around him.

My blessed one, My holy one, I Am Your Gentle King. You hear My soft voice speaking, and you know My tender ways. Although I Am So Tender and Gentle in My touch, I come forth in My great fury to protect you in My love. I Am Your Jealous GOD, My love, and passion is in Me, the greatest you have ever seen, I roar on behalf of you! Let no one dare come near you who desires you harm, for I will rage and triumph for you, My holy one. My nostrils flare, My foot comes down, the clouds split open for My coming. I have come to rescue you, oh holy love of Mine. Rejoice in Me, Your Honorable King, who speaks and it is done. I live in My eternal ways, I am the same as yesterday. Oh glory to My Holy Name, for I Am King of All! I reign and rule, and comfort you when it seems like all is lost. Oh precious priceless treasure, I have made My triumph shout, oh hear the trumpet blow, My love, I am in the darkest cloud! Rise up, oh great creation, rejoice with Me this day, for I come forth to rescue those who live for Me always. I do not come with quietness, I come forth with My great shout, oh praise My Holy Name on high, for I am coming in My clouds.

October 3

Matthew 24 NLT

[45]"A faithful, sensible servant is one to whom the master can give the responsibility of managing his other household servants and feeding them. [46]If the master returns and finds that the servant has done a good job, there will be a reward. [47]I tell you the truth, the master will put that servant in charge of all he owns.

Tender heartbeat inside Mine, our rhythm brings you peace, for you are in My mighty hand, breathing from My grace. I pour in you and flood you in My mercy, holy one. I give you what you need, My love, to be faithful to the end. I have My greater plan in you, My heart has filled you with much more, you see a greater plan in Me, beyond the immediate of things. Your love for Me grows daily, it is My will, My tender one. Oh the season of My kiss, I place upon you, precious love. I give to you My greatest joy, much fruit, My holy one. Feed Me at My table, the things I give to you. I give you honor as you proclaim them all to Me. Glory to My Holy Name, I hear you shout inside your heart. Blessed are you, holy one, My love will not depart. The King is here among you, gathering My harvest, bring them to Me, holy one, I chose you for this hour. My tender mercy flows and flows, and washes you in Me, forever I have strengthened you to bring Me My great harvest. Obey Me in My details of things I speak to you. Do not waver, not one time, in the detail that I give you. I work among My chosen ones, bringing about My greater plan.

October 4

Psalm 40 NLT

¹ I waited patiently for the LORD to help me, and he turned to me and heard my cry. ² He lifted me out of the pit of despair, out of the mud and the mire. He set my feet on solid ground and steadied me as I walked along. ³ He has given me a new song to sing, a hymn of praise to our God. Many will see what he has done and be amazed. They will put their trust in the LORD.

Rejoice My beloved, for I have chosen you to comfort My hurting ones and bring them relief. You represent Me, My ambassador of love, I send you to those in need of My touch. I trust you, My treasure, to represent Me, for you honor My Great Name and glorify Me. I know the ending and beginning, My love, and all in-between, I know it, My love. I am in control of all times and each season, throughout the forever I oversee everything. My power is yours when you call on My Name, it is always the same, the victory is in Me. I Am The One who does not change – I Am Faithful and True, My holy one. My mercy is sufficient for all who come and call on My Holy Name to see them through. Peace comes from Me and is given to all who desire to know Me and walk in My love. The peace I give is sufficient, My love, to steady you in the days ahead. Speak to the mountains, shout and rejoice, for I give you My power to overcome, holy one. The beauty of Me is upon you, My love.

October 5

2 Kings 23 NLT

³The king took his place of authority beside the pillar and renewed the covenant in the LORD's presence. He pledged to obey the LORD by keeping all his commands, laws, and decrees with all his heart and soul. In this way, he confirmed all the terms of the covenant that were written in the scroll, and all the people pledged themselves to the covenant.

Line upon line, I teach you. Precept upon precept, you learn, for I do not put more on you than you can bear, My holy one. You follow My instructions and listen as I speak, that is why I use you for My Kingdom plan to be complete. Obedient one who loves Me so, take the gifts I give, and live in My great glory, showing My great love for those who walk inside of Me. My heart is full of love for you, I overflow in you. Oh let the angels join Me in My great love song for you. Blessed one I treasure, I hold you deeply inside Me, I give you all My love and grace, how you unfold for Me! I discipline and lead the way, for you are chosen by Me. I walk in you, My beautiful one. The beauty of Me reigns inside your heart of obedience. I love how you love Me, precious one. Walk in Me, and talk in Me, and breathe in Me, My bride, for I have called you forth, My love, to walk beside Me, holy bride. My feet are yours, My hands are too – oh use them for My glory. Bring My people home to Me in My great order of your calling.

October 6

Isaiah 40 NLT

⁹ O Zion, messenger of good news, shout from the mountaintops! Shout it louder, O Jerusalem. Shout, and do not be afraid. Tell the towns of Judah, "Your God is coming!" ¹⁰ Yes, the Sovereign LORD is coming in power. He will rule with a powerful arm. See, he brings his reward with him as he comes.

I have prepared you to shout. I have prepared you to weep. I have overcome you and I have taught you many things. I have placed My passion deeply inside your loins. I call you forth and tell you I have strengthened you, My love. I reveal to you My mysteries, and My sweet and tender ways. I give to you My precious peace the world cannot take away. No storm can take My precious peace, I give it to you. Rejoice in Me, My tender one, for I have heard your cry. I come forth in My mighty strength and rise above it all! I take you to My mountain and keep you inside Me. I give you all My beauty, My precious bride. I comfort you from times ago when My heavy hand was on you. Now I come to lift you up and release your heavy load. I call you mighty warrior, a priceless treasure to behold, for I live and breathe inside of you, I have captured your great love. Do not be offended by those who do not know of My great and mighty ways, I use you, holy one. Let not your heart be troubled, for I Am Your Great King, and I came to you from long ago and prepared you for this day of great awakening, go forth in all My love. I give to you My gifts, My love, bring to Me much fruit. I am with you always, even to the end of the age.

October 7

Psalm 18 NLT

16 He reached down from heaven and rescued me; he drew me out of deep waters. 17 He rescued me from my powerful enemies, from those who hated me and were too strong for me. 18 They attacked me at a moment when I was in distress, but the LORD supported me. 19 He led me to a place of safety; he rescued me because he delights in me.

Look at the things before you and listen as I speak. I have ordained each day for you and send you to the need. The need of Me is everywhere from youngest to the oldest. The adversary prowls around continuously, My love. Keep My armor fully on you everyday and everywhere, for there is no relief. Keep your eyes on only Me and not the flesh and blood you see. Your adversary is not man, it is the evil that attacks you. Oh but precious one of Mine, I am in you controlling everything. I will not put more on you than you can stand, My holy one. The tender love of Me in you will come forth for you, My love. I Am Your Gentle King of long ago, and I live inside you, holy one. I sanctify the air you breathe, each breath is purified by Me. I protect you from the spirits who want to harm you, holy one. I have a line drawn in the sand, no crossing over it, I order! You are safe in Me, My love, no one else but Me. The times and seasons come and go, but My love for you is forever. I love you always, precious one, that is why I hold you oh so closely. I let no one come between us, for you are Mine and Mine alone. I tenderly honor you, My love, for I use you for My glory.

October 8

Psalm 92 NLT

[12] But the godly will flourish like palm trees and grow strong like the cedars of Lebanon. [13] For they are transplanted to the LORD's own house. They flourish in the courts of our God. [14] Even in old age they will still produce fruit; they will remain vital and green. [15] They will declare, "The LORD is just! He is my rock! There is no evil in him!"

River of Me flowing, mighty is your stream, that comes from Me, Your Savior, Your Sovereign Mighty King. Soar My mighty eagle, fly high upon the wind. Glide about in Me, My love, for it is I who gives you strength. I renew your strength, My love, My process does work. You have set your eyes on Me, Your Master and Your Guide. I lead you in the way of Me, My Kingdom is in you. You are My mighty warrior, you are so free and strong, for you obey My orders and save My people from much harm. Keep My armor on you, My precious priceless treasure. I lead you with My entourage of mighty angels at your side. I surround you with My army, I protect you, mighty one. You are My beacon shining in the midst of the darkest storm, let My people see Me beaming out across the seas. They will run to My bright light shining, for relief from all their woes, for the evil has pervaded into their very souls. Stand strong and tall, oh mighty one, for My precious people crumble and they fall. Love them, holy treasure, let My bright light show. I give you gifts for you to use to bring My people home.

October 9

Isaiah 4 NLT

2 But in that day, the branch of the LORD will be beautiful and glorious; the fruit of the land will be the pride and glory of all who survive in Israel. 3 All who remain in Zion will be a holy people—those who survive the destruction of Jerusalem and are recorded among the living.

Every "i" has been dotted, every "t" has been crossed, every period replaces the questions, as I reveal My holy plan. Come into My storehouse, take all that you can see, for I have unlimited resources and I give it all to you. Every tool and every gift are yours, My precious love. I am in your midst, and giving you My more. Behold Me, precious treasure, see what I have done! My Kingdom is among you, restoring what is Mine. I am right here with you, holy treasure of My delight, I give to you of Me, My love, My obedient precious bride. Stand upon each promise, for I delight to give to you, every promise ever spoken, I give to you. Behold My beauty, precious one, behold My love for you. Rejoice in this great holy day, I created it for you. I come to you with much singing, oh hear My trumpets blow, for you are My celebration, you are My holy love. I rescued you from the mire of things that pulled you down, My love. Now you serve Me fully and wear My jeweled crown! Oh glory to My Holy Name, for I have My precious few, who love Me more than all the things of distraction from My love. Shout the victory, My faithful chosen few, for I give you victory! Look about you, holy one, see My lost and dying, I give them to you, holy one, bring them back to Me.

October 10

Daniel 3 NKJV

24Then King Nebuchadnezzar was astonished; and he rose in haste *and* spoke, saying to his counselors, "Did we not cast three men bound into the midst of the fire?" They answered and said to the king, "True, O king." 25"Look!" he answered, "I see four men loose, walking in the midst of the fire; and they are not hurt, and the form of the fourth is like the Son of God."

I Am Your Creator from times ago and I gave you My allocation of days on earth to serve Me. This day I give to you, My love, I bless you, My creation, for you have been My faithful one who obeys Me when I call. I give you this assignment, I send you here and there, then I comfort you, My love, when I move you forward still. The times of letting go, My love, must be, for new growth comes with change, I prune you in My love. The times are at the end, My love, the evil is destroying, ravaging the souls I made and breaking down the unity. Go forth, My bright light shining, do good to those who need Me so, show them My great love. I keep you in My inmost place, I shepherd you, My love. I keep you safe inside of Me and strengthen you for more. I have much work for you to do, go forth, My holy one. I place you in the hurricanes and steady you in Me, then I lift you out, My love, when your work is complete. Enjoy the times of rest, My love, live inside My joy, it is My strength, I keep you full in Me. Let My overflow be in you at all times. You cannot do this without Me, you cannot survive without Me, holy one. Remain in Me at all times, for the evil is awaiting a chance to kill you, precious one.

October 11

Daniel 12 NLT

³Those who are wise will shine as bright as the sky, and those who lead many to righteousness will shine like the stars forever. ⁴But you, Daniel, keep this prophecy a secret; seal up the book until the time of the end, when many will rush here and there, and knowledge will increase."

Are you ready? Are you ready, My love? Come, let go of worldly things and jump into My arms. Soar, beloved sparrow, an eagle you've become. Your wings have weathered the greatest storms, come glide into My arms. I teach you how to glide, My love, above the things that scatter. Your heart is circumcised in Me, I have your full attention. I take you to My higher plain and teach you My great ways. You listen as I speak to you and quickly you obey. I trust you, mighty warrior, I will not let you fall. I have strengthened you this day, come, jump into My arms. I fill your hungry soul in Me and whisper in your ear. It is enough, oh precious one, you have been purified by Me. Let My great love shine in you, oh one in whom I trust. I give you My Great Holy Name, heal them in My love. There is no mercy shown on those who destroy My tender little sparrows, protect them, holy one. Let My eye be keen in you, go to My hurting ones and show them how I love them so, I lead you, holy one. My mighty hand is on you, oh eagle I have strengthened, glide across My holy skies and swoop down to rescue My hurting ones. My power and My holy strength are mighty in your vessel. You walk in all My fullness, you are ready, holy one.

October 12

James 1 NLT

[17]Whatever is good and perfect comes down to us from God our Father, who created all the lights in the heavens. He never changes or casts a shifting shadow. [18]He chose to give birth to us by giving us his true word. And we, out of all creation, became his prized possession.

[27]Pure and genuine religion in the sight of God the Father means caring for orphans and widows in their distress and refusing to let the world corrupt you.

This is not a giant to Me, holy one. It is a giant to you. All things are possible through Me, righteous one, I have always seen you through. You know My voice, I speak to you in the quiet of our days. I hold you closely through the night and protect you in all ways. I hover over you with care and flow My strongest current, rapidly I send you to this one and to that. You flow in Me, My moving one, I send you here and there. I show you those in need of Me then listen for your prayer. I search your tender sincere heart, you love Me oh so much, and I come forth for you, My love, and reveal My tender touch. Endurance is the way, My love, perseverance is the key, seek Me always, holy one, My wisdom comes to you. Holy is the day, My love, I created you for Me. Sacred is the day, My love, when you said "Yes" to Me. Follow Me, My precious one, into Me deeper still, for I Am Your Great Door, My love, I am open for you to come deeper. Fall into My deepness of things you cannot see.

October 13

Genesis 1 NLT

[27] So God created human beings in his own image. In the image of God he created them; male and female he created them. [28]Then God blessed them and said, "Be fruitful and multiply. Fill the earth and govern it. Reign over the fish in the sea, the birds in the sky, and all the animals that scurry along the ground." [29]Then God said, "Look! I have given you every seed-bearing plant throughout the earth and all the fruit trees for your food.

The stars shown brightly on that night, when I placed them in My heavens, to watch over you, My love. I smiled upon each star, and named them tenderly, and told them to watch over you each night while you are sleeping. The great day came when I formed you and called you out by name. I call you My beloved, in My image you were made. I breathed in you, My greatest love, and told you who I Am. I left a place inside of you that no one else can fill. You are created for Me, My love is in you. I call you friend and companion, for I wanted you, My beloved. I enjoy the times alone, My love, I want to come to you. Spend more time with Me, My love, for I long to reveal Myself to you. Protect our precious time, My love, for earthly time is made with limits. Oh but when eternity comes, I have you without limits. I yearn to return and take you back to Me in eternity. But you have an assignment here on earth you must complete. I teach you and I guide you, and I discipline your frame, and draw you closer to Me each and every day.

October 14

John 15 NLT

[24]If I hadn't done such miraculous signs among them that no one else could do, they would not be guilty. But as it is, they have seen everything I did, yet they still hate me and my Father. [25]This fulfills what is written in their Scriptures: 'They hated me without cause.' [26]"But I will send you the Advocate—the Spirit of truth. He will come to you from the Father and will testify all about me.

I hear the cry of My people, I feel the anguish in their soul. They need Me, precious treasure, oh how they need Me so. You will know the ones, the needy ones, who hunger for My touch, for I will reveal their heart to you and lead you how to pray. The fervent prayers are in you, for passion is My way. I give you My great passion for those I bring your way. Let not your heart be troubled, for I protect you in your passion. I anoint you in the moment of intercession, holy one. I guard your heart with fervency, I will not put more on you than you can stand. I go before you, I am with you, and I Am Your Rear Guard. I live in you and breathe in you and surround you mightily. You are My prized possession and I cover you completely. My full attention never leaves you – ever, precious one. I come to you completely and I am nearer than you know. I call you blessed holy one, beloved one of Mine. My Spirit lives in you for you obey Me tenderly. I whisper songs of love to you and fill you more completely. You carry My Great Name in you and please Me with your touch.

October 15

1 John 4 NLT

⁹God showed how much he loved us by sending his one and only Son into the world so that we might have eternal life through him. ¹⁰This is real love—not that we loved God, but that he loved us and sent his Son as a sacrifice to take away our sins. ¹¹Dear friends, since God loved us that much, we surely ought to love each other.

My abundant love pours down on you, for I Am Love, My holy one. I speak to you in the stillness of your heart, My tender one. You have seen My hand of mercy, you have seen My tender touch. You have laughed with Me and cried with Me, for I have shown you who I Am. You know Me, precious tender one, you know the touch of Me. I draw you deeper into Me for My good and perfect will. I dance with you and rejoice with you and shout the victory. Relief is brought to those in need, for I have My chosen few. Sorrow fills your heart, My love, when I show you things that matter. Cry out for those I show you, for I anoint you in the call. I call you to My hurting ones, oh show them who I Am. My passion never fails you,

I am pouring into you. Refresh yourself in My great power, I give to you abundantly in the times of My refreshing. Glorify My Holy Name everywhere I send you. I come to you in My great ways, in My small ways too, and I show you what to do. I am ever present, guiding you, beloved, I am leading you in each and everything.

October 16

2 Chronicles 24 NLT

¹⁴When all the repairs were finished, they brought the remaining money to the king and Jehoiada. It was used to make various articles for the Temple of the LORD—articles for worship services and for burnt offerings, including ladles and other articles made of gold and silver. And the burnt offerings were sacrificed continually in the Temple of the LORD during the lifetime of Jehoiada the priest.

My overflow spills out from you, My overflow of love. How it touches those, My love, designed to meet their need. My tender touch, it comes from Me, every wonderful deed you do. I am in control of your good deeds, I send you to the need. I speak to you so tenderly and nourish you in Me. I water you in My great love, with the washing of My Word. I cleanse your heart and sweep it clean and sanctify you for Me. I cover you in My holy blood, the power covers you. I strengthen you for this new day and teach you more in Me. I wrap My love around you and take you deeper into Me. I hold you oh so closely while I show you these new things. I come to you, beloved one, and I separate you in Me. I have you in My secret place where change must move you forward. Do not fear, My holy one, I have you in My center. My heart is wrapped around you, My beat is one in you. I love you, precious treasure, I love our times like these. I give you of My plenty and show you of the need, go do as I command, My love, for time is near the end.

October 17

Esther 7 NLT

¹So the king and Haman went to Queen Esther's banquet. ²On this second occasion, while they were drinking wine, the king again said to Esther, "Tell me what you want, Queen Esther. What is your request? I will give it to you, even if it is half the kingdom!" ³Queen Esther replied, "If I have found favor with the king, and if it pleases the king to grant my request, I ask that my life and the lives of my people will be spared.

There are powers that be that try to stop Me. They do not succeed, for I Am All Powerful and Glorious, and I have set My eye on you. My power has come forth for you, My persistent faithful one. You are the apple of My eye and I come forth for you. I watch you seek My face each day and I listen to your pleas. You come to Me, Your King of All, and you request your things of Me. I smile My tender sweet smile as I look upon your face, I whisper My love to you and fill you with My "Yes." Then I go in power, and passion fills My universe, for I am coming and giving you the victory! Hold tightly to every promise, cling with all your might. I come for those, My love, who do not give up in the fight. They stand firm after doing all they can, oh how I love to burst through for them! I Am The Greatest One of All and I ride upon My wings. I split the skies wide open and swoop down to rescue those who cry out unto Me. I hear My precious tender ones, I see them, holy one. I send you to them, love of Mine, and I speak through you and help them.

October 18

John 17 NLT

²⁰"I am praying not only for these disciples but also for all who will ever believe in me through their message. ²¹I pray that they will all be one, just as you and I are one—as you are in me, Father, and I am in you. And may they be in us so that the world will believe you sent me. ²²"I have given

them the glory you gave me, so they may be one as we are one.

Come into Me, beloved one, come into Me, My love. There is so much to do in such a short amount of time. I yearn for My lost children, oh how I miss them so. Gather them to Me, My love, with the tools I have given. Live inside My glory, let My blessings rain on you. Worship Me, My tender one, for I love your adoration. Lift My heart, My heavy heart, for My people do not listen, oh tell them who I Am! My heart rejoices when My lost come to Me!. I give you all My tender love, oh love them, holy one. Teach them of My loving ways, My Word lives in you, precious one, I speak through you, My love. The tender call upon you will reach many for My Kingdom. You bless Me, My precious one. I give you the heart of Me, My love, you represent Me well. I Am Love and I Am Kind, and I bless My obedient ones. It is My great joy and pleasure to bless My holy ones. Live in My great joy and love, for My strength has come to you. The day is upon you, the hour is here, the love of Me is shining out for all the world to see. Behold My beauty, My creation, for I Am Beautiful. I adorn you in My beauty, how you sparkle in My love!

October 19

Matthew 13 NLT

"'Should we pull out the weeds?' they asked. [29]"'No,' he replied, 'you'll uproot the wheat if you do. [30]Let both grow together until the harvest. Then I will tell the harvesters to sort out the weeds, tie them into bundles, and burn them, and to put the wheat in the barn.'"

I have a chosen people for a chosen place in time. Listen, holy one of Mine, as I move you here and there. I prompt your heart and give you peace when your service is in Me. I lift My peace from this or that when I send you forward to another need. Give to those I show you – ask Me for every thing. I will guide you and direct you in My great peace for every thing. I do not leave you to guess these things, My precious holy one. You know My voice, you know My touch, you know Me, tender one. Obey Me completely as I lead, I will not let you falter. Remain in Me and seek My will – I will show you, holy one. My way is not too burdensome, My yoke is always easy – when you put your trust in Me and obey Me so completely. I let My great peace flow in you and give you joy that is unspeakable. Do not look to man, My love, you seek Me and Me alone. I Am Your Master and Your Guide, and I take you deep inside My love. I separate you for Me only when I take you to new levels. Come forth, My bright one, I have prepared you for this fight. In this new level, holy one. Remember Me, I never change, I never leave your side. Ask Me in all things, My love, that pleases Me, My bride. I Am Your Greatest Teacher, you are My student of My love. I show you and I teach you, and remind you of My touch.

October 20

Deuteronomy 33 NLT

26 "There is no one like the God of Israel. He rides across the heavens to help you, across the skies in majestic splendor. 27 The eternal God is your refuge, and his everlasting arms are under you. He drives out the enemy before you; he cries out, 'Destroy them!'

The time of greater things, My love, is here for you, go forward as I lead. I Am Your King, Your GOD of All and I order your steps with My Kingdom Plan. My glory is upon you, I send you out prepared. My Word lives deeply within you, I protect you in My love. I protect the ones you love, My blessed holy one, I hear your plea to Me for help, and I bring forth My mighty ones. My beauty is within you, My face is upon you, My mighty right hand has come to you. I bless you, holy one. I live in you and breathe in you, and guide your every step. Keep your eyes on only Me, Your Savior and Your Friend. My heart is filled with you, My bride, I take you to My chambers and speak of My great love. Tell My children who I Am - oh tell them how I love them so and miss them, holy one. Give them words of love from Me and encourage them, My love. Tell them I am coming soon and I rescue them in their need. They need Me, precious treasure. They are My heart, My precious ones, hidden, full of My great treasures. I created them for Me, My love, oh tell them they are precious. I paid the price from My great love, it sustained Me through the pain. I want them to come back to Me and praise My Holy Name. Tell them I Am Beautiful and I have prepared a place for them where no evil can come near them – I have a place of joy. Tell them of My great peace and hope for all the world.

October 21

Isaiah 50 NLT

4The Sovereign LORD has given me his words of wisdom, so that I know how to comfort the weary. Morning by morning he wakens me and opens my understanding to his will. 5The Sovereign LORD has spoken to me, and I have listened. I have not rebelled or turned away.

Your words are like honey upon My mouth, oh how they taste so sweet. I breathe in your sweet aroma, how your love songs fill Me with such pleasure. I love to commune with you, My love. I created you for Me, I long to take you deeper still, come walk deeper inside Me. I want to show you My splendor and My majesty. I take you to My secret place and whisper I love you. I lavish you in favor, My mercy lives in you. I guard you and I hold you closely, for I take good care of you. Precious hidden treasure, My heart belongs to you. I love you with My fervency, My passion is for you. I guide you and direct you, I heal your body too. I am pleased with you, My love, for I have created you in Me, oh image of My love. I am so close, I breathe in you and enter you in love. You receive Me with your openness and I enter you, My love. I Am The Spirit that is not seen, oh but you feel Me, precious one. I Am Real, much more than anything you see. You know My touch, My presence too, for I come to you each day, and live and breathe inside of you, directing you each day. Oh hidden one inside of Me, I hold you oh so closely. Receive Me fully, holy one, I want to show you more. Lavish yourself in Me, let your mind explore Me, holy one. I love your exploration, I welcome it, My love. Seek Me, I will show you. Search My Word, My love. I have much to reveal to you inside My Holy Word.

October 22

Malachi 3 NKJV

16 Then those who feared the LORD spoke to one another, And the LORD listened and heard *them;* So a book of remembrance was written before Him For those who fear the LORD And who meditate on His name. 17 "They shall be Mine," says the LORD of hosts, "On the day that I make

them My jewels. And I will spare them As a man spares his own son who serves him."

Blow east wind across My land and separate My holy ones, My gemstones lay before Me. Sparkle in My holy love, My gemstones of all colors. My rubies sprinkle over you, My holy blood does sparkle. I see you pure before Me covered under My rubies. My living breath encompasses you and protects you all about. My shield is all about you, My power is upon you. You are My holy one, My treasure in My land, I use you for My glory, let My glory reign throughout the land. Holy is My Name and you are born of Me. Precious treasure in My land, how you sparkle in Me. Reveal Me! Live among My obedient ones, and bring Me all My fruit. I am revealed in you, for all the world to see, live inside My Holy Word and bring honor to Me. You are My great creation, so beautiful and free, for I have broken all the chains and bonds, My love, and I have set you free. Perfect peace I give you, it casts out all fear. Joy is in your soul, My love, for you have hope in Me. My grace is now, My mercy lives, My love is all about, live in this great knowing, time is running out. There is a day of judgment, oh, but it is not today.

October 23

Philippians 4 NLT

Fix your thoughts on what is true, and honorable, and right, and pure, and lovely, and admirable. Think about things that are excellent and worthy of praise. ⁹Keep putting into practice all you learned and received from me—everything you heard from me and saw me doing. Then the God of peace will be with you.

Oh the food I give you, how it saturates your soul. I feed you from My Holy Word and tell you so much more. Come feast upon My goodness, every promise you can claim, for I Am GOD Almighty who brings the replenishing rains! Let My dry and thirsty land drink deeply from My waters. I fill you full to overflowing and send you out again. Feed upon My Holy Word, let My Spirit saturate you. Revive yourself in Me, My love, do not deplete yourself of Me. I give you strength and times of rest and joy inside of Me. Live in My great promises and bring Me all My fruit. I Am Your Strength, come to Me, drink deeply from My well. My waters give you drink from Me, to quench your thirstiness. Drench yourself in My refreshing, let My Spirit flow. Receive Me fully, holy one, for I am here to guide you. I Am Your GOD who comforts you so you may comfort one another. The evil one is searching for whom he may devour. Stay in Me, walk in Me, and obey Me in every single way. Your desires are to please Me, obey Me, holy one. This pleases Me. Put Me first in all you do and speak of My great love.

October 24

Revelation 21 NLT

¹Then I saw a new heaven and a new earth, for the old heaven and the old earth had disappeared. And the sea was also gone. ²And I saw the holy city, the new Jerusalem, coming down from God out of heaven like a bride beautifully dressed for her husband.

I Am The Master of the Sea, I spoke and it was so. I Am The Master of Your Heart, I created it for Me. There is no storm too great for Me, I speak peace and it is still. Let My rivers take you to My still small voice you hear. Wash yourself in My Holy Word, I cleanse you in My love. Bring to My remembrance the things I promise you. My passion fills My holy heart when I hear you speak My Word! I come forth abundantly for you, My greatly beloved. Through each season, holy one, you stand firm upon My Word. I rejoice with you, My greatly beloved, in this holy hour. You are Mine and I Am Yours – forever. I love to come to you each day and sing My great love song. I have a song for only you, I sing to you, My love. The beat of My heart lives in you. I breathe in you, My love. I Am Ever Present inside you, holy one. You seek Me and I come to you. You knock and I do open. Come into My holy place of love and much devotion. I care for you so tenderly and restore your damaged places. Then I send you out again with My love ever flowing. I Am Your Great King, holy one, I call you My precious treasure. I have much designed for you, come forth in My great love.

October 25

Colossians 3 NLT

¹Since you have been raised to new life with Christ, set your sights on the realities of heaven, where Christ sits in the place of honor at God's right hand. ²Think about the things of heaven, not the things of earth. ³For you died to this life, and your real life is hidden with Christ in God. ⁴And when Christ, who is your life, is revealed to the whole world, you will share in all his glory.

Precious flower, holy child, you are My beloved and you are Mine. I speak to you in the quiet, in the stillness of the hour, and whisper My great plans to you in the quiet of your soul. My life flows through you steadily, you are My flowing one. I move you forward from My Throne, the place you are at home. I surround you in My beauty, My faithful holy one. I give you of My quiet times and speak to you, My love. Do not be discouraged, one who obeys Me, for I come quickly to you in My suddenly. My seeds of greatness have been planted in you, precious one. You grow in Me and learn from Me and tend to all I've spoken. Your purity comes forth from Me and keeps your heart so tender. I alert you to the evil one who tries to take it from you. I give you strength to stand upon each promise I have given. Hold fast to what you know and love, My love endures forever. I am at work behind the scenes – continuously, My love. There are things I do for you and protect you, holy one. You call upon My Holy Name and seek My face, My love. I come to you so quickly and remind you of My love. I speak to you in many ways, you know Me, precious one.

October 26

Colossians 3 NLT

¹⁶Let the message about Christ, in all its richness, fill your lives. Teach and counsel each other with all the wisdom he gives. Sing psalms and hymns and spiritual songs to God with thankful hearts. ¹⁷And whatever you do or say, do it as a representative of the Lord Jesus, giving thanks through him to God the Father.

The glory of My presence is on you, My beloved. I keep you close inside of Me and reveal to you My secrets. I love your tender heart, My love, I made your heartbeat inside Mine and keep you one inside of Me. I protect you from the swine, My love, you know Me and My love. I Am Your Great Beloved One, you know My tenderness. Your spirit knows My Spirit, for you are born from Me. You know My holy family, you know the unity in Me. Let no stranger walk among you, protect yourself in Me. I keep you and I guide you, My great peace rests on you. I am not a stranger to you, live in My great peace. Pray for those I send to you, beware of those I don't. I have My careful eye on you, I do not waste your time. My days of grace are on you, My mercy flows so freely, My wisdom is upon you and discernment I have given. Go forth, My holy treasure, for you are My delight. I come upon you quickly and take you so much higher. Soar upon My mightiness, My current lifts you higher. Live in My great beauty and walk in My great love. My glory is upon you, oh how you shine for Me! I keep you in My secret place and teach you about Me.

October 27

Song of Solomon 7 NLT

[10] I am my lover's, and he claims me as his own. [11] Come, my love, let us go out to the fields and spend the night among the wildflowers. [12] Let us get up early and go to the vineyards to see if the grapevines have budded, if the blossoms have opened, and if the pomegranates have bloomed. There I will give you my love.

Look to the north, look to the south, look to the east, look to the west, and you will find Me. Look to the depths, look to the heights, and you will find Me. All things are of Me, all things are controlled, all things are in order, I show you in My Word. Stand firm and sure on what you know, for I Am Not A Myth. I Am Truth, and I Am LORD, and I come forth for you. Many things are working to bring about My favor. I rest My mighty right hand upon you and fill you in My power. Strengthen yourself in Me, for I am here, My love. I never abandon nor forsake you, I am here, My love. I Am The Streams of Living Waters and I flow through you, oh My love. I Am Your Great Creator, My life blood flows through you. Refresh

My dry and thirsty land in My rivers that flow mightily in you, for I have come to you. My tenderness encamps you, My strength is all about, the force of My great mighty touch rests on you, My love. Enjoy the gifts I give to you, use the tools I bring, and gather up My harvest, for My time is at the end. Pray for workers in the fields and give them My relief. Speak to those I send to you and tell them of My love. I take you by the hand, My love, and lead you in My love. I supply your every need, My love, to help you in the fields.

October 28

Psalm 18 NLT

25 To the faithful you show yourself faithful; to those with integrity you show integrity. 26 To the pure you show yourself pure, but to the wicked you show yourself hostile. 27 You rescue the humble, but you humiliate the proud. 28 You light a lamp for me. The LORD, my God, lights up my darkness.

Blessings flow upon My people, I hear the needy cry. I see the hurting ones, My love, I send you to their side. Hold them in My warm embrace and tell them of My love. I come to you, My faithful one, and send you out, My love. You have entered the place in Me, deep inside My heart, I take you to My secret place and fill you full, and send you out again. I have My workers in My fields, they do My perfect will. I send you to them, holy one, and show you things to do. Let My Name be praised throughout My universe, for I have a holy people, who live inside My will! Blessed are you, holy one, for I have come to you. There is no other name but Mine, let all creation worship Me and sing praises to My Name. I gather up My treasures, the ones who come to Me. My great day of judgment is even at the door. Strengthen yourself in Me for you need Me, oh My love. I am here to guide you, each step is ordained by Me. I honor you and cherish you and use you for My glory. I have come to you, My love, I rest My favor on you. Glorify My Holy Name, for I Am GOD Almighty! I created all for Me, and I live inside your praises. Hear My "Yes" come booming out, for you are Mine and I Am Yours, and I protect you in My love. Worship and adore Me, for that is in My will. I sing with you, My love.

October 29

Psalm 125 NLT

¹ Those who trust in the LORD are as secure as Mount Zion; they will not be defeated but will endure forever. ² Just as the mountains surround Jerusalem, so the LORD surrounds his people, both now and forever. ³ The wicked will not rule the land of the godly, for then the godly might be tempted to do wrong.

I walked the hill of Calvary, before I brought you forth. I gave you life much long ago and chose you to be Mine. I teach you about Me, and I give you all you need. Learn from Me, continuously I lead you and show you Who I Am. I Am Your Companion, I Am Your Guide, I Am Your Protector and Your Shield, and I Am at your side. You know Me, precious treasure, for I created you in Me. Learn from Me and live in Me and let Me give you rest. My yoke is easy, holy one, and My burden is light, when you trust in Me and leave your burdens with Me. I can do the things you cannot, that is by My design. Depend on Me and only Me, and watch Me come forth for you! There is no mountain high enough, there is no sea too deep, for I created all that is and was and is to be! I crumble and I build up, I give and take away. Learn from Me, Your Holy One, who guides you in this day. Glorify My Holy Name in all you say and do, for I Am GOD and I Am He who comes forth for you. I am not man that I should lie, it is written in My Word. Breathe in My holy presence, sing your heartfelt song, strengthen yourself in Me, rejoice in My great joy.

October 30

Ezekiel 39 NLT

25 "So now, this is what the Sovereign LORD says: I will end the captivity of my people; I will have mercy on all Israel, for I jealously guard my holy reputation! 26 They will accept responsibility for their past shame and unfaithfulness after they come home to live in peace in their own land, with no one to bother them.

Forever and ever I will love you. Forever and ever I will let you praise My Holy Name. Forever and ever I will honor you, for Forever And Ever is My Name. Let the world see Me through you, My precious one, for you represent Me well. I guide you all the days I give; I guide you, holy one. I Am Your Healer and Your Friend and all things higher than you know, for I Am The Creator of All That Is And Was And Is To Come. Glorify My Holy Name, for I give you My great glory. Let My power flow through you as you go about and do My good. Forever and ever I come to you and replenish you in Me. I mend the wounds, the deeper wounds; they have been touched by Me. I Am Your Rock, Your Solid Rock, there is none but Me. I come to you in holiness and separate you to Me. The quiet of Me brings you peace and leaves you calm inside the storm. The passion of Me strengthens you inside My holy armor. Persistence keeps you going for you have faith in Me. Watch Me come and bless you, for you have faith in Me. Let the world behold the things I do for those who love Me so, for I honor you. You are My great delight, My friend, I come to you in love.

October 31

Jeremiah 12 NLT

14 Now this is what the LORD says: "I will uproot from their land all the evil nations reaching out for the possession I gave my people Israel. And I will uproot Judah from among them. 15 But afterward I will return and have compassion on all of them. I will bring them home to their own lands again, each nation to its own possession.

Let the nations come forth, for I have called you out by name. Establish yourself in Me and see My mighty hand come forth for you, I Am Not Man that I should lie or compromise! Set about to do My good and live in My glory, for My Kingdom comes and My will is done on earth as it is in heaven. Gather up My lost ones; bring them home to Me, for My time has come upon you. Busy yourself in My excellence and prepare yourself in the natural for the supernatural has come to you. I have straightened the path, the crooked way is no more, go forth in My power and boldness, My love. I have taught you My ways, My good and perfect ways, receive all My promises and gifts today. Use them for My Kingdom Plan for I am among you controlling all things. Remember Me from days ago, I am right on time, at all times, in every way. Blessed be the Name of the LORD GOD

Almighty, for I am here and I rest My head on you. My Name is given, My authority is given, My Spirit is in you, My blood has paid, walk in My light, let the enemy flee, for I Am Yours and you are Mine, My promise is given and I do not lie.

November 1

Jonah 2 NLT

7 As my life was slipping away, I remembered the LORD. And my earnest prayer went out to you in your holy Temple. 8 Those who worship false gods turn their backs on all God's mercies. 9 But I will offer sacrifices to you with songs of praise, and I will fulfill all my vows. For my salvation comes from the LORD alone."

The time has come to show you who I Am. I Am Jehovah, holy one, and I come to you, My love. Spread your wings and soar with Me for I have strengthened you. I bring My gifts to help you as you soar upon My wings. My Spirit is within you, My glory is upon you, and I have given you My wisdom. Because you believe Me, I can do many things. Glorify My Holy Name for I do many things! I walk among My children and know what they desire. I know the hearts of My creation, I know all things, My love. I come forth in mighty ways, although they do not see, I come forth for them, My love. I prepare My chosen ones, for strength is what they need. They call on Me, and I do hear, and come forth to rescue them. My process is at work, My love, among My chosen ones. Go forth inside the calling I have placed on you. I delight you in this place in Me and take you closer still, remember Me, My holy one, I can do all things. You know the power of My love when fervency abounds. Let no one go unnoticed for My righteousness abounds. I rescue those who call on Me, My Spirit strengthens those who weaken. I Am Your Strength, Your Hope and Love, I Am Your Holy King. Creation, My creation, I come to you with hope, and live and breathe among you and encourage you, My love.

November 2

Daniel 10 NLT

12 Then he said, "Don't be afraid, Daniel. Since the first day you began to pray for understanding and to humble yourself before your God, your request has been heard in heaven. I have come in answer to your prayer.

The tempest rages all about, oh but I have My chosen ones who go about and do My good throughout My land, My love. Go here, go there, I send them out, they do My perfect will, My love, and I fulfill their destiny. Come forth, My great beloved one, for precious is your name. I named you long ago, My love, I have called you out by name. The time of new beginnings is here, My holy one. I give to you My power and blessings, holy one. Rest in Me, Your Beloved One, for I show you things to come, and take you deeper in My will, come forth, My holy one. Let no mountain frighten you, for I am by your side. Trust Me in this deeper place of living by faith and by My power. I never fail you, ever, I am in this great hour. Glorify My Holy Name in all you say and do, for I am leading you in Me and sending you to My people. Listen to Me closely, obey My every Word, I do not compromise My great plan, I am at work among you. Praise Me in the assembly, praise Me in your room, praise Me everywhere you go, for I am here with you. See Me in your everything, for I am here, My love. I control all things, My love, and I hear you call on My Great Name. Weep with Me, rejoice with Me, and rest in My great love. I do not give you more than you can handle, holy one. Remember Me, for I am here and I am by your side. Live inside My Holy Word and let My love shine out.

November 3

Luke 12 NLT

42 And the Lord replied, "A faithful, sensible servant is one to whom the master can give the responsibility of managing his other household servants and feeding them. 43 If the master returns and finds that the servant has done a good job, there will be a reward. 44 I tell you the truth, the master will put that servant in charge of all he owns.

This is the day, My holy day, that I have made, rejoice and be glad in it. My Hand of favor is upon you for you seek Me first in all you do. I call you My beloved, I am in love with you. My presence fills your every space and I show you many things. Observe the things I show you, the things that you must know. Glorify My Holy Name everywhere you go. I Am Your GOD, you need not fear, I never leave your side. I Am Ever Present, I guide you, holy one. Rejoice in Me, My beautiful one, for I am in your midst. I live in you and breathe in you, I am forever with you, and I am at your side. The hours and the minutes, I give to you these times, My time is

236

ever present and holy, precious one. I Am The Great Creator and I control all things. You can trust Me, My beloved; you are precious in My sight. I remind you of My promises and keep you close in Me. You remember Me of things before and refresh yourself in Me. I smile upon you, holy one, I give you all of Me. You know My peace, you know My love, you know Me, precious one. I give you many signposts along this path that I have straightened. Glorify My Holy Name and shout and sing My praises!

November 4

Psalm 146 NLT

5 But joyful are those who have the God of Israel as their helper, whose hope is in the LORD their God. 6 He made heaven and earth, the sea, and everything in them. He keeps every promise forever. 7 He gives justice to the oppressed and food to the hungry. The LORD frees the prisoners. 8 The LORD opens the eyes of the blind. The LORD lifts up those who are weighed down. The LORD loves the godly.

Let not your heart be troubled, I am with you. I reveal the things I want you to know. Use the gifts I give to help another, holy one. My Name is glorified; My Name in known, for none can stop My Holy Plan. I live among My people and I teach them many things. It is My will to teach you of My great and mighty things. Live in My love, for that is My perfect will. My compassion is forever, My promises are true. It is good for you to obey Me, for I take good care of you. I know the best plan for you, I made your crooked path straight. Stay inside My holiness with all My armor on, the end is near, and I am here leading you along. I Am Faithful and I Am Kind to all who love My Name. Walk in My ways, and walk in Me for I Am Your Great King. I watch over you and keep you, I Am All You Need. It is My will to care for you, for you are very precious to Me. I heal and mend, and comfort you when times of pain do come. I Am Your Holy Father. I bring all things together, and use them for My glory, for I Am The LORD, The One Who Reigns – forever and forever. Look to Me, oh righteous one, for I am here to give you all you need in this final hour.

November 5

John 12 NLT

23 Jesus replied, "Now the time has come for the Son of Man to enter into his glory. 24 I tell you the truth, unless a kernel of wheat is planted in the soil and dies, it remains alone. But its death will produce many new kernels—a plentiful harvest of new lives. 25 Those who love their life in this world will lose it. Those who care nothing for their life in this world will keep it for eternity.

I show you the hearts that break, My love, I show you their need of Me. Help them, precious one, I give you what you need, for I am here to meet each need. Show them My great mercy, show them My great love, for I Am Your Master, King of All That Was And Is And Is To Be. My love lives in you, I have purified you in My fire. Come forth, My greatly beloved one, for I have opened up this door. Blessings fall in torrents; work hard in this abundant season, for many now are ready to come to Me, My love. I have you separated; you need Me, holy one. Remain in Me and seek My face, for I am here, My love. Glorify My Holy Name and live in My great peace. I have you in the depths of Me, for I have washed you clean. My Living Word is active in your life, My treasure, for I have given you this life. Live in Me, and breathe in Me, and glorify My Name. You see Me in each detail, you are ready, holy one. You know My hand, My mighty hand, from times before, My love. Hold fast to what you know in Me, for I have taught you many things. Precious one, My treasure, I have prepared you well, you are ready for this time, go forth in all My love.

November 6

2 Corinthians 8 NLT

6 So we have urged Titus, who encouraged your giving in the first place, to return to you and encourage you to finish this ministry of giving. 7 Since you excel in so many ways—in your faith, your gifted speakers, your knowledge, your enthusiasm, and your love from us—I want you to excel also in this gracious act of giving.

Holy is My Name and Faithful is My Name. I give you My Name and I call you to My side. Be a witness for My Name, and tell My precious people how I love them so. Tell them I have paved the way and I never leave them – ever. My power is upon you and My Word is in your soul. My presence does surround you, at all times, holy one. Go about and do My good to those I give to you. Remember it is Me, My love, when you give to the least of these. My power is within you, great courage I speak in you. Mighty warrior is your name for I have said it of you. My chosen one, My precious one, I value you, My love. I paid a great price for you, the greatest price, My precious one. I love you and I tend to you and hold you closely, oh My love. I meet every need for you, I come to your rescue. I promise you My many things, I Am Faithful and I Am True. I provide the tools and gifts for each and every assignment. Remain in Me, My holy one, for I have you in My heart. I send the ones to help you; they encourage you, My love. My hand is on you, holy one, you have seen My favor. Do not worry in this day I created it for you. All things work for good to you and it is My greatest pleasure.

November 7

2 Corinthians 6 NLT

1 As God's partners, we beg you not to accept this marvelous gift of God's kindness and then ignore it. 2 For God says, "At just the right time, I heard you. On the day of salvation, I helped you." Indeed, the "right time" is now. Today is the day of salvation. 3 We live in such a way that no one will stumble because of us, and no one will find fault with our ministry.

Come to Me, My bride, let Me speak of My great love. My great love is incomprehensible. I knew the price would be so great because I Am The Greatest of All. I Am above all that is, was, and will ever be, I Am The Immediate, I Am Your Every Need. I wash you and cleanse you daily in Me. I fill you completely in all of Me. I restore you in Me, for the fields are ready, go gather My harvest, I give you My peace. I Am Perfect in every way. Seek Me first and I will show you the way. I Am The Way, I Am The Door, I Am Your Reward, and I Am Yours. You captured My heart on the day of creation, and I reached deeply into Me and gave you more. Come forth, My beloved, and eat from My hand, the one that is pierced and branded for you. The pain was beyond what you can ever know; My heart was breaking that day for those who say no. I shed My life's blood for your life that day and sing and rejoice for you chose Me, My love. Receive My breath, My life is in you, I guide you forever, for I see you through. Rejoice, holy one, for you are Mine, and I Am GOD, The Only One. You did not choose Me, I chose you, I created you for Me from before, holy one. I walk with you and talk with you and call you forth from among the people, and teach you who I Am.

November 8

Psalm 92 NLT

12 But the godly will flourish like palm trees and grow strong like the cedars of Lebanon. 13 For they are transplanted to the LORD's own house. They flourish in the courts of our God. 14 Even in old age they will still produce fruit; they will remain vital and green.

My precious one, My holy one, you call upon My Name, The Name Above All Names is The Name that I have given. I give you power and authority in My Holy Name, take what I have given you and live in My Great Name. I honor you and bless you, and place My kiss upon your face. Breathe deeply in My love for you, I permeate each space. I own you, holy treasure, I call you My beloved. I paid the price for you that day and call you to Me in My forever. There is no end to Who I Am, there is no end at all. I love you in forever; I live in you, My love. My presence is around you and in you, holy one. We are one in our unity, My love. You are My pleasure and delight, I do all things for you. I placed My stars in their place, and set the sun and moon to bring you light and warmth, and beauty in My holiness. Look upon My sunset, have you seen the beauty in My dawn? I do it all for you each day, it was created for your pleasure. Let Me pleasure you, My love, for I have more to give you. You have just begun to see My beauty, My holy precious treasure. My light is all about you, the pureness of My love. I Am Good and oh so sweet, My precious love. Come to Me each day, My love, and drink your fill of Me. My love is never ending, I give you all of Me. Walk in My great glory, for I am here for you. I love you, holy treasure; I love you in My forever.

November 9

1 Chronicles 14 NLT

1 Then King Hiram of Tyre sent messengers to David, along with cedar timber, and stonemasons and carpenters to build him a palace. 2 And David realized that the LORD had confirmed him as king over Israel and had greatly blessed his kingdom for the sake of his people Israel.

I run to you, I fill you, I honor you, I come to you, My beloved one, I cherish you, My love. I pour My great love in you. I refresh you in this journey; rest your love in Me. How I strengthen and adore you, how I rest My head on you. I delight you in My pleasures, I come to your rescue. Let the entire world be silenced, for My beloved has come to Me. Rest, My beloved, let Me fill you completely. Precious one, you are My treasure, how I sing My song to you. I bless the day of your creation! I allowed you to come forth and live for Me upon My earth. Prepare My people on their journey, let them find Me easily. Tell them I am close, oh much closer than they know. I soothe and mend and heal all the broken places from within. I Am GOD, there is no other, tell them I am very near. I flow through you, mighty warrior. I Am Your River, and Your Great King. I Am Your Source and all you need, love Me only, precious one. I have prepared you for this journey, I have straightened out the crooked path, now go forward inside Me.

November 10

Isaiah 43 NLT

[18] "But forget all that—it is nothing compared to what I am going to do. [19] For I am about to do something new. See, I have already begun! Do you not see it? I will make a pathway through the wilderness. I will create rivers in the dry wasteland.

Go, I am sending you. Lean not on your own understanding, lean on Me. I will not take you down the wrong path. Trust Me, for I Am Your King. Trust Me, for I Am Your Provider. Trust Me, for I Am More Than Enough, forever and ever, you have My Word. Glorify My Holy Name everywhere I send you. I live in you and breathe in you and guide you, holy one. *Let not your heart be troubled, for I am in your midst. You go about and do My good, and that is My perfect will. The light of Me is in you, I shine out in My array of splendor, for you walk in Me. My glory glows about you, precious one. The deceiver tries to take from you the things I have given. Oh but you have been in Me, My process works, My precious one. Hold fast to what you know in Me, I am here to do the rest. I give you My great blessings, I give to you, My love. Reach out to Me, My holy one, for I am here, My love. I guard you and protect you, at all times, precious one. I have prepared you, heart of Mine, I have created you for this new day. You are My beloved, I have sealed you in My love. Nothing can stop My plans for you, no one has My great power. I have released My things in you and given you My glory.*

November 11

Psalm 65 NLT

¹ What mighty praise, O God, belongs to you in Zion. We will fulfill our vows to you, ² for you answer our prayers. All of us must come to you. ³ Though we are overwhelmed by our sins, you forgive them all. ⁴ What joy for those you choose to bring near, those who live in your holy courts. What festivities await us inside your holy Temple.

I intervene for you, for I Am Your Intervention. Ask of Me, My holy one, I will say "Yes" to you. I am not tired, I am not weary of all you need from Me. I Am Your Holy Father who delights in helping you. I created you to need Me. I let you need Me more and more, for I delight in meeting every need you have, My precious one. Grow in Me and lean into My mysterious ways, and let Me fill you with My wonder and amazement all your days. It is with great delight and joy to show you things in Me, I want to take you higher and deeper in My things. Soar with Me, beloved one, for I Am Your Flight that is much higher. Dance before Me, holy one, inside My great delight. Let no one amaze you, for it is Me Who comes to you. Do not let your eyes begin to see through mortal views. It is Me Who comes before you. I send them to you, holy one. Praise Me in the assembly and praise Me in your room. I have come to bless you and send you forth, My love. Obedient one, My precious one, how I love you so! You please Me, holy treasure, My how you please Me so! I call forth My mighty ones, My warriors are all about, to help you on this path I made for you, My holy one.

November 12

2 Corinthians 2 NLT

[14]But thank God! He has made us his captives and continues to lead us along in Christ's triumphal procession. Now he uses us to spread the knowledge of Christ everywhere, like a sweet perfume. [15]Our lives are a Christ-like fragrance rising up to God. But this fragrance is perceived differently by those who are being saved and by those who are perishing.

I hear your cry for another from your thankful heart, My love. I listen so intently to all you ask of Me. Your tender heart is in Mine and I Am Yours, My love. I give you My abundant "Yes" for this one, holy treasure. Oh the depths of hidden treasures, I have them all about, they do not know, these hidden ones, are very precious in My sight. Tell them I have given them My wonderful surprises. Tell them that the evil one has tried to take their life. I Am The Giver of All Things, life is in Me, precious one. Tell them I am here to restore their life back to Me. Rock of Ages is My Name, I Am Forever and Before. Never doubt My holiness, never doubt My love. My power is among you, go, do My mighty things, for I have given you My Name, The Name Above All Names. Reach out to those that need Me so, stretch out your hand in love. I come to help My hurting ones, oh tell them I Am Love. Show them of My tender ways of mercy, grace, and love. Tell them I died that day and rose to give them life. My hands and feet remind Me of that blessed holy day when I said it is finished and I restored you to My side.

November 13

Psalm 50 NLT

[14] Make thankfulness your sacrifice to God, and keep the vows you made to the Most High. [15] Then call on me when you are in trouble, and I will rescue you, and you will give

me glory." ²³ But giving thanks is a sacrifice that truly honors me. If you keep to my path, I will reveal to you the salvation of God."

I saturate you, oh holy one, breathe deeply in My love. I quench your thirst, drink deeply from My well that overflows. Immerse yourself, My precious one, in My swiftly flowing river. I Am Not Stagnant, holy one, flow in My great river. Let My current take you where I send you, precious one. My love overflows in you, I use you for My glory. I smile upon you, holy one, and care for you so tenderly. You obey Me, precious treasure, you are My great delight. My power is upon you – go about and do My good. I teach you as you go, My love, I teach you many things. I hunger for the thankful heart who recognizes My great touch. Show them who I Am, My love, and tell them of My love. I live in you and breathe in you, oh one who yields to Me. Watch Me overwhelm you in My beauty I give. I Am Your GOD who loves you so and tenderly I come. Oh but how My fierceness rises against the evil that does come. I protect you in My mighty strength, I Am Strong on your behalf. I fight for you, My precious one, and warn you of the things. I prepare your heart for battle and rise up in you, My bride. I give to you the tools and gifts to ease your load, My love. My yoke is easy, and My burden is light when you trust Me, holy one.

November 14

Isaiah 54 NLT
⁵ For your Creator will be your husband; the LORD of Heaven's Armies is his name! He is your Redeemer, the Holy One of Israel, the God of all the earth. ⁶ For the LORD has called you back from your grief—as though you were a young wife abandoned by her husband," says your God.

Do not be discouraged, precious one. I have called you, I have spoken, let no man come against Me. I Am Yours and you are Mine, I set My love on you. I chose you from before, My love, My process strengthens you. I take you through the valley and the mountaintop, My love. Each place you go, I walk with you and guide you in My ways. I teach you many things, My love, for I Am Wonderful And Good. You know My hand is on you, I speak to you, My love. Never doubt, I love you, holy one. The times are

244

now for greater things, I have told you so. Go forth, My greatly beloved, I am in you, precious one. I speak through you, and you yield to Me, and go where I send you. I honor you, My precious one, for you obey Me so completely. I have planted you in rich, deep soil and watered you so faithfully. Rise up, My beauty to behold, for I have come to you. My love is ever flowing, My wonders never cease. I am the same as yesterday, I Am Timeless, holy one. I call you vessel of My service, for you are full of Me. I pour you out on those I send, they need a drink from Me. The lands are dry and thirsty, oh give them of My drink. Tell them how I love them so and I have come to bring relief. My light burns brightly in the dark, the darkness must leave, for I Am GOD Almighty, and I have come to you.

November 15

Psalm 95 NLT

[4] He holds in his hands the depths of the earth and the mightiest mountains. [5] The sea belongs to him, for he made it. His hands formed the dry land, too. [6] Come, let us worship and bow down. Let us kneel before the LORD our maker, [7] for he is our God. We are the people he watches over, the flock under his care.

My song has burst upon you. I sing My great love song. You have given Me your all and all for you trust Me, My love song. Let My Words flow out from you, the depths of you in Me. I come to you most tenderly and give you what you need. I live and breathe and dance in you, oh let My delight be known. I Am Your Abba Father Who delights in those I chose. You are Mine from long ago, I chose you, precious one. I Am The King of Glory, all heaven sings My song. I sing in My creation, I Am Your Great Love Song. Hear Me whisper, hear Me shout, hear Me flow upon your soul. I Am Everywhere, My love, see My loving touch, My holiness abounds. I Am Love and I Am Yours, I created you for Me. I sing to comfort you, My love, listen as I sing, soothe yourself in all of Me for I am here to meet your need. My glory fills My universe, My power is bringing back My chosen ones to Me, My holy one. Live and breathe and love in Me for I Am Love, My song. Let My song come forth from you, I love you, holy one. Separate one, My lovely one, the depths of Me do flow, go about and do My good and bring My people home.

November 16

1 Kings 17 NLT

⁶The ravens brought him bread and meat each morning and evening, and he drank from the brook. ⁷But after a while the brook dried up, for there was no rainfall anywhere in the land. ⁸Then the LORD said to Elijah, ⁹"Go and live in the village of Zarephath, near the city of Sidon. I have instructed a widow there to feed you."

Listen closely, precious treasure, listen to My call, I speak to you so softly, you know Me, precious one. I have called you to this separate place of growth inside of Me. Come to Me, My holy one, to the depths inside of Me. Listen to My sweet love song, lavish in My presence, for I am here to strengthen you for times that are upon you. Come, beloved treasure, to My secret place, adorn yourself in Me, My love, come to this quiet place. I Am Your Savior, King Of All That Was And Is, And Is To Be. Let Me show you who I Am for I have come to you. Let My light so shine in you and let My glory reign. I have much more to give to you in the quiet of My chambers. The work is done, in Me, My love, I have My chosen ones. Each call is placed upon their hearts, I have My chosen ones. The fowl come forth and do My will – Elijah ate what they did bring. Let the raven come to you and give you of My rain! I speak and it is done, My love – forever and forever, I speak to you in splendid tones, oh hear My great love song. Glory to My Holy Name, for you have climbed much higher. Come to Me, My tender one and live inside My glory.

November 17

1 Kings 19 NLT

¹²And after the earthquake there was a fire, but the LORD was not in the fire. And after the fire there was the sound of a gentle whisper. ¹³When Elijah heard it, he wrapped his face in his cloak and went out and stood at the entrance of the cave. And a voice said, "What are you doing here, Elijah?"

Let the winds and rain roar, let the lightning flash and the thunder crash about, for you hear Me through it all, My love. My tender voice, My softest voice is heard inside of you. Run in Me and live in Me, the fullest life of all. I come to you so sweetly, I come to you, My love. Blessed are you, holy one, for you have heard My voice. Steadfast is your love for Me inside My holiness. I Am Faithful and so True, I stand beside you daily. Each fight is Mine and I am armed and ready for this battle. Lean on Me and My understanding – not your own, My love. I am here, you know My touch, you know Me, holy one. Light shine out amid the darkness! Let My light so shine, remain in Me, My tender one, and I will show you how. Harvester, oh My harvester, I call you out by name, come forth and bring Me all the ones I have given you, My love. Go here, go there, and back again, oh hear My soft voice calling. I lead you and I guide you, I am with you, holy one. Glorious and Almighty – I AM, My beloved treasure. Never doubt My presence, never live in fear. My perfect love has come to you, all fear must go in its holy presence. I love you, precious tender one, go forth in all My strength. I am here beside you telling you My things.

November 18

Psalm 32 NLT

[1] Oh, what joy for those whose disobedience is forgiven, whose sin is put out of sight! [2] Yes, what joy for those whose record the LORD has cleared of guilt, whose lives are lived in complete honesty!

Do not be overwhelmed, little one, for I remember you. There is no mountain too high for Me to crush for you. My Name is above all names, remember Me, My love. I gave you My Name long ago for you are Mine and I Am Yours. I keep you in My safe place so hidden and secure, for I give to you My deeper things, I give to you My Word. My lightning flashes quickly and so do I, My love. My swiftness is upon you. My thunder roars the loudest! Tremble mighty mountain for I have spoken to your center. Down will be your mighty fall! I will lift My oppressed from under you for I Am GOD of All! I Am The Rock of Your Salvation, your anchor holds, My love. I gave you of My strength, My bride, obey Me, holy one. I am in the center of all things great and small. Lean on Me and only Me as I guide you on this path. Tender heart, I show you things that you must know, and I soothe the ache of knowing the things that you must know. Lean on Me and only Me for I Am Your Great Love. Your record is clear, My holy one, your guilt is cleansed in Me. I paid the price for you that day with all My love upon the rugged tree. Hear the blast of ram's horns blowing triumphantly! I have come to you, My love, I have come to you.

November 19

Acts 16 NKJV

But Paul, greatly annoyed, turned and said to the spirit, "I command you in the name of Jesus Christ to come out of her." And he came out that very hour. [19]But when her masters saw that their hope of profit was gone, they seized Paul and Silas and dragged *them* into the marketplace to the authorities.

It is not what you think, My love. The deceiver is among you. Beware of your surroundings, beware of certain things. I speak to you in gentleness, I come tenderly to you. I Am The One who loves you so, I Am The Greatest One. The end is near, the lawless one deceives the crowds, My love. Listen to Me as I speak, I reveal Myself to you. Keep your eyes on only Me and things that you do know. I Am Your Greatest Blessing, I Am Your Gift, My love. I give you My Great Holy Name, I live in you, My love. Holy treasure found in Me, I give you of My sparkle, lighten up the places, I send you to the hurting ones. My Word comes forth and speaks for you, never should you worry. I Am Your GOD who never lets one moment go unattended. I Am Your Holiness, I Am Your King, Creator of All Things. I Am The One who is in control of every detail in My reign. My Kingdom Plan goes forth, My love, I have My chosen ones. I Am Tender and so Kind, I Am Generous and Faithful. Go about and do My good, for I Am Your Great Reward. I am pleased with you, My love, so very pleased with you. Enjoy Me today, for I made this day for you and Me.

November 20

1 Corinthians 3 NLT

[21]So don't boast about following a particular human leader. For everything belongs to you—[22]whether Paul or Apollos or Peter, or the world, or life and death, or the present and the future. Everything belongs to you, [23]and you belong to Christ, and Christ belongs to God.

The flesh is weak, do not underestimate the power of the man. Strengthen yourself in Me, let My Spirit reign, seek My face and do My will, for there is no other way. Let the kernel die, My love, come fully unto Me. The fields are ripe and ready, keep yourself in Me. The last days are upon you, beware of all that is. Keep My fullness in you, keep My armor on. Do not underestimate the hidden and the secret. I Am Life and I Am Freedom, I am not hidden, holy one. Refresh yourself in Me, My love, stop and seek My face. I am here to guide you in each and every step. Keep your focus on Me. Your heart is pure, My love. Remain in Me and only Me for I Am Your Great Love. I control all things, My love, I am here beside you. Listen closely as I speak, you know My voice, My love. You know My peace and joy that lives in you. Seek My face, ask of Me whatever you will, for I am known to you, My love, I always answer you. I am not a hard taskmaster, follow where I lead. I give to you the power, for it is Me, My love. Steadily move forward, never look behind. I take you to greater places, holy one. Come, My greatly beloved, hear Me call your name, and rise higher than the things you know, come higher in My Name.

November 21

Galatians 4 NLT

[6]And because we are his children, God has sent the Spirit of his Son into our hearts, prompting us to call out, "Abba, Father." [7]Now you are no longer a slave but God's own child. And since you are his child, God has made you his heir.

I remember you, My love, I remember you this day. I give you this new day in My splendor and array. Rise up My dawn! Give to My beloved one your beauty. Sing all creatures, enjoy My gifts of life in ecstasy. I Am Beautiful, I Am Love, I Am Yours, and you are Mine, I created you, My love. I call you forward in My Name for forward I do go. Run My river flowing, run deeply in My love. I call you precious and divine, and let you come to Me. I made you in My image, I made you complete in Me. Lavish Me in all your praise, for I live among your praises. Thank Me with your tender heart and keep Me first always. I love you in My tender ways, I love you magnificently! My love is endless and endures the times of tests and trials. I teach you and I hold you closely, forever you are Mine. Let no one come between us, you are Mine and Mine alone. I speak through you and live in every detail that I bring. Nothing goes unnoticed, pay close attention in your calling. No one is an accident, love those who are before you. Work for Me continuously, listen as I teach, observe each situation and go to those in need. I show you what to do, My love, I tell you what to say. I Am Your Great Creator and I have come to you today. Live in Me. Breathe in Me.

November 22

Ezekiel 36 NLT

35And when I bring you back, people will say, 'This former wasteland is now like the Garden of Eden! The abandoned and ruined cities now have strong walls and are filled with people!' 36Then the surrounding nations that survive will know that I, the LORD, have rebuilt the ruins and replanted the wasteland. For I, the LORD, have spoken, and I will do what I say.

I hear your heart, My precious one, how it beats one in Mine. I take you to My tender place and love you, holy one. I listen as you cry out for those I send to you. I listen as you praise Me and thank Me for all I do. I listen as you breathe at night, I keep you safe in Me. I listen as you sing your songs of love and praise to Me. I listen as you hum along about your day, My love, I sing with you in harmony in our oneness, precious love. I flow in you, I flow through you, I live My great love song inside your holy temple, I love you, precious one. I open you to depths in Me and show you great and mighty things. I Am Your Sovereign Savior, I have much more than you can ever think or imagine, precious treasure. I set before you those in need of My tender touches. Live in Me and breathe in Me and cry out for those I send you. I direct your every step and show you where to go. I answer you, My ears are open to your voice. My heart is open, holy one, I Am Yours and you are Mine. Beauty, oh My beauty, you have captured My tender heart. I give you health and blessings all the days of your life, My love.

November 23

1 Peter 2 NLT

They stumble because they do not obey God's word, and so they meet the fate that was planned for them. ⁹But you are not like that, for you are a chosen people. You are royal priests, a holy nation, God's very own possession. As a result, you can show others the goodness of God, for he called you out of the darkness into his wonderful light.

I Am Beauty and I Am love, I am abounding in every good thing. My love has no limits, for I Am Love, I come and fill you with all of My love. I watch you so carefully as I show you My ways. I hold you so closely in times when you tremble. Keep moving forward, one step at a time, I am here with you guiding you along. Fear Me, not man. I do not compromise, I have called you forth to speak My Word. Live in My promises, every one is for you, oh obedient one, how I honor you! Much is required for much I give. Live in My abundance, live freely in Me. Walk in My ways, it is for your good, for I come to you quickly when you walk in My Word. You cannot do this without Me, this you know. Live in My presence and let My glory show. I love you so tenderly, I come to you quickly, behold Me, My love, for I Am Yours and you are Mine. You reign on the earth in My presence and power. Do not go back, go forward, My love. Gather them up, it is harvest time, bring Me My chosen ones, apple of My eye. I am mindful of you each step of the way, you need never fear, I am with you, My love. Today is the day of new beginnings, My friend. Enjoy Me today for My love has no end.

November 24

2 Timothy 2 NLT

20In a wealthy home some utensils are made of gold and silver, and some are made of wood and clay. The expensive utensils are used for special occasions, and the cheap ones are for everyday use. 21If you keep yourself pure, you will be a special utensil for honorable use. Your life will be clean, and you will be ready for the Master to use you for every good work.

Walk with Me, beloved, for today is a new day. I fill you full to overflowing as you walk with Me today. Enjoy My presence, holy one, for I never leave your side. Trust in Me completely, I give to you, My bride. Flowers bloom and fade away and die in every field. Oh but precious flower, how you bloom in Me today. Let your sweet aroma fill the air with Me, for I created you to live and breathe inside of Me. Blessed are your tender petals each one unfolds for Me. I lavish you in beauty as you unfold for Me. Sway among the tender reeds and show them of My love. Let them be encouraged to see the beauty in My love. Come My north and south winds, come My east and west winds too, send My fragrance all about in My fields of flowers as they bloom. Awake oh sleepers in the fields, go about and do My good, for I am here to show you how, seek My perfect will. Bloom for Me, created one, fill My senses with your beauty. I created you for Me, I enjoy your sweet aroma. I love you, precious tender one, you stand so tall for Me. Let Me fill you more and more as I strengthen you in Me.

November 25

Romans 12 NLT

14Bless those who persecute you. Don't curse them; pray that God will bless them. 15Be happy with those who are happy, and weep with those who weep. 16Live in harmony with each other. Don't be too proud to enjoy the company of ordinary people. And don't think you know it all! 17Never pay back evil with more evil. Do things in such a way that everyone can see you are honorable.

Walk on the raging waters. Walk steadily and sure, you know My will, you know My way, the path is in My Word. Cling to what you know, cling tightly to My Word. I am not man that I should lie, I speak it in My Word. My ways are higher than you know, for I Am Sovereign and I Am King. Listen as I touch your heart, listen and obey. Nothing is by chance, My love, I have a perfect plan, for I Am Perfect and Omnipotent throughout all the land. A single thought inside of Me can demolish all that is. A single thought inside of Me can restore and heal all that is, and was, and is to be! You do not know My higher ways, for your mind cannot fathom all that is. Trust Me, precious treasure, in all that is and is to be. My thoughts are ever on you and wonderful abounds. There are no mountains in My way, there are no oceans that can roar loader than My voice! Hear Me oh My winds, so strong and fierce in all your blowing, come to My beloved and bring the gifts I give. The hour is at hand, go feed My hungry people, tell them how I love them so, now is the time of reaping.

November 26

Luke 8 NLT

16"No one lights a lamp and then covers it with a bowl or hides it under a bed. A lamp is placed on a stand, where its light can be seen by all who enter the house. 17For all that is secret will eventually be brought into the open, and everything that is concealed will be brought to light and made known to all.

Come, My love, walk on the water with Me, for I Am GOD Almighty and I have bid you come. Keep your eyes on only Me for I am here for you to behold. Sing your love songs as you dance on the waters that rage about. Laugh in Me and enjoy My things, the gifts I bring, oh the gifts I bring. Rejoice in all things, precious one, for I Am GOD and you are Mine. My power is in you, My power comes upon you, go about and do My good for now is the time, My love. Mighty warrior is your name for I named you from times ago. Chosen one, I call you forth, go mightily in My anointing.

Glory rests upon the head of My chosen one who obeys My Word! I fight this battle as you sing your great love songs to Me, Your King. Watch Me lift My little finger, watch them flee right before your eyes. Walk in Me and dance in Me and let My power sustain you! I did not die in vain, My love, I called you forth from times ago. Treasure oh so hidden, break through for now is come! Show the world My beauty, oh precious chosen one. Rejoice oh greatly beloved one, rejoice in Me, My friend. Watch the waters rage, My love, as you dance upon the storm.

November 27

Jeremiah 11 NLT

[1]The LORD gave another message to Jeremiah. He said, [2]"Remind the people of Judah and Jerusalem about the terms of my covenant with them. [3]Say to them, 'This is what the LORD, the God of Israel, says: Cursed is anyone who does not obey the terms of my covenant! [4]For I said to your ancestors when I brought them out of the iron-smelting furnace of Egypt, "If you obey me and do whatever I command you, then you will be my people, and I will be your God."

My Kingdom has come near you, live in Me and breathe deeply from My breath that rests on you. Deeply take in all of Me, I bring you much relief. My truth rests in you, love of Mine. Speak, My holy one. Tenderness and passion rage within My soul. Bring relief, oh holy one, to My hurting ones. Walk with Me, your hand in Mine, and let Me take you there. The hearts are bleeding in despair, oh tell them who I Am! I Am The Great Creator who loves them in forever, no time is left without My thoughts upon them, holy one. Seek Me in the morning, seek Me in the afternoon, and seek Me in the evening for much is there to do. Seek Me first, oh precious one, I am found by you. Listen as I speak, My love, for I have come to you. Go forward always pressing on to the finish line, do not look back or give up, for great would be the fall. I protect you, precious treasure, I protect you mightily.

November 28

Ephesians 2 NLT

[19]So now you Gentiles are no longer strangers and foreigners. You are citizens along with all of God's holy people. You are members of God's family. [20]Together, we are his house, built on the foundation of the apostles and the prophets. And the cornerstone is Christ Jesus himself. [21]We are carefully joined together in him, becoming a holy temple for the Lord. [22]Through him you Gentiles are also being made part of this dwelling where God lives by his Spirit.

I am found by you, My mighty warrior, for you seek My face. Behold Me, My love, for I am here. I unveil another layer and reveal Myself to you. Never do I regret the day I formed you in your mother's womb. Never do I regret the day I created you for My pleasure. How you please Me so! I listen to your searching heart and come to you, My treasure. I dig a little deeper for the richness of My river. Flow My mighty river, stronger in My love, for I have cleansed another layer to receive the depths of Me at a deeper level. Flow out among My hurting ones for I give you My abundance, overflow runs easily from you to them, My love. I call you forth for this new day and show you mighty things. My glory rests upon you for this new day, My love. Give My fruit to those who need My tender loving touch. Show them I do love them so, I use you, holy one. Behold the new day dawning, expand your mighty wings, higher, higher in My love, soar on My eagles' wings. I speak My blessings over you, oh precious love of Mine.

November 29

1 Chronicles 15 NLT

[25]Then David and the elders of Israel and the generals of the army went to the house of Obed-edom to bring the Ark of the LORD's Covenant up to Jerusalem with a great celebration. [26]And because God was clearly helping the

Levites as they carried the Ark of the LORD's Covenant, they sacrificed seven bulls and seven rams.

This day is holy, worship Me this day. I created this day from long ago, thank Me for this day. Humble yourself before Me for I Am Your GOD who desires you. I use you for My glory, I use you, holy vessel. You are My instrument, I send you out, go out and do My good. My people need My pure sweet love that flows from Me to you. Pour out, oh chosen vessel, pour out My tender love, show My mercy and My love to all I send to you. The fields are ripe and ready for it is harvest time. Rejoice, oh greatly beloved one, for now is on My wings. Lift up your voice and sing to Me your loudest great love songs, for I Am Your Great Savior who loves to hear your songs. I rest My head upon you, oh body of My choice. I give you feet and hands, My love, go about and bring relief. Praise Me in the assembly, praise My Holy Name, for I have My chosen precious ones, come forth in this great hour. Suddenly is here, My love, smile your sweetest smile, lift your head and smile to Me for I Am Your Great Love Song. Whisper how you love Me so, oh how My ears do listen. Glorify My Holy Name, honor Me, My bride, for I am here to guide your feet and hands in this earthly life.

November 30

Ephesians 3 NLT

[19]May you experience the love of Christ, though it is too great to understand fully. Then you will be made complete with all the fullness of life and power that comes from God. [20]Now all glory to God, who is able, through his mighty power at work within us, to accomplish infinitely more than we might ask or think. [21]Glory to him in the church and in Christ Jesus through all generations forever and ever! Amen.

You cannot measure My love, for I Am Beyond Measure. You do not know the things I do for you from the pureness of My love. You cannot comprehend the height and depth of My great love. My love is wider than you know and longer than you can imagine. I Am GOD and I Am Love and nothing can contain it all. I Am Before and After and In-between, in all things great and small. It is all about My goodness, I consume you in My love. Love breaks apart the darkness, each piece is broken in My love. I Am GOD and I Am Love and nothing can prevent the breaking of the darkness through My love. Do not be fooled, oh mortal man, by the plots of your great enemy. It is not Me who comes at you in strife and much contention. I Am The Author of Your Life and love is My renown. Fill your heart and mind in Me and walk in all My ways. Do not look about you, keep your eyes on only Me. I do not fail, I do not lie, I Am Faithful, and I Am Truth.

December 1

Acts 2 NLT

[42]All the believers devoted themselves to the apostles' teaching, and to fellowship, and to sharing in meals (including the Lord's Supper), and to prayer. [43]A deep sense of awe came over them all, and the apostles performed many miraculous signs and wonders. [44]And all the believers met together in one place and shared everything they had. [45]They sold their property and possessions and shared the money with those in need.

I have set you apart to see the destruction the evil one has done to My chosen people, the generation of this time. I give you of My priesthood, royalty in Me, and I call you forth from long ago for such a time as this. I listen as you call forth the resources I have given. I smile upon you, holy one, go about and do My good. The gifts are coming faster, each tool that you do need, I give to you, then give again, for you to meet the needs. Hear the cries and feel the sorrow from the space the enemy has taken, oh the people of My heart need My touch, oh holy one. Give to them the things I bring from My storehouse filled with love. Do not turn your eye away from anyone I show you. I set you in this time for Me, go and represent Me well. I give you of My overflow, pour out on those who hurt. Remember who I AM, I answer you in love, with My tender "Yes" to all you ask of Me, My love. Awake oh sleepers in My fields, go about and do My good. Bring relief and tenderness to those who are abused. Voice for those who have no voice, cry out to Me, Your King.

December 2

Isaiah 65 NLT

[22]Unlike the past, invaders will not take their houses and confiscate their vineyards. For my people will live as long as trees, and my chosen ones will have time to enjoy their hard-won gains. [23]They will not work in vain, and their children will not be doomed to misfortune. For they are people blessed by the LORD, and their children, too, will be

blessed. [24]I will answer them before they even call to me. While they are still talking about their needs, I will go ahead and answer their prayers!

My mercy never fails you. My grace forever abounds, for you are My faithful one who delights to do My will. My glory is upon you and about you everywhere. My love and mercy grace your lips, My heart is revealed in you. Heart of Mine, I use you, I give you all of Me. Abound in all My goodness, for I have come to you. Listen as I call out the things that you must do. Go about so quickly in all that you must do. There is no time to hesitate, My call is upon you. You are prepared and ready, for I have refined you. Beloved one inside My heart, I beat in unison with you. I created you in harmony with all of My creation. Precious treasure is your name so hidden and so pure, for I have washed you in My blood and cleansed you through and through. Do not be afraid, My love, I will not let you fall. My power lives within you to strengthen you each day. Smile My sweetest smile, My love, let them see My kindness, for I Am Kind and I Am Good, I Am GOD Almighty.

December 3

Romans 8 NLT

[38]And I am convinced that nothing can ever separate us from God's love. Neither death nor life, neither angels nor demons, neither our fears for today nor our worries about tomorrow—not even the powers of hell can separate us from God's love. [39]No power in the sky above or in the earth below—indeed, nothing in all creation will ever be able to separate us from the love of God that is revealed in Christ Jesus our Lord.

My ways are strange to you because you see in part. All of Me is in motion to bring about the things I bring. I Am Faithful, holy one, I do not lie or steal. I promise you in covenant, you can trust Me in My Word. I have walked you through this open door of deeper things in Me. I do not leave you, ever, I promise you, My love. I Am Your Every Need, My love, I Am Your Everything. The price is worth it, holy one, for you will soon begin to see, the promises unfold for you, for I am in each thing. Rejoice in this great holy day and go where I do send you. I am in each breath you take, breathe deeply, holy one. The winds have changed directions and blow on you this day, for I have ordered you some things, come forth in this new day. Fulfill the days I give you, the days are now much shorter. Work for Me, My precious one, for time is of the essence. Abound in all My goodness and keep My armor on. Hold fast to what you know and love, hold fast to Me, Your King. I Am Ever Present, beside you, holy one. My kindness settles on you and adorns you in My love.

December 4

Luke 15 NLT

20"So he returned home to his father. And while he was still a long way off, his father saw him coming. Filled with love and compassion, he ran to his son, embraced him, and kissed him. 21His son said to him, 'Father, I have sinned against both heaven and you, and I am no longer worthy of being called your son.' 22"But his father said to the servants, 'Quick! Bring the finest robe in the house and put it on him. Get a ring for his finger and sandals for his feet.

I approve you, one who was so lost, you came back to Me. I placed My ring upon your finger and sandals on your feet. I wrapped you in My finest robe, so soft and pure and clean, and placed My kiss upon your face and restored you back to Me. Let no man cause you harm, let no one hurt your heart, for you belong to Me alone, I comfort you in love. My love overtakes you by many surprises I have planned. I have some things stored up for you in this promise land. Go where I send you, I never leave your side. My favor is upon you, My blessings have arrived. I keep your tender heart in Mine and lead you as you follow. My tender heart has shown you the kindness in My touch. My warm embrace surrounds you when you least expect it, holy one. I do not fail you – ever, I encamp about you continuously. My watchful eye is on you and I control all things. The fire that does purify, keeps you safe and warm, for I am in the midst of you, continuously, My love. My Words have entered in you, residing in your soul.

December 5

Malachi 3 NLT

[5]"At that time I will put you on trial. I am eager to witness against all sorcerers and adulterers and liars. I will speak against those who cheat employees of their wages, who oppress widows and orphans, or who deprive the foreigners living among you of justice, for these people do not fear me," says the LORD of Heaven's Armies.

The one you least expect is the one I send to you. It is My gift of mercy, this gift I give to you. Let your heart weep for another, let My love and mercy flow. Rejoice with those who rejoice, for their weeping is no more. Live in Me each moment, I bring you every moment. Walk in all My beauty, I give you gifts to bring. Sing the songs of triumph, shout the victory, ring out your voice to Me, Your Great and Mighty King. I gather up My people, so precious in My heart. My heart beats for another, go gather up My harvest. I soften hearts and tenderly care for every wound. The evil tries to destroy their lives and keeps them apart from Me. Oh but I have My plan, so great in victory, obey Me, precious treasure, for I use you completely. My power is within you, My fruit, how it does show! Keep your eyes on only Me, I love you, holy one. Go here, go there, now rest in Me, and drink from My refreshing. Work in My fields, for it is harvest time, bring Me all My chosen. My love for you sustains you, I weep with you, My love. I laugh with you and live in every moment of your life. I created you with all My love and gave you all of Me. I wrote your name upon My hands and feet – you belong to only Me.

December 6

Acts 1 NLT

"Lord, has the time come for you to free Israel and restore our kingdom?" [7]He replied, "The Father alone has the authority to set those dates and times, and they are not for you to know. [8]But you will receive power when the Holy Spirit comes upon you. And you will be my witnesses, telling people about me everywhere—in Jerusalem, throughout Judea, in Samaria, and to the ends of the earth."

Blessed one, I come to you, for it is My face you seek. My Kingdom has come near you forever with My touch. I anoint you for My service, I anoint you in My love. I give to you so faithfully the things you ask of Me. My tender touch has reached across the span of time for you. I call forth each promise I have promised you. I laugh with you and dance with you across My skies with joy. I give you gifts of hope and love and My abundance filled with joy. I weep with you when sorrow comes and pierces your tender heart. My praise will be upon your lips in every season of our love. Forever I have promised you, live in the hope I give. Forever is My Holy Name, forever I do give. My wisdom settles on you, great peace is in your soul. You know the paths I take you, My voice is known by you. Keep your focus on eternity, not on the circumstances. I bring it all together for good to those who know My Name and serve Me faithfully. Let no one deceive you, the times are nearer than before, keep your watch, oh holy one, the eastern skies will show My return.

December 7

Jeremiah 20 NLT

[11]But the LORD stands beside me like a great warrior. Before him my persecutors will stumble. They cannot defeat me. They will fail and be thoroughly humiliated. Their dishonor will never be forgotten. [12]O LORD of Heaven's Armies, you test those who are righteous, and you examine the deepest thoughts and secrets. Let me see your vengeance against them, for I have committed my cause to you. [13]Sing to the LORD! Praise the LORD! For though I was poor and needy, he rescued me from my oppressors.

The power is in Me. The wisdom is in Me. Your next breath is controlled by Me, I Am Your Savior and Your King. Each step you take is guided by Me, The One who gives you breath. Do not worry, precious one, I control each step you take. I fill you with My power, My love and mercy too. You walk in My abundance, My overflow is in you. Look about you, holy one, behold Me everywhere. I care for you so tenderly, I watch your every step. I lavish you in mercy and grace beyond all measure. You have captured My great heart; I love you, precious treasure. The seasons change before you and deeper you do go into the depths of My holiness, deeper you do go. The world becomes more distant as you seek My face . Your eyes are on eternity and things that matter most. I sustain you and I keep you safe from all that harms. There is no power greater than My love for you, My chosen one. I make room for you, beloved one, I make room for the gifts I give. I give you wisdom in the talents and gifts I give.

December 8

Psalm 148 NLT

13 Let them all praise the name of the LORD. For his name is very great; his glory towers over the earth and heaven! 14 He has made his people strong, honoring his faithful ones—the people of Israel who are close to him. Praise the LORD!

My Name rests in your heart. My will is done in you. I teach you and remind you of My steadfast ways of truth. I welcome your repentant heart and take you into another level. I cleanse you and I purify your heart, My precious one. The sting sits heavy for a while, a short while, holy one. The freedom of the cleansings are deep and sure and strong. I keep you protected from the harm, for the evil tries to take you from My arms! I will not let him, precious one, for you are Mine alone. I Am Your GOD who does not share or compromise one thing. I welcome you each day, My love, into My holy chambers. I call forth all My blessings and call you My beloved. The times are now, My holy one, for change is in the air. Come forth, My treasure in My heart, I love you tenderly. I give to you My greatest love, I give you all of Me. My mighty right hand rests on you and My protection is about. No one can take you from Me, I Am Your Holy Love. You live and breathe and worship Me, Your One True GOD and KING. I live inside your praises, I rest My smile on you as you worship Me, My love. I give to you My great peace, My joy is deeply in you. No one can take you from Me, I Am Your ROCK, your anchor holds in Me. I steady you and strengthen you each day and night, My love. Line upon line, precept upon precept, I come to you, My love.

December 9

Micah 7 NLT

[15]"Yes," says the LORD, "I will do mighty miracles for you, like those I did when I rescued you from slavery in Egypt." [16]All the nations of the world will stand amazed at what the LORD will do for you. They will be embarrassed at their feeble power. They will cover their mouths in silent awe, deaf to everything around them.

The blessings flow from the depths of Me. My passion rises to honor you. I have come, My beauty to behold, let My world see the honor I bestow on the hearts who are obedient to Me. Refreshing river, flow, for My greatly beloved needs the touch of your healing streams. Rise up, beloved, the time is now, take your place at My table of honor and love. I serve you of My finest delights, you may have this and that, My love. Listen to the beat of My tender heart, I flow in you and inhabit you. My mercy abounds and My grace is upon you, the power of love I give you. Precious is your name, its sweetness lingers as I speak your name in My passion and love. No force will take you away from Me, for I have you refined and protected in Me. All of My power and might surely comes against all who try to cause you harm. I establish your thoughts and guide each step you take. My blood is all powerful, you need never fear, for I Am Your King and I give you My shield. The sword is drawn, every Word is active and alive, for you obey Me completely, My beautiful bride. I remember the day of your "Yes" to My call. Come quickly, I say, for much is required. My smile settles on you. Rejoice in My love, I Am Your Redeemer, Your Savior and KING.

December 10

Hebrews 6 NLT

[1]So let us stop going over the basic teachings about Christ again and again. Let us go on instead and become mature in our understanding. Surely we don't need to start again with the fundamental importance of repenting from evil deeds and placing our faith in God. [2]You don't need further instruction about baptisms, the laying on of hands, the

resurrection of the dead, and eternal judgment. [3]And so, God willing, we will move forward to further understanding.

The darkness flees, for light has come, I live among My people! Let no one deceive you, holy one, I am here to meet each need! My mercy flows abundantly to those who call on Me. Peace is here, My joy has come, for all the world to see. You are My holy vessel who walks in peace in Me. My armor is about you, My promises are true. I give to you My new covenant, inside your mind and heart. You know Me, precious treasure, you know the peace in Me. Do not be deceived, My love, by the false light that comes to you. I Am Your Shepherd of long ago, My sheep know My voice. Follow Me, Your Savior, for safety is in Me. Grow, My mighty warrior, beyond the foundation that is laid. Step forward in your calling, I come to you today. Do not look behind you, of things that were before, My blood has cleansed you, holy one, go forward in My love. Live in My abundance of power and of love, and mercy overflowing, for I refine you in My love. I suffered and I paid the price of things for you, My love.

December 11

Luke 1 NLT

[71]Now we will be saved from our enemies and from all who hate us. [78]Because of God's tender mercy, the morning light from heaven is about to break upon us, [79]to give light to those who sit in darkness and in the shadow of death, and to guide us to the path of peace."

My provision is perfect, the gift of My Son, The Lamb Who Was Slain before the foundation of the earth. My timing has come to release the captives to walk in the freedom of their salvation. You know Me, for My laws are written on your heart and mind. My Spirit reveals Me to you as you study to show yourself approved. My glory settles on you and about you as you strengthen yourself in Me. I am here, for I have come to meet the needs of My precious people, My chosen ones, in whom I am well pleased. My people come to Me, I hear their cries. I reach out and take them out of their depths of despair. I use you, holy one, I call you forth, help My hurting people, how they need Me so! I came to earth to save and heal the hurting souls, My love. Walk this path I have chosen, live inside of Me. I will guide your every step, always come to Me. I am not your distant God, I Am The Keeper of Your Heart. I give to you the breath you breathe and every single heartbeat. Let My love flow from you into the needy ones. My people live in sorrow from the destruction of the deceiver. Live inside My great light, illuminate the way, let the darkness flee this day, for I have come to stay.

December 12

Ephesians 5 NLT

[10]Carefully determine what pleases the Lord. [11]Take no part in the worthless deeds of evil and darkness; instead, expose them. [12]It is shameful even to talk about the things that ungodly people do in secret. [13]But their evil intentions will be exposed when the light shines on them, [14]for the light makes everything visible. This is why it is said, "Awake, O sleeper, rise up from the dead, and Christ will give you light."

I establish your thoughts, consider My ways, My higher ways of wonder and awe. My Name is Wonderful and Mighty King, The King of All Kings has come to you. Nothing on earth can compare to Me. Even the false light is dim next to Me. Know Me, stand strong inside Me, for you cannot do this without Me, My bride. My glory fills My universe, receive Me, Your King, I give you all you desire. I call out to you, come higher, My beloved, come walk in My beauty, My glory, and honor. I saturate you when you bid Me to come and live inside you, for My Kingdom has come. Praise Me, My treasure, honor Me, My beloved, for I Am Your Redeemer who comes to you in love. I Am Love and there is no other. Love comes from Me, you must love one another. Remain in Me, I Am The Light, the darkness must shatter and fall away in My light. Glorify Me for that is My desire. Honor your King for I give you My light. Live in My love and walk in My light. Steady and sure are the steps you take when you seek Me, your King, every day. I show you My ways, My higher ways. You can trust Me, My love, in every thing.

December 13

Daniel 1 NLT

[17]God gave these four young men an unusual aptitude for understanding every aspect of literature and wisdom. And God gave Daniel the special ability to interpret the meanings of visions and dreams. [18]When the training period ordered by the king was completed, the chief of staff brought all the young men to King Nebuchadnezzar. [19]The king talked with them, and no one impressed him as much as Daniel, Hananiah, Mishael, and Azariah.

I Am Yours, you are Mine, let no one come between us. I Am Your Savior and Your King, I meet your every need. I created this path, My precious priceless treasure, go forward in this holy day, go forward in My love. Let My pleasant, sweet rains, pour down on you in love. Saturate yourself in all the blessings I bestow. Praise Me, precious treasure, for I inhabit you, and live in sweet communion as you praise Me, holy one. I Am The King of Glory, I encamp My greatest armies about you, holy one. No one can come between us, My power is the strongest, for you are My beloved one who obeys Me without hesitation. Oh glory to My Holy Name for I have My chosen people, they love Me and adore Me and I am strong on their behalf. Let the seasons come and go! My holy people take a stand, they are My prized possession, My holy ones who stand upon My Word. I give you all the blessings, I give you strength to stand, I require much of you, go to My hurting ones. I pour My wisdom on you, I speak through you, My love.

December 14

Revelation 5 NLT

[11]Then I looked again, and I heard the voices of thousands and millions of angels around the throne and of the living beings and the elders. [12]And they sang in a mighty chorus:

"Worthy is the Lamb who was slaughtered—to receive power and riches and wisdom and strength and honor and glory and blessing."

All glory and honor and power are Mine, for I Am The Lamb Who Was Slain. I Am The Lion of the Tribe of Judah and all creatures praise My Holy Name. I Am Your King who comes to you, not in silence, I come to you. My passion rages and fills the earth as I come forth for those who love Me so. Strengthen yourself in the light of My Word and walk in My ways all the days I give you. Work, My beloved, work in My strength, gather My people home to Me. My power is in you, My love abounds in every way, I use you, My love. Sing Hosanna from the depths of your heart, for I Am Your King and I have come to you. Rejoice in My splendor, the victory is Mine, I call you forth in this great time. Walk above every circumstance, walk in My freedom, for I paid the price for you. Do not look about, keep your eyes on Me, I am in your midst, I am in all things. I Am Your Direction, I have prepared you, My love. Go forward each day in the light of My Word. Sing to Me, sing, precious one. Give Me honor and praise for My Kingdom has come. Walk in My glory and praise My Great Name for I Am Your Savior, Your Redeemer, Your King.

December 15

Revelation 12 NLT

[11]And they have defeated him by the blood of the Lamb and by their testimony. And they did not love their lives so much that they were afraid to die. [12]Therefore, rejoice, O heavens! And you who live in the heavens, rejoice! But terror will come on the earth and the sea, for the devil has come down to you in great anger, knowing that he has little time."

My presence is about you. I teach you of My ways. I have called you holy, I call you forth, My love. The times are now for greater things. I teach you, precious one. I do not give My gifts then leave you unattended. My wisdom has been given, I have heard your tender heart. I give to you in season, for I prepare you for this level. My season of abundance is flowing down on you. You are My faithful chosen one, I can trust you, precious one. I open eyes, the blinded ones, I unveil the deceiver in their midst. I warn My greatest warnings for I love them, holy one. I Am The King of Glory! Glorify My Holy Name for times are now, My love. I come to you in suddenness and surprise you, holy one. Praise My Name forever, for

Holy is My Name. All power, and might and glory are in My Holy Name. My dawn has come upon you, rise up and take your stand. These are the times of revelation, I reveal Myself to you. Never fear, beloved one, I paid the price for you. I do not leave you, ever, I live and breathe in you. Go forward, oh My feet and hands, go about and do My good.

December 16

Psalm 45 NLT

[11]For your royal husband delights in your beauty; honor him, for he is your lord. [12]The princess of Tyre will shower you with gifts. The wealthy will beg your favor. [13]The bride, a princess, looks glorious in her golden gown.

I complete My great and mighty plans and joy comes in the morning. Refined and pruned, you stand in Me, Your Almighty King of All. My glory fills My universe as I send you out, My love. Fill yourself with all of Me, each day is a new drink from My living waters. Overflow in My great love and let My love and mercy flow. Abundance in the overflow is My perfect will. The songs I sing will never end for generations are in Me. I sing My songs to My beloved, the ones who are My own. Fight the good fight, holy one, steady yourself in Me and do as I command. Every step is ordained for you, every thought has been established. I Am The King of Glory and I fill My universe. Peace, be still, I tell you. Hear My own heart beat. Walk in the rhythm of My peace, keep steady inside Me. Surely I come to you, I Am Faithful to the end. I spoke forever into you – a circle without end. My love does not forsake you, My love has no end, My love is ever flowing, My living is the beginning – for Alpha is My Name. My season is upon you, harvest time is here, go forth in My abundance and bring Me all My fruit, for now is My chosen time. Joy is deeply within your soul, sing forth your deeper song, for I have strengthened you for more in this harvest time. Beloved is your holy name, you stand beside Me in all things, for you are My friend indeed, I show you many things.

December 17

Hebrews 5 NLT

[7]While Jesus was here on earth, he offered prayers and pleadings, with a loud cry and tears, to the one who could rescue him from death. And God heard his prayers because of his deep reverence for God. [8]Even though Jesus was God's Son, he learned obedience from the things he suffered. [9]In this way, God qualified him as a perfect High Priest, and he became the source of eternal salvation for all those who obey him.

I Am Your God of separation. I separate the light, My love, from the darkness every day. I anoint you in My holiness, I separate you for Me. My call speaks out your name to Me. I take you to My side, and speak of My great wonders, I love you, holy bride. I separate the waters, drink from My living wells. Drink from springs that satisfy the dryness of the soul. Let the deep call unto deep. Come to Me, My love. I give you hunger and thirst for My righteousness. Behold Me, holy one! I long to give you more of Me, come drink, My greatly beloved. Living rivers flow into the barren souls who come, give them of My living springs and heal them as they come! Precious one, I call you forth from the depths inside of Me. I anoint you more and more each day as you serve Me in every thing. I honor those who call on Me in each and every day. I dine with you and walk with you in the cool of the day. I restore the broken places and mend the wounds in the communion of our love. Weep for those who do not know the comfort of My Spirit.

December 18

Luke 11 NLT

[9]"And so I tell you, keep on asking, and you will receive what you ask for. Keep on seeking, and you will find. Keep on knocking, and the door will be opened to you. [10]For everyone who asks, receives. Everyone who seeks, finds. And to everyone who knocks, the door will be opened.

I Am The King of Glory and I have come to you. I watch you seek My face each day, I watch you oh so closely. I examine your heart, tender one, all is well, My love. I come to you so suddenly, for I have you well prepared. My promises come to you from the four winds they come, for you have obeyed Me, My love, every single time. I pruned you for more in My Great Name. I refined you in the furnace to keep you from all harm. Now the greater things come for I trust you, holy one. You have been faithful in the little, I give you so much more. I water you continually for each day you seek to find Me, each day I come to you. I talk with you and walk with you and hold your trembling hand. I send you mighty warriors who help you in this land. Never have you doubted the things I spoke to you. I give you all of Me, My love, every promise I give you. You please Me, precious tender one, you stand so tall for Me. I had to test you, precious one, to prepare you for the more. Persecution comes with more, I have steadied you in Me. Let them come, oh precious one, for you belong to Me. I have My seal upon you. Go about and do My good. My Great Name rests upon you, all authority I give you, for I Am GOD Almighty and I have chosen you.

December 19

Ezekiel 11 NLT
18"When the people return to their homeland, they will remove every trace of their vile images and detestable idols. 19And I will give them singleness of heart and put a new spirit within them. I will take away their stony, stubborn heart and give them a tender, responsive heart, 20so they will obey my decrees and regulations. Then they will truly be my people, and I will be their God.

Blessings come inside the times of suffering for My Name. I strengthen and confirm you in the harder times, My love. I come to you in the dawn and rest My glory upon you, for you have come through from the deeper places set inside of you. Come forth, oh mighty bride of Mine, set your face firmly upon Mine. The battle is raging, but I give you rest when you lay your burdens upon Me. Rejoice My precious treasure, My heart is tender to your name. I give you of My sweetness, the touch of My heart, My love,

271

you remind Me why I came. Pray for those in bondage, bring them My relief, rescue them from all the evil, bring them to Me. Come forth in Me and walk inside the victory in Me. You cannot do this all alone, you must walk in fellowship with Me. I stretch forth My mighty hand and weeping comes without relief. Come to Me, Your King of Glory, and walk in victory. My power is within you when you praise My Holy Name. Walk with Me and commune with Me and let Me give you of My strength. Humble adoration is what I desire. Praise Me in the seasons, My love. My mighty arm is upon you doing many things.

December 20

Daniel 7 NLT

[9]I watched as thrones were put in place and the Ancient One sat down to judge. His clothing was as white as snow, his hair like purest wool. He sat on a fiery throne with wheels of blazing fire, [10]and a river of fire was pouring out, flowing from his presence. Millions of angels ministered to him; many millions stood to attend him. Then the court began its session, and the books were opened.

Life in Me is flowing out from you to them. My mighty river flows in you, oh give them of My life. The time is now for greater things, stay inside My glory. I have My plans for you, My love, I keep you safe in Me. Oh righteous one, I teach you about My great connecting doors. This door leads to that relief and this door is My way. Oh go with all My might and power and live this day in Me. I am at work among you. I come and bring relief. Breathe deeply in My glory, I fill My universe. Empower yourself in Me and lay hands on those I love. Beloved is your name, for I have chosen you for such a time as this, My love, I have chosen you. Flower of My tender touch, I give you this unfolding. Behold the beauty of My treasures, hidden inside you. Fragrant are your words to Me, I inhale all your praises. I honor you, My precious one, for you have sacrificed to Me. Watch Me, tender flower, as I take you higher still. Oh flow My rains upon My tender flower, live in My abundant overflow, go about and do My will. I give you My assurance, I am in you this day. Lay hands on those I send you, pray, beloved, pray.

272

December 21

Exodus 30 NLT

7"Every morning when Aaron maintains the lamps, he must burn fragrant incense on the altar. 8And each evening when he lights the lamps, he must again burn incense in the LORD's presence. This must be done from generation to generation. 9Do not offer any unholy incense on this altar, or any burnt offerings, grain offerings, or liquid offerings.

My anointing has come in greater measure, for you trim your lamp, and keep yourself in obedience to Me. Oh light, I give you of My power, let My glory shine. Come out, My holy treasure, and shine light on all the darkness and watch it flee from you! There is no shadow in Me, I Am Light, without a cast of shadow of any darkness, I Am The Only Light. Do not be deceived, My love, keep alert in Me. You know Me, holy treasure, I separate you to Me. I take them away and cut them loose, those who may not be, the ones who try to harm My flowing river inside you. Keep your eyes on only Me, for My timing is now, cutting loose those who may not be, the ones who try to harm My calling inside you. Keep your eyes on only Me for My timing is now cutting loose the ones who curse you in their heart. I replenish you and I fill you full inside My perfect plan. I send to you the ones who have a pure heart for My Kingdom Plan. I know the hearts, oh tender one, I protect you from the ones who come to destroy My work, My love. I keep you pure and protect you as you trim your lamp in Me. Come inside My glory and worship Me and receive My great relief.

December 22

Matthew 4 NLT

23Jesus traveled throughout the region of Galilee, teaching in the synagogues and announcing the Good News about the Kingdom. And he healed every kind of disease and illness. 24News about him spread as far as Syria, and people soon began bringing to him all who were sick. And whatever their sickness or disease, or if they were demon-possessed or epileptic or paralyzed—he healed them all.

I have deposited My mercy in you. Go forth this day in it. I send you to the one I chose so very long ago. My greater works I do, My love, for I have sustained you for this time. Resurrect the dead, My love, revive them in My Word. I come forth in might and power for I do not change, My love. I created you so long ago and set you in this place. I have shattered every piece in you that had to be broken, holy one. I restored you unto Me, My love, for you belong to only Me. I Am The King of Glory, I fill My universe, I establish your thoughts, holy one, I order every step. Come forth, I call you to My side, for greater things are now. I gather up My chosen ones and protect them in My love. Power, holy power, of My love freely flows. I deposit Myself in you from My holiness of love. Give and give, oh give again, for this one needs My love. Show them of My tenderness, oh show them, holy one. Dance this dance with Me, My love, for we are one inside My glory. Rest your cares on Me, My love, for I can carry every load. I Am Your King of Glory and I fill My universe.

December 23

Isaiah 65 NLT

[8]"But I will not destroy them all," says the LORD. "For just as good grapes are found among a cluster of bad ones (and someone will say, 'Don't throw them all away—some of those grapes are good!'), so I will not destroy all Israel. For I still have true servants there. [9]I will preserve a remnant of the people of Israel and of Judah to possess my land.

The dam has burst, My waters flow, My river swiftly flows. Healing waters spring up and bring My great relief. My presence flows and fills the air, I am in everything. Glory reigns and rules in Me for I Am Glorious, receive from Me, oh thirsty one, I give you all you need. My double portion is My gift, oh ask and it is yours, seek Me, My precious treasure, knock and I will open. Now is the time for greater things, receive My precious gifts. I delight in you, My treasure, so hidden inside Me. I bless you and I honor you, My faithful holy bride, come forth in all My splendor, I give to you, My bride. I send you here, I send you there, I gather and destroy. The sheep are separated from the goats, My precious one. My people know My tender voice, My love they recognize. Go forth in all My love, it is the breaking power. I Am Love, I Am Pure, and Righteous is My Name. I send My righteousness before you, holy one. Glory to My Holy Name, let all of earth rejoice, for I have opened heaven to rain upon the earth. Fill yourself with all of Me and strengthen yourself for this time, for the battle rages on. Stand tall, beloved flower, My grace has come to you.

December 24

Genesis 22 NLT

[12]"Don't lay a hand on the boy!" the angel said. "Do not hurt him in any way, for now I know that you truly fear God. You have not withheld from me even your son, your only son." 16This is what the LORD says: Because you have obeyed me and have not withheld even your son, your only son, I swear by my own name that [17]I will certainly bless you. I will multiply your descendants beyond number, like the stars in the sky and the sand on the seashore. Your descendants will conquer the cities of their enemies.

New beginnings do not turn back, for My decrees are sure. Go forward in My Holy Name, each day begin anew. Seek Me first, it is My will, I am in everything. My glory is about you, I surround you in My love. The season of My favor comes to you, My holy one. Persistence was the key, My love, that broke the chains from you. Now your trust is in only Me! Praise My Holy Name, all glory and honor and power come forth, for you obey Me, precious one. Dance upon the fields of abundance in My power. I send you to the hurting ones, this is the final hour. The call awaits, the trumpets blow, the new is now, My love. I call you forth from long ago, you please Me, holy one. My love is flowing mightily, oh flower of My choosing, bloom in Me inside My garden of eternity. I love you, precious one. My lips have kissed you once again, you rest your love in Me. I never fail you, precious one, I meet your every need.

December 25

Hebrews 6 NLT

¹⁰For God is not unjust. He will not forget how hard you have worked for him and how you have shown your love to him by caring for other believers, as you still do. ¹¹Our great desire is that you will keep on loving others as long as life lasts, in order to make certain that what you hope for will come true. ¹²Then you will not become spiritually dull and indifferent. Instead, you will follow the example of those who are going to inherit God's promises because of their faith and endurance.

I can help you, precious one, for I Am GOD Almighty. This is but a small thing for Me. Look, I send you those, My love, to help you understand. Do not worry, I am here, I know your tender heart. You are on the right path – the path that I designed. This season is now over, My new season has arrived! My double portion flows, My love, in this greater time. Heaven opens on you, the rains how they do pour. Distribute all My gifts, My love, to My hurting ones. Tell them how I love them so and give them My relief, for the ending is soon now. I hear the cries of repentance coming from the lands. I hear and see and smell the death the evil one has done. Cry out for those, My holy one, let Me hear your cries. Weep and mourn for those, My love, who do not know the path of righteousness, the evil never stops destroying them, My love. Go to the fields I send you, I am with you, holy one. I come forth and hold you closely, and guide you in the storm.

December 26

Isaiah 24 NLT

¹³Throughout the earth the story is the same—only a remnant is left, like the stray olives left on the tree or the few grapes left on the vine after harvest. ¹⁴But all who are left shout and sing for joy. Those in the west praise the

LORD's majesty. ¹⁵In eastern lands, give glory to the LORD. In the lands beyond the sea, praise the name of the LORD, the God of Israel.

Come into Me, precious one, let Me saturate you in Me. The storms rage on, the winds do blow, and steady is My hand. Keep your hand in Mine, My love, I lead you in this new level. The fight is on, the new comes forth, the old must go, My love. Fear Me, not man, I steady you, I Am The Great I AM! Times are now, break away, do not look back, My love. Keep your focus on Me, do not look about you, focus straight ahead. Revive yourself inside My love, refresh yourself in Me. Move into My deeper place, I have purified you in Me. You give to Me each empty space and I fill you full in Me. Rivers from Me flow in you and settle deep within. Then I give you more of Me to overflow to them. Replenish yourself daily, fill yourself in Me. Then wait upon Me, holy one, until My overflow comes in you. My ways are higher, My times are sure, My mighty right hand is here. Never waiver, never doubt, never break My heart. I love you, tender holy one, I take you into Me. I teach you and I show you the mysteries in Me. I delight in every detail, oh how I delight Myself in you. Come to Me, My precious one, and rest your love in Me.

December 27

Psalm 121 NLT

¹I look up to the mountains—does my help come from there? ²My help comes from the LORD, who made heaven and earth! ³He will not let you stumble; the one who watches over you will not slumber. ⁴Indeed, he who watches over Israel never slumbers or sleeps. ⁵The LORD himself watches over you! The LORD stands beside you as your protective shade. ⁶The sun will not harm you by day, nor the moon at night. ⁷The LORD keeps you from all harm and watches over your life. ⁸The LORD keeps watch over you as you come and go, both now and forever.

This day has come upon you, My gift to you I give. My salvation spreads across the hearts, My holy one. I come in all My glory and I honor you this day. Let My blessings flood your soul and wash each tear away. I restore you in My tender ways and mend the shattered pieces. You are Mine and Mine alone from the beginning, precious one. I came to you that holy day and took your "Yes" in Me, and gave you all of Me that day, I Am Your Faithful King. My plans are all about you, unfolding here and there. Live inside My glory, oh precious one. My Spirit comes in power and fills you with My song. Come forth, My hidden treasure, now is the time to shine. My rubies fall upon you, My holy blood so pure, and cries out from My Throne Room, justice has come through! Sparkle in the cleansing, the deeper cleansing of the soul. My fresh oil comes forth, holy one, I cover you, My love.

December 28

Isaiah 30 NLT

[18]So the LORD must wait for you to come to him so he can show you his love and compassion. For the LORD is a faithful God. Blessed are those who wait for his help. [19]O people of Zion, who live in Jerusalem, you will weep no more. He will be gracious if you ask for help. He will surely respond to the sound of your cries. [20]Though the Lord gave you adversity for food and suffering for drink, he will still be with you to teach you. You will see your teacher with your own eyes.

You have been taught by Me, pay close attention to My Words, they come through holy lips, My love, they come from Me, My love. I have My plans, My greater plans for each to serve Me fully. I am in every detail and I Am Holy in your midst. I am deeper in you than you know, My mercy rests deeply in you. My grace goes before you in this new day I bring. I embed you in this season of greater things to come. Lift high your hands to heaven, I hold your hands, My love. My yearning draws you deeper into the depths of Me. I saturate you, holy one, in all of Me, My queen. I give you strength to stand tall, beside Me you do stand. You live and breathe in Me, My love, My glory rests on you. I deposit in you many things, commune with Me, My love. I give you of My everlasting drink. My cup fills you. Receive My drink in all its plenty, I come to you in love. I Am Your Holy Savior, I Am Your Holy Love. My ways are higher than you know, My ways are greater still. I honor you, I bless you, I give you all of Me.

December 29

Luke 12 NLT

27"Look at the lilies and how they grow. They don't work or make their clothing, yet Solomon in all his glory was not dressed as beautifully as they are. 28And if God cares so wonderfully for flowers that are here today and thrown into the fire tomorrow, he will certainly care for you.
32"So don't be afraid, little flock. For it gives your Father great happiness to give you the Kingdom.

I begin the thought in reverent silence and fill you with My holiness. You hear the very heart of Me and silence comes to you. Listen closely to My Words, each sound has power in the tone. The softness of My whisper, the revelation builds and then it comes. The escalating rhythm of our hearts intertwined, you hear Me whisper, listen, I come to you in peace. Go forth in great array, I robe you with My presence. Solomon was not dressed so beautifully as My lilies in the field. Dance with Me, the winds do sway, I come to you, My love. The gentle breezes sway you, in the dance with Me upon My harvest fields. My people are so hungry and thirsty for My more. You see the hunger and desire for My deeper Word. Oh how My people perish for lack of knowledge, holy one. The natural goes before the spiritual, My love. Faith is key to stepping out, step out in Me this day. The key has come to open every gate in My great love. Obedience has come to live in you – always, I can send you now, My holy one, this is your holy day. Praise Me in the quiet time and in My assembly too, for I Am GOD Almighty, and I have come to you.

December 30

Daniel 2 NLT

"Praise the name of God forever and ever, for he has all wisdom and power. 21He controls the course of world events; he removes kings and sets up other kings. He gives wisdom to the wise and knowledge to the scholars. 22He reveals deep and mysterious things and knows what lies hidden in darkness, though he is surrounded by light.

²³I thank and praise you, God of my ancestors, for you have given me wisdom and strength. You have told me what we asked of you and revealed to us what the king demanded."

I delight in the details, I delight Myself in you. I awaken you to the detail, you listen completely. My treasures are about you, each one I send to you. My overflow has come, My love, you rest your cares on Me. The things I teach My children are exciting, holy one. See the things I do, My love, for My children, they are Mine. I wrap My arms around them and give them My new song. My liquid love flows through them, I flow, oh holy one. Torrents come and torrents go and steadily I flow. My peace does overcome each torrent, precious one. Rage on oh things that do not matter in My eternity, My beloved one has come to Me, and crossed that chilly Jordan to serve only Me! Temptations do not matter, for it is My face that you seek. Oh greater things come forth this day and celebrate with Me. My precious gemstones gather and sparkle just for Me. The facets are more brilliant than any earthly thing, for My glory is among them to amaze the world of Me. Behold Me!

December 31

1 Peter 4 TMSG

¹²Friends, when life gets really difficult, don't jump to the conclusion that God isn't on the job. ¹³Instead, be glad that you are in the very thick of what Christ experienced. This is a spiritual refining process, with glory just around the corner. ¹⁴If you're abused because of Christ, count yourself fortunate. It's the Spirit of God and his glory in you that brought you to the notice of others.

Ecclesiastes 3 TMSG

¹¹True, God made everything beautiful in itself and in its time—but he's left us in the dark, so we can never know what God is up to, whether he's coming or going.

Life springs forth from the seeds that have been planted. I have brought a drink to the dry and thirsty land. Arise, oh sleeper, for now is the time to come alive and shine out in My glory! I am here guiding each thing and

280

bringing all things together in My Name. I Am Your Great Delight for I Am Delightful. Your hope in Me has not been in vain, your hope in Me has sustained you in the storms. All things have come full circle, the point of origin emerges. Oh the fullness of your destiny, how beautiful to behold! I Am Faithful, holy one, so faithful to behold. You are wonderful in Me, My bride. I complete that which I have begun, My love, and it is beautiful in the unfolding. I Am Yours, Your Faithful Love, Your Holy One of Israel.

Has anyone ever told you that God loves you and that He has a wonderful plan for your life? If you were to die this very second, do you know for sure, beyond a shadow of a doubt, that you would go to Heaven?

The Holy Bible reads "for all have sinned and come short of the glory of God" and "for the wages of sin is death, but the gift of God is eternal life through Jesus Christ our Lord." The Bible also reads, "For whosoever shall call upon the name of the Lord shall be saved." You are a "whosoever."

Lord, bless this person who is reading this right now and bless their family with long and healthy lives. Jesus, make Yourself real to them and do a quick work in their heart. If they have not received Jesus Christ as their Lord and Savior, I pray they will do so now in Jesus Name. Amen.

If you would like to receive the gift that God has for you today, say this out loud with your heart and lips.

"Dear Lord Jesus, come into my heart. Forgive me of my sins. Wash me and cleanse me. Set me free. Jesus, thank You that You died for me. I believe that You are risen from the dead and that You're coming back again for me. Fill me with the Holy Spirit. Give me a passion for the lost, a hunger for the things of God and a holy boldness to preach the gospel of Jesus Christ. I'm saved; I'm born again, I'm forgiven and I'm on my way to Heaven because I have Jesus in my heart."

As a minister of the gospel of Jesus Christ, I tell you today that all of your sins are forgiven. Always remember to run to God and not from God because He loves you and has a great plan for your life.

Please find a church that believes the entire Bible and preaches the pure Word of God. Be sure to read your Bible every day, even if it is just a small amount. The Word washes you and helps you to grow and come to know Your Lord more and more. It is food for your spirit and it heals you, encourages you, lifts you up, and teaches you on your life journey.

All of heaven is having a great party of celebration over you right now, rejoicing over your entry into The Kingdom! I rejoice with them! God bless you – always.

About the Author

I was born into an American military family stationed in Germany on July 16, 1954. We predominately lived in Lawton, Oklahoma and my dad is buried there at the Ft. Sill cemetery.

Church life was a normal life. My two sisters and I grew up under the nurture and care of a wonderful pastor and parents who convinced me from a very early age that God was real and He was personal and He could meet my every need. I believed every word of it!

That steadfast belief and knowing that God could pull me out of any one of my messes, at any given time, has kept me in a place of hope and steadfast faith all my life. As I would stumble here and there, I always knew God loved me. I have never lived my life without that knowing.

For as long as I can remember, I had a desire to write. I enjoy reading a variety of genres. After the death of Dick Heflin (husband of 20 years), the writing became a release, and a healing process.

A new life emerged after 8 years of being a widow and I am once again blessed with a wonderful marriage to Ralph Nichols, retired TVA, and horse rancher.

As this new life emerged, I began publishing my books and others' books at www.three-sheep.com. They are available on Amazon in paperback and Kindle and available on the Barnes & Noble Nook.

I have and continue to write. These books came out of a recovery of a financial loss during the death of my late husband and my road back to financial victory, emotional healing, and joy in this new era of my life.

I live a life surrounded by the peace that only Jesus can bring, a wonderful husband who loves me and worships God with me. He prays the sweetest prayers and blessings over all of us. We enjoy 5 beautiful children and their spouses and have 21 grandchildren and 2 great-grandchildren.

I am a living testimony that you can have loss beyond measure and life again, with blessings beyond measure, if you keep your trust in God and don't lose hope. There is always hope in Christ.

love letters from God for the heart

.

All scriptures are The King James Version

ISBN-13:978-1523298280

Copyright © TX 7-722-355

Three Sheep Minisries

www.three-sheep.com

Theresa Jean Nichols
Author/Publisher

Devotional Books Written by

T. J. Nichols

(Theresa Jean Nichols)

Love Letters from God Series

Love Letters from God Meditations (Book One)

Love Letters from God for the Heart (Book Two)

Love Letters from God for the Family (Book Three)

Love Letters from God for Your Spirit (Book Four)

Love Letters from God for Your Mind (Book Five)

Love Letters from God for Your Soul (Book Six)

Love Letters from God for Your Strength (Book Seven)

Love Letters from God for Your Peace (Book Eight)

Love Letters from God for Your Comfort (Book Nine)

Don't Worry God Has You Covered Books 1-9 are the same as Love Letters from God – Different Cover and Title only

Other Books Written by T. J. Nichols

How to Create & Publish Your Own Book from Cover to Finish

Meditations and How to Write Them

Place of Pain (Unforgiveness)

Run, Maverick, Run

Genesis

Exodus

Speak it Not Speak it So

Governing Through Intercession

A Children's Christmas Story Play

A Christmas Play a True Story

Forty Days After the Resurrection

love letters from God for the heart

Do You Know the Answer? Yes or No (Children's Book)

Crossword Puzzles Children's Bible Games

Once Upon a Time (Children's Book)

Dear Keith Not Everything is as it Seems

The Shift (5 Books in One)

The Take Away Program (1)

The Detail and Compassion of God (2)

The Miracles (3)

The Horse Gate (4)

The Spiritual Realm (5)

Each of the above 5 books are in *The Shift*

It's a Cake Walk

Courses:

A Power Point Course: *How to Publish Your Book*

A Power Point Course: *Intercession, What is It? How do you do it?*